Cultural Poetry

" The Poetry of Different Cultures & Nations "

Edited by Paul F. Kisak

Contents

Chapter 1

National poetry

This is a list of articles about poetry in a single language or produced by a single nation.

World languages will tend to have a large body of poetry contributed to by several nations (Anglosphere, Francophonie, Latin America, German-speaking Europe), while for smaller languages, the body of poetry in a particular language will be identical to the national poetry of the nation or ethnicity associated with that language.

1.1 Contemporary

1.1.1 Asia

Middle East

- Persian poets
- Piyyut
- Modern Hebrew poetry

Near East

- Arabic poetry
- Azerbaijani literature
- Persian poetry
- Turkish poetry

South Asia

- Afghan poetry
  - Pashto literature and poetry
- Bangladeshi poetry
  - New Age Poetry of Bangladesh
- Indian poetry

- Assamese Poetry
- Bishnupriya Manipuri poetry
- Gujarati poetry
- Hindi poetry
- Kannada poetry
- Kashmiri poetry
- Malayalam poetry
- Marathi poetry
- Nepali poetry
- Rajasthani poetry
- Sindhi poetry
- Tamil poetry
- Telugu poetry
- Urdu poetry
- Indian Poetry in English
- Pakistani poetry
  - Urdu poetry

East Asia

- Chinese poetry
- Japanese poetry
- Korean poetry
- Vietnamese poetry

Southeast Asia

- Javanese poetry
- Thai poetry
- Filipino poetry
- Singaporean Poetry
- Southeast asian poetry

1.1.2   Europe

- Albanian poetry
- British poetry
  - Cornish poetry
  - English poetry
    - Old English poetry

- Manx poetry
- Scottish poetry
- Welsh poetry
  - Anglo-Welsh poetry
- Catalan poetry
- Finnish poetry
- French poetry
- German poetry
- Icelandic poetry
- Irish poetry
- Italian poetry
- Japanese poetry
- List of Polish language poets
- Portuguese poetry
- Romanian poetry
- Russian poetry
- Bulgarian poetry
- Serbian epic poetry
- Slovak poetry
- Spanish poetry
- Ukrainian poetry

1.1.3 Americas

- Brazilian poetry
- Canadian poetry
- Latin American poetry
- Mexican poetry
- Peruvian poetry
- United States poetry

1.1.4 Africa

- Malagasy poetry
- South African poetry
- Swahili poetry
- Yoruba Ewi

1.2   Historical

Further information: Epic poetry and History of poetry

- Rhapsode

- Rishi

- Sanskrit poetry

- Indian epic poetry

- Bard

- Skald

- Germanic poetry

- Old Norse poetry

- Biblical poetry

- Hebrew and Jewish epic poetry

- Ghazal

- Latin poetry

1.3   See also

- Ethnopoetics

- Latin American poetry

Chapter 2

The History of English Poetry

This article is about the book by Thomas Warton. For a historical survey of English poetry, see English poetry.
The History of English Poetry, from the Close of the Eleventh to the Commencement of the Eighteenth Century (1774-1781) by Thomas Warton was a pioneering and influential literary history. Only three full volumes were ever published, going as far as Queen Elizabeth's reign, but their account of English poetry in the late Middle Ages and Renaissance was unrivalled for many years, and played a part in steering British literary taste towards Romanticism. It is generally acknowledged to be the first narrative English literary history.[1][2][3]

2.1 Composition and content

Warton probably began researching the *History* in the 1750s, but did not actually begin writing in earnest until 1769.[4] He conceived of his work as tracing "the transitions from barbarism to civility" in English poetry, but alongside this view of progress went a Romantic love of medieval poetry for its own sake.[5][6] The first volume, published in 1774 with a second edition the following year,[7] is prefaced with two dissertations: one on "The Origin of Romantic Fiction in Europe", which he believed to lie in the Islamic world, and the other on "The Introduction of Learning into England", which deals with the revival of interest in Classical literature.[8][9] Then begins the *History* proper. Warton decided to give no account of Anglo-Saxon poetry, ostensibly because it lay before "that era, when our national character began to dawn", though doubtless really because his knowledge of the language was too slight to serve him.[10] Instead he began with the impact of the Norman Conquest on the English language, before moving on to the vernacular chronicles. Then follow a series of studies of various Middle English romances, of *Piers Plowman*, and of Early Scots historical writing. The volume ends with a long and detailed look at the works of Geoffrey Chaucer. The second volume appeared in 1788. It deals with John Gower, Thomas Hoccleve, John Lydgate, and the controversy over the authenticity of Thomas Rowley's poems (actually forgeries by Thomas Chatterton, as Warton shows), before moving on to Stephen Hawes and other poets of the reigns of Henry VII. He studies the Scottish Chaucerians in some detail, then returns to England and John Skelton. The volume ends with chapters on the mystery plays, and on continental humanism and the Reformation. The third volume, published in 1791, begins with a dissertation on the Gesta Romanorum, one of many sections of the *History* to fall out of chronological sequence.[11] He moves on to the Earl of Surrey, Thomas Wyatt, *Tottel's Miscellany*, John Heywood, Thomas More, and another out-of-sequence study, this time of the Middle English romance of *Ywain and Gawain*. Then come *The Mirror for Magistrates*, Thomas Sackville, Richard Edwardes, and finally a general survey of Elizabethan poetry. His fourth volume was never published complete, though 88 pages of it were printed in 1789.[7] It is often said that attacks on the *History* by the antiquary Joseph Ritson were the cause of Warton's publishing no more, but other theories have been suggested: that he found the wide variety of 16th century literature difficult to bring within a simple narrative structure; that he found himself unable to reconcile his Romantic and Classical attitudes towards early poetry;[12] that the further he left his greatest love, the era of romance, behind him the less interested he became;[6] that an alternative project of editing Milton had captured his interest; or that he was just congenitally lazy.[4]

THE

HISTORY

OF

ENGLISH POETRY,

FROM THE

CLOSE of the ELEVENTH

TO THE

COMMENCEMENT of the EIGHTEENTH CENTURY.

TO WHICH ARE PREFIXED

TWO DISSERTATIONS.

I. On the Origin of ROMANTIC FICTION in EUROPE.
II. On the Introduction of LEARNING into ENGLAND.

V O L. II.

By THOMAS WARTON, B. D.

Fellow of Trinity College, Oxford, and of the Society of Antiquaries, and
late Professor of Poetry in the University of Oxford.

L O N D O N:

Printed for, and fold by, J. Dodsley, Pall-Mall; J. Walter, Charing-Crofs; J. Robson,
New Bond-Street; G. Robinson, and J. Bew, Pater-nofter-Row; and
Meffrs. Fletcher, at Oxford.   M.DCC.LXXVIII.

Title page of the first edition of volume 2

2.2 Later editions

As the state of medievalist scholarship advanced the need for revision in Warton's *History* became increasingly felt. In 1824 a new and expanded edition of the *History* was published, with additional notes by, among others, Joseph Ritson, George Ashby, Francis Douce, Thomas Park, and the editor, Richard Price. The 1840 edition, by Richard Taylor, contained further notes by Frederic Madden, Thomas Wright, Richard Garnett, Benjamin Thorpe, J. M. Kemble and others. Finally, William Carew Hazlitt edited the *History* afresh in 1871. The contributors to this version included Frederic Madden, Thomas Wright, Walter Skeat, Richard Morris and Frederick Furnivall.[13][14]

2.3 Critical reception and influence

Warton's *History* had all the advantages and disadvantages of a pioneering work. Being almost the first work to give general readers any information on Middle English poetry it had the attraction of novelty, leading to a generally favourable response to the first edition. *The Gentleman's Magazine*, reviewing the first volume, called it "this capital historical piece", and had no doubt that "every connoisseur will be curious to view the original, and impatient for the completion of it". Of the third volume the same magazine wrote that it "does equal credit to Mr. Warton's taste, judgment, and erudition, and makes us impatiently desirous of more".[4][15] Edward Gibbon mentioned the *History* in *The Decline and Fall of the Roman Empire*, saying it had been accomplished "with the taste of a poet and the minute diligence of an antiquarian".[13] But the praise was not unanimous. Horace Walpole and William Mason both professed themselves annoyed by Warton's habit of throwing in illustrative material indiscriminately.[13] A more dangerous attack came from Joseph Ritson, whose pamphlet *Observations on the Three First Volumes of the History of English Poetry*, bitterly tore into Warton for the many mistranscriptions, misinterpretations, and errors of fact that his book, as the very first attempt to map the Middle English world, inevitably contained.[16] This led to a long and sometimes ill-tempered correspondence in the journals between Warton, Ritson, and their respective supporters. Ritson kept up the attack in successive books through the rest of his life, culminating in the viciously personal "Dissertation on Romance and Minstrelsy" in 1802.[17][18]

By the time the dust had settled from this controversy everyone was aware that the *History* could not be implicitly trusted, but it continued to be loved by a new generation whose taste for the older English poetry Warton's book, along with Percy's *Reliques*, had formed. The influence of those two books on the growth of the Romantic spirit can be illustrated by Robert Southey, who wrote that they had confirmed in him a love of Middle English that had been formed by his discovery of Chaucer; and by Walter Scott's description of the *History* as "an immense commonplace book…from the perusal of which we rise, our fancy delighted with beautiful imagery and with the happy analysis of ancient tale and song".[19][20][4]

In 1899 Sidney Lee wrote that

> Even the mediæval expert of the present day, who finds that much of Warton's information is superannuated and that many of his generalisations have been disproved by later discoveries, realises that nowhere else has he at his command so well furnished an armoury of facts and dates about obscure writers.[21]

The 1911 *Encyclopædia Britannica* confirmed that "his book is still indispensable to the student of English poetry".[11] Though Warton's *History* no longer enjoys the same position as an authority on early poetry, it is still appreciated. Arthur Johnston wrote that

> To the modern scholar reading Warton, it is not his errors in transcripts or dating which attract attention; it is rather the richness of his information, the wealth of documentation, the multitude of his discoveries, his constant alertness to the problems and awareness of the ramifications of his subject.[22]

2.4 Notes

[1]Fairer, David (1981)."The Origins of Warton's*History of English Poetry*".*Review of English Studies***32**: 37–63.doi:10.1093/r. Retrieved 29 June 2014.

[2] Wellek, René (1941). *The Rise of English Literary History*. Chapel Hill: University of North Carolina Press. pp. 199–200.

[3] Mee, Jon (2009). "Warton, Thomas (1728-90)". *An Oxford Companion to the Romantic Age*. Oxford University Press. Retrieved 29 June 2014.

[4] Reid 2004.

[5] Matthews 1999, pp. 30, 32.

[6] Bronson 1938, pp. 316-317.

[7] Rinaker 1916, p. 234.

[8] Matthews 1999, p. 33.

[9] Johnston 1964, p. 108.

[10] Matthews 1999, pp. 30-32.

[11] Encyclopædia Britannica 1911, p. 337.

[12] Matthews 1999, pp. 31-32.

[13] Allibone 1871, p. 2593.

[14] Matthews, David (2000). *The Invention of Middle English: An Anthology of Primary Sources*. University Park, PA: Pennsylvania State University Press. p. 79. ISBN 0271020822. Retrieved 29 June 2014.

[15] Bronson 1938, pp. 316, 318.

[16] Matthews 1999, pp. 36-37.

[17] Burd, Henry Alfred (1916). *Joseph Ritson: A Critical Biography*. Urbana: Illinois University Press. pp. 59–61, 63–64. Retrieved 29 June 2014.

[18] Bronson 1938, pp. 332-344.

[19] Ousby, Ian (1996) [1993]. *The Cambridge Guide to Literature in English*. Cambridge: Cambridge University Press. p. 995. ISBN 0521440866. Retrieved 29 June 2014.

[20] Agrawal, R. R. (1990). *The Medieval Revival and its Influence on the Romantic Movement*. New Delhi: Abhinav. pp. 11, 164. ISBN 8170172624. Retrieved 29 June 2014.

[21] Lee, Sidney (1899). "Warton, Thomas (1728-1790)". In Lee, Sidney. *The Dictionary of National Biography. Volume 59*. London: Smith, Elder. p. 434. Retrieved 29 June 2014.

[22] Johnston 1964, p. 117.

2.5 References

- Allibone, S. Austin (1871). *A Critical Dictionary of English Literature and British and American Authors. Volume 3*. London: Trübner. Retrieved 29 June 2014.

- Bronson, Bertrand H. (1938). *Joseph Ritson, Scholar-at-Arms*. Berkeley: University of California Press.

- *Encyclopædia Britannica* **28**. Cambridge: Cambridge University Press. 1911.

- Johnston, Arthur (1964). *Enchanted Ground: The Study of Medieval Romance in the Eighteenth Century*. London: University of London, Athlone Press.

- Matthews, David (1999). *The Making of Middle English, 1765-1910*. Minneapolis: University of Minnesota Press. ISBN 0816631859. Retrieved 29 June 2014.

- Reid, Hugh (2004). "Warton, Thomas (1728–1790)". *Oxford Dictionary of National Biography*. Oxford University Press. Retrieved 29 June 2014.

- Rinaker, Clarissa (1916). *Thomas Warton: A Biographical and Critical Study*. Urbana: University of Illinois Press.

2.6 External links

- *The History of English Poetry* at the Internet Archive

Chapter 3

History of poetry

For a more in-depth table of the history of poetry, see List of years in poetry.

Poetry as an art form may predate literacy.[1] The earliest poetry is believed to have been recited or sung, employed as a way of remembering oral history, genealogy, and law. Poetry is often closely related to musical traditions, and the earliest poetry exists in the form of hymns (such as the work of Sumerian priestess Enheduanna). Many of the poems surviving from the ancient world are recorded prayers, or stories about religious subject matter, but they also include historical accounts, instructions for everyday activities, love songs,[2] and fiction.

Many scholars, particularly those researching the Homeric tradition and the oral epics of the Balkans, suggest that early writing shows clear traces of older oral traditions, including the use of repeated phrases as building blocks in larger poetic units. A rhythmic and repetitive form would make a long story easier to remember and retell, before writing was available as an aide-memoire. Thus many ancient works, from the Vedas (1700 - 1200 BC) to the *Odyssey* (800 - 675 BC), appear to have been composed in poetic form to aid memorization and oral transmission, in prehistoric and ancient societies.[3] Poetry appears among the earliest records of most literate cultures, with poetic fragments found on early monoliths, runestones and stelae.

The oldest surviving speculative fiction poem is the *Tale of the Shipwrecked Sailor*,[4] written in *Hieratic* and ascribed a date around 2500 B.C.E. Other sources ascribe the earliest written poetry to the *Epic of Gilgamesh* written in *cuneiform*; however, it is most likely that *The Tale of the Shipwrecked Sailor* predates *Gilgamesh* by half a millennium. The oldest epic poetry besides the *Epic of Gilgamesh* are the Greek epics *Iliad* and *Odyssey* and the Indian Sanskrit epics *Ramayana* and *Mahabharata*. The longest epic poems ever written were the *Mahabharata* and the Tibetan *Epic of King Gesar*.

Ancient thinkers sought to determine what makes poetry distinctive as a form and what distinguishes good poetry from bad, resulting in the development of "poetics", or the study of the aesthetics of poetry. Some ancient societies, such as the Chinese through the *Classic of History*, one of the Five Classics, developed canons of poetic works that had ritual as well as aesthetic importance. More recently, thinkers struggled to find a definition that could encompass formal differences as great as those between Chaucer's *The Canterbury Tales* and Matsuo Bashō's Oku no Hosomichi, as well as differences in context that span from the religious poetry of the Tanakh to love poetry to rap.[5]

Context can be critical to poetics and to the development of poetic genres and forms. For example, poetry employed to record historical events in epics, such as *Gilgamesh* or Ferdowsi's *Shahnameh*,[6] will necessarily be lengthy and narrative, while poetry used for liturgical purposes in hymns, psalms, suras and hadiths is likely to have an inspirational tone, whereas elegies and tragedy are intended to invoke deep internal emotional responses. Other contexts include music such as Gregorian chants, formal or diplomatic speech,[7] political rhetoric and invective,[8] light-hearted nursery and nonsense rhymes, threnodies to the deceased and even medical texts.[9]

The Polish historian of aesthetics, Władysław Tatarkiewicz, in a paper on "The Concept of Poetry," traces the evolution of what is *two concepts of poetry*. Tatarkiewicz points out that the term is applied to two distinct things that, as the poet Paul Valéry observes, "at a certain point find union. Poetry [...] is an art based on *language*. But poetry also has a more general meaning [...] that is difficult to define because it is less determinate: poetry expresses a certain *state of mind*."

The Deluge tablet, carved in stone, of the Gilgamesh epic in Akkadian, circa 2nd millennium BC.

3.1 Classical and early modern Western traditions

Classical thinkers employed classification as a way to define and assess the quality of poetry. Notably, Aristotle's *Poetics* describes the three genres of poetry: the epic, comic, and tragic, and develops rules to distinguish the highest-quality poetry of each genre, based on the underlying purposes of that genre.[10] Later aestheticians identified three major genres:

epic poetry, lyric poetry and dramatic poetry, treating comedy and tragedy as subgenres of dramatic poetry. Aristotle's work was influential throughout the Middle East during the Islamic Golden Age,[11] as well as in Europe during the Renaissance.[12] Later poets and aestheticians often distinguished poetry from, and defined it in opposition to, prose, which was generally understood as writing with a proclivity to logical explication and global trade. In addition to a boom in translation, during the Romantic period numerous ancient works were rediscovered.

3.2   History and development of Chinese poetry

The *Classic of Poetry*, often known by its original name of the *Odes* or *Poetry* is the earliest existing collection of Chinese poems and songs. This poetry collection comprises 305 poems and songs dating from the 10th to the 7th century BC.The stylistic development of Classical Chinese poetry consists of both literary and oral cultural processes, which are conventionally assigned to certain standard periods or eras, corresponding with Chinese Dynastic Eras, the traditional chronological process for Chinese historical events. The poems preserved in written form constitute the poetic literature. Furthermore, there is or were parallel traditions of oral and traditional poetry also known as popular or folk poems or ballads. Some of these poems seem to have been preserved in written form. Generally, the folk type of poems they are anonymous, and may show signs of having been edited or polished in the process of fixing them in written characters. Besides the *Classic of Poetry*, or *Shijing*, another early text is the *Songs of the South* (or, *Chuci*), although some individual pieces or fragments survive in other forms, for example embedded in classical histories or other literature.

3.3   Modern developments

The development of modern poetry is generally seen as having started at the beginning of the 20th century and extends into the 21st century. Among its major practitioners are Robert Frost, Wallace Stevens, and Anne Carson.

The use of verse to transmit cultural information continues today. Many Americans know that "in 1492, Columbus sailed the ocean blue". An alphabet song teaches the names and order of the letters of the alphabet; another jingle states the lengths and names of the months in the Gregorian calendar. Some writers believe poetry has its origins in song. Most of the characteristics that distinguish it from other forms of utterance—rhythm, rhyme, compression, intensity of feeling, the use of refrains—appear to have come about from efforts to fit words to musical forms. In the European tradition the earliest surviving poems, the Homeric and Hesiodic epics, identify themselves as poems to be recited or chanted to a musical accompaniment rather than as pure song. Another interpretation is that rhythm, refrains, and kennings are essentially paratactic devices that enable the reciter to reconstruct the poem from memory.

In preliterate societies, these forms of poetry were composed for, and sometimes during, performance. There was a certain degree of fluidity to the exact wording of poems. The introduction of writing fixed the content of a poem to the version that happened to be written down and survive. Written composition meant poets began to compose for an absent reader. The invention of printing accelerated these trends. Poets were now writing more for the eye than for the ear.

3.4   Lyric poetry

The development of literacy gave rise to more personal, shorter poems intended to be sung. These are called lyrics, which derives from the Greek *lura* or lyre, the instrument that was used to accompany the performance of Greek lyrics from about the seventh century BC onward. The Greek's practice of singing hymns in large choruses gave rise in the sixth century BC to dramatic verse, and to the practice of writing poetic plays for performance in their theatres. In more recent times, the introduction of electronic media and the rise of the poetry reading have led to a resurgence of performance poetry in the lyric genre.

3.5   References

[1] http://www.yukon-news.com/arts/poet-goes-from-newsprint-to-verse/

[2] http://www.nytimes.com/2006/02/14/international/europe/14poem.html

[3] For one recent summary discussion, see Frederick Ahl, *The Odyssey Re-Formed* (1996). Others suggest that poetry did not necessarily predate writing. See, for example, Jack Goody, *The Interface Between the Written and the Oral* (1987).

[4] UCSC Daniel Seldon Professor of AfroAsiatic studies

[5] See, for example, Ribeiro, Anna Christina. 'Intending to Repeat: A Definition of Poetry'. Journal of Aesthetics and Art Criticism 65:2, 2007.

[6] Abolqasem Ferdowsi, Dick Davis trans., *Shahnameh: The Persian Book of Kings* (2006) ISBN 0-670-03485-1

[7] For example, in the Arabic world, much diplomacy was carried out through poetic form in the 16th century. See *Trickster's Travel's*, Natalie Zemon Davis (2006).

[8] Examples of political invective include libel poetry and the classical epigrams of Martial and Catullus.

[9] For example, many of Ibn Sina's medical texts were written in verse.

[10] *Aristotle's Poetics*, Heath (ed) 1997.

[11] Ibn Rushd (Averroes) wrote a commentary on Aristotle's *Poetics*, replacing the original examples with passages from Arabic poets. See for example, W. F. Boggess, 'Hermannus Alemannus' Latin Anthology of Arabic Poetry,' *Journal of the American Oriental Society,* 1968, Volume 88, 657-70, and Charles Burnett, 'Learned Knowledge of Arabic Poetry, Rhymed Prose, and Didactic Verse from Petrus Alfonsi to Petrarch', in *Poetry and Philosophy in the Middle Ages: A Festschrift for Peter Dronke,* 2001. ISBN 90-04-11964-7.

[12] See, for example, Paul F Grendler, *The Universities of the Italian Renaissance,* Johns Hopkins University Press, 2004. ISBN 0-8018-8055-6 (for example, page 239) for the prominence of Aristotle and the *Poetics* on the Renaissance curriculum.

The Oldest Love Poem at the Istanbul Archaeology Museums

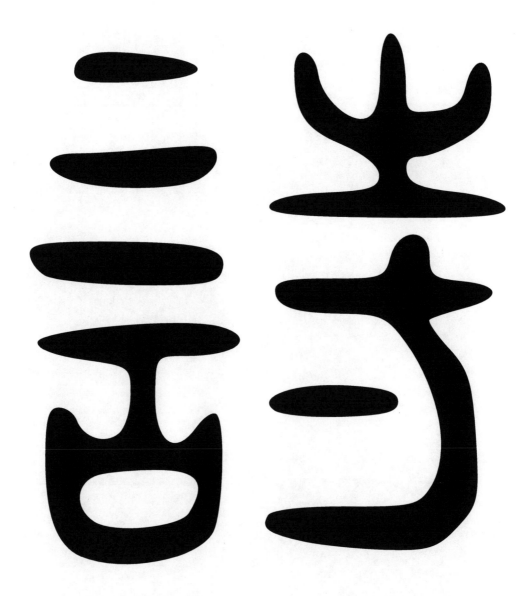

The character which means "poetry", in the ancient Chinese Great Seal script style. The modern character is 詩/诗 (shī).

Manuscript of the Rig Veda, Sanskrit verse composed in the 2nd millennium BC.

Chapter 5

List of years in poetry

This page gives a chronological **list of years in poetry** (descending order). These pages supplement the List of years in literature pages with a focus on events in the history of poetry.

5.1 21st century in poetry

5.1.1 2010s

- **2015 in poetry**

- **2014 in poetry** Death of Madeline Gins, Amiri Baraka, Juan Gelman, José Emilio Pacheco, Maya Angelou

- **2013 in poetry** Death of Thomas McEvilley, Taylor Mead, Seamus Heaney

- **2012 in poetry** Günter Grass's poem "What Must Be Said" leads to him being declared *persona non grata*; Death of Adrienne Rich, Wisława Szymborska

- **2011 in poetry** Tomas Tranströmer awarded the Nobel Prize in Literature; Liz Lochhead succeeds Edwin Morgan as The Scots Makar; Death of Josephine Hart, Václav Havel, Robert Kroetsch

- **2010 in poetry** Seamus Heaney's *Human Chain*; Death of Tuli Kupferberg, Peter Orlovsky, P. Lal, Edwin Morgan

5.1.2 2000s

- **2009 in poetry** Turkish government posthumously restores Nâzım Hikmet's citizenship, stripped from him because of his beliefs; Ruth Padel the first woman elected Oxford Professor of Poetry, only to resign in controversy before taking office; Carol Ann Duffy succeeds Andrew Motion as the UK's Poet Laureate; Elizabeth Alexander reads "Praise Song for the Day" at presidential inauguration of U.S. President Barack Obama; Death of Dennis Brutus, Jim Carroll, Nicholas Hughes (son of Ted Hughes and Sylvia Plath)

- **2008 in poetry** Death of Harold Pinter, Jonathan Williams

- **2007 in poetry** Death of William Morris Meredith, Jr., Emmett Williams

- **2006 in poetry** Seamus Heaney's *District and Circle*; Death of Stanley Kunitz

- **2005 in poetry** Harold Pinter awarded the Nobel Prize in Literature; Death of Philip Lamantia, Robert Creeley

- **2004 in poetry** Seamus Heaney reads "Beacons of Bealtaine" for 25 leaders of the enlarged European Union; Edwin Morgan named as The Scots Makar; Death of Janet Frame, Jackson Mac Low, Czesław Miłosz

- **2003 in poetry** John Paul II's *Roman Triptych (Meditation)*; Kenneth Rexroth's *Complete Poems* (posthumous)

- **2002 in poetry** Death of Kenneth Koch

- **2001 in poetry** Seamus Heaney's *Electric Light*; First-ever Griffin Poetry Prize in Canada; Death of Gregory Corso

- **2000 in poetry** Death of Yehuda Amichai, Ahmad Shamlou

5.2   20th century in poetry

5.2.1   1990s

- **1999 in poetry** Andrew Motion succeeds Ted Hughes as the UK's Poet Laureate; Death of Edward Dorn

- **1998 in poetry** Ted Hughes's *Birthday Letters*; Death of Zbigniew Herbert, Ted Hughes, Octavio Paz

- **1997 in poetry** Death of William Burroughs, Allen Ginsberg, James Dickey, Denise Levertov, David Ignatow, James Laughlin, William Matthews

- **1996 in poetry** Seamus Heaney's *The Spirit Level*; Wisława Szymborska awarded the Nobel Prize in Literature; Death of Joseph Brodsky

- **1995 in poetry** Seamus Heaney awarded the Nobel Prize in Literature; Death of May Sarton, Sir Stephen Spender CBE, David Avidan

- **1994 in poetry** Death of Charles Bukowski

- **1993 in poetry** Maya Angelou reads "On the Pulse of Morning" at the inauguration of U.S. President Bill Clinton

- **1992 in poetry** Derek Walcott awarded the Nobel Prize in Literature; Death of Eve Merriam

- **1991 in poetry** Death of Dr. Seuss, James Schuyler, Howard Nemerov

- **1990 in poetry** Octavio Paz awarded the Nobel Prize in Literature; Death of Lawrence Durrell

5.2.2   1980s

- **1989 in poetry** Death of Samuel Beckett, Robert Penn Warren, May Swenson

- **1988 in poetry** Death of Máirtín Ó Direáin, Miguel Piñero, Robert Duncan

- **1987 in poetry** Joseph Brodsky awarded the Nobel Prize in Literature; Ezra Pound and Louis Zukofsky, *Pound/Zukofsky: Selected Letters of Ezra Pound and Louis Zukofsky*, edited by Barry Ahearn (Faber & Faber)[1]

- **1986 in poetry** Wole Soyinka awarded the Nobel Prize in Literature; Death of John Ciardi, Jean Genet, Jaroslav Seifert

- **1985 in poetry** Death of Robert Graves, Philip Larkin

- **1984 in poetry** Jaroslav Seifert awarded the Nobel Prize in Literature; Ted Hughes succeeds John Betjeman as the UK's Poet Laureate (on the refusal of Philip Larkin); Death of George Oppen

- **1983 in poetry** Death of Ted Berrigan, Edwin Denby

- **1982 in poetry** Death of Kenneth Rexroth, Archibald MacLeish, Djuna Barnes

- **1981 in poetry** Death of Christy Brown

- **1980 in poetry** Czesław Miłosz awarded the Nobel Prize in Literature; Death of Muriel Rukeyser

5.2.3 1970s

- **1979 in poetry** Death of Elizabeth Bishop; Jacqueline Osherow is awarded the Chancellor's Gold Medal for an English Poem

- **1978 in poetry** Death of Micheál Mac Liammóir

- **1977 in poetry** Death of Robert Lowell, Vladimir Nabokov, Seán Ó Ríordáin

- **1976 in poetry**

- **1975 in poetry**

- **1974 in poetry** - Death of Miguel Ángel Asturias, Anne Sexton; Philip Larkin's *High Windows*

- **1973 in poetry** - Death of W. H. Auden, Pablo Neruda, J. R. R. Tolkien

- **1972 in poetry** - John Betjeman succeeds Cecil Day-Lewis as the UK's Poet Laureate; Death of John Berryman, Kenneth Patchen, Padraic Colum, Marianne Moore, Richard Church, Cecil Day-Lewis, Ezra Pound, Mark Van Doren, Paul Goodman

- **1971 in poetry** Pablo Neruda awarded the Nobel Prize in Literature; Death of Jim Morrison, Ogden Nash

- **1970 in poetry** Death of Nelly Sachs, Charles Olson, Paul Celan, Leah Goldberg

5.2.4 1960s

- **1969 in poetry** Samuel Beckett awarded the Nobel Prize in Literature; Death of Jack Kerouac, André Salmon

- **1968 in poetry** Leonard Cohen, *Selected Poems, 1956-1968*

- **1967 in poetry** Cecil Day-Lewis selected as the UK's new Poet Laureate (succeeding John Masefield); Death of Patrick Kavanagh, John Masefield, Carl Sandburg

- **1966 in poetry** Seamus Heaney's *Death of a Naturalist*; Death of Anna Akhmatova, André Breton, Frank O'Hara, Basil Bunting's *Briggflatts*

- **1965 in poetry** Death of T. S. Eliot

- **1964 in poetry** John Lennon's *In His Own Write*, containing nonsensical poems, sketches and drawings (a best seller by the member of The Beatles); Something Else Press founded by Dick Higgins in 1963 (publishes concrete poetry by several authors, starting in 1964), Philip Larkin's *The Whitsun Weddings*; Death of Brendan Behan, Dame Edith Sitwell DBE

- **1963 in poetry** Bob Dylan's album *The Freewheelin' Bob Dylan* released (with his most influential early song-writing); Death of Nâzım Hikmet, Louis MacNeice, Sylvia Plath, Robert Frost, William Carlos Williams, Tristan Tzara, Jean Cocteau

- **1962 in poetry** Death of E. E. Cummings

- **1961 in poetry** Allen Ginsberg's *Kaddish and Other Poems*; death of H. D.

- **1960 in poetry** Death of Boris Pasternak

5.2.5   1950s

- **1959 in poetry** Death of Edgar Guest

- **1958 in poetry** Boris Pasternak awarded the Nobel Prize in Literature; Death of Alfred Noyes, Robert W. Service; Ezra Pound's indictment for treason is dismissed.[2] He is released from St. Elizabeths Hospital, an insane asylum in Maryland, after spending 12 years there (starting in 1946)

- **1957 in poetry** Howl obscenity trial in San Francisco, Ted Hughes's *The Hawk in the Rain*; Death of Oliver St. John Gogarty

- **1956 in poetry** Allen Ginsberg's *Howl and Other Poems*, a signature of the Beat Generation published by City Lights Books, United States; Birth of Cathal Ó Searcaigh

- **1955 in poetry** Discovery of the *Hinilawod* by F. Landa Jocano; Death of Wallace Stevens; Birth of Paula Meehan, William Wall

- **1954 in poetry**

- **1953 in poetry** Death of Dylan Thomas; Birth of Frank McGuinness

- **1952 in poetry** Death of Paul Éluard, George Santayana; Birth of Nuala Ní Dhomhnaill

- **1951 in poetry** Birth of Paul Muldoon

- **1950 in poetry** Death of Edna St. Vincent Millay; Birth of Mary Dorcey, Medbh McGuckian

5.2.6   1940s

- **1949 in poetry** Birth of Gabriel Rosenstock

- **1948 in poetry** T. S. Eliot awarded the Nobel Prize in Literature

- **1947 in poetry** Cleanth Brooks's *The Well Wrought Urn: Studies in the Structure of Poetry* (a classic statement of the New Criticism); Birth of Dermot Healy

- **1946 in poetry** "On Raglan Road" first published, with the title "Dark Haired Miriam Ran Away"; Ezra Pound brought back to the United States on treason charges, but found unfit to face trial because of insanity and sent to St. Elizabeths Hospital in Washington, D.C., where he remained for 12 years; Death of Gertrude Stein

- **1945 in poetry** Death of Paul Valéry, Robert Desnos, Zinaida Gippius; Birth of Van Morrison, OBE

- **1944 in poetry** Birth of Eavan Boland, Paul Durcan

- **1943 in poetry** Death of Stephen Vincent Benét, William Soutar in Perth; Birth of Jim Morrison; T. S. Eliot's *Four Quartets* published as a whole

- **1942 in poetry** Birth of William Matthews, Eiléan Ní Chuilleanáin; Death of Konstantin Balmont

- **1941 in poetry** Death of James Joyce, Marina Tsvetaeva; Birth of Bob Dylan, Derek Mahon

- **1940 in poetry** Birth of Joseph Brodsky, John Lennon

5.2.7   1930s

- **1939 in poetry** Death of W. B. Yeats; Birth of Seamus Heaney, Michael Longley

- **1938 in poetry** Death of Osip Mandelstam

- **1937 in poetry** *Lahuta e Malcís* - Gjergj Fishta; First-ever Governor General's Literary Awards in Canada; Birth of Diane Wakoski

- **1936 in poetry** Killing of Federico García Lorca, Death of Rudyard Kipling; Birth of John Giorno

- **1935 in poetry** Charles G. D. Roberts knighted for his poetry; Anna Akhmatova begins publishing her cycle of poems *Requiem*

- **1934 in poetry** Death of Andrei Bely; Birth of Leonard Cohen, Wole Soyinka

- **1933 in poetry** *The Winding Stair* - W.B. Yeats; Death of Sara Teasdale; Birth of Yevgeny Yevtushenko

- **1932 in poetry** Death of Hart Crane; Birth of Christy Brown, Michael McClure, David Antin, Sylvia Plath

- **1931 in poetry** Death of Vachel Lindsay, Kahlil Gibran; Birth of Tomas Tranströmer

- **1930 in poetry** John Masefield succeeds Robert Bridges as the UK's Poet Laureate; Death of Robert Bridges, D. H. Lawrence, Vladimir Mayakovsky; birth of Gary Snyder, Adunis, Harold Pinter, Derek Walcott

5.2.8   1920s

- **1929 in poetry** Pulitzer Prize for Poetry awarded to Stephen Vincent Benét for *John Brown's Body*; Birth of Ed Dorn, John Montague

- **1928 in poetry** *The Tower (book)* - W.B. Yeats; Birth of Maya Angelou, Thomas Kinsella; Death of Thomas Hardy

- **1927 in poetry** William Soutar creates his *Epigram form* of the Cinquain; Birth of John Ashbery

- **1926 in poetry** Death of Rainer Maria Rilke, Birth of Allen Ginsberg, Robert Creeley, Frank O'Hara

- **1925 in poetry** Death of Sergei Yesenin, Birth of Ahmad Shamlou

- **1924 in poetry** Birth of Yehuda Amichai, Janet Frame, Zbigniew Herbert

- **1923 in poetry** W. B. Yeats is the first Irishman awarded the Nobel Prize in Literature; Edna St. Vincent Millay is the first woman to win the Pulitzer Prize for Poetry; Birth of Brendan Behan, Wisława Szymborska

- **1922 in poetry** T. S. Eliot's "The Waste Land"; Rainer Maria Rilke completes both the *Duino Elegies* and the *Sonnets to Orpheus*; Birth of Jack Kerouac, Máire Mhac an tSaoi

- **1921 in poetry** Death of Alexander Blok

- **1920 in poetry** The *Epic of Manas* is published; approximate date of Mikhail Khudiakov's *Dorvyzhy*; *The Dial*, a longstanding American literary magazine, is re-established by Scofield Thayer, with the publication becoming an important outlet for Modernist poets and writers (until 1929), with contributors this year including Sherwood Anderson, Djuna Barnes, Kenneth Burke, Hart Crane, E. E. Cummings, Charles Demuth, Kahlil Gibran, Gaston Lachaise, Amy Lowell, Marianne Moore, Ezra Pound, Odilon Redon, Bertrand Russell, Carl Sandburg, Van Wyck Brooks, and W. B. Yeats; Birth of Paul Celan, Charles Bukowski

5.2.9   1910s

- **1919 in poetry** Birth of - Lawrence Ferlinghetti, Robert Duncan, May Swenson, William Meredith

- **1918 in poetry** Death of Guillaume Apollinaire, Wilfred Owen; Gerard Manley Hopkins's *Poems* published posthumously by Robert Bridges

- **1917 in poetry** Birth of Robert Lowell; T. S. Eliot's *Prufrock and other Observations*

- **1916 in poetry** The Dada movement in art, poetry and literature coalesced at Cabaret Voltaire in Zurich, Switzerland, where Hugo Ball, Emmy Hennings, Tristan Tzara, Hans Arp, Richard Huelsenbeck, Sophie Täuber and others discussed art and put on performances expressing their disgust with World War I and the interests they believed inspired it; Death of Patrick Pearse, Joseph Mary Plunkett; Birth of Tom Kettle

- **1915 in poetry** Death of Rupert Brooke

- **1914 in poetry** Death of Adelaide Crapsey; Birth of William Burroughs, Octavio Paz, Dylan Thomas

- **1913 in poetry** Robert Bridges succeeds Alfred Austin as the UK's Poet Laureate; The launch of Imagism in the pages of *Poetry* magazine by H.D., Richard Aldington and Ezra Pound, Robert Frost's *A Boy's Will*; Death of Alfred Austin, Lesya Ukrainka; birth of R. S. Thomas

- **1912 in poetry** Adelaide Crapsey creates her *couplet* form

- **1911 in poetry** Adelaide Crapsey creates the *American Cinquain* form; Birth of Leah Goldberg, Czesław Miłosz

- **1910 in poetry** Death of Julia Ward Howe; Birth of Charles Olson, Jean Genet

5.2.10   1900s

- **1909 in poetry** Death of Sarah Orne Jewett; Birth of Stephen Spender

- **1908 in poetry**

- **1907 in poetry** Rudyard Kipling awarded the Nobel Prize in Literature; Birth of W. H. Auden, Louis MacNeice

- **1906 in poetry** Alfred Noyes publishes *The Highwayman*; Birth of Samuel Beckett

- **1905 in poetry**

- **1904 in poetry** Birth of Cecil Day-Lewis, Patrick Kavanagh, Pablo Neruda

- **1903 in poetry**

- **1902 in poetry** Death of Shiki the haiku poet; Birth of Langston Hughes ; Giles Lytton Strachey is awarded the Chancellor's Gold Medal for an English Poem

- **1901 in poetry** Birth of Jaroslav Seifert

- **1900 in poetry** Death of Oscar Wilde

5.3   19th century in poetry

5.3.1   1890s

- **1899 in poetry** Birth of Hart Crane, Micheál Mac Liammóir, Vladimir Nabokov

- **1898 in poetry** Death of Stéphane Mallarmé, Lewis Carroll; Birth of Stephen Vincent Benét, Federico García Lorca, William Soutar

- **1897 in poetry**

- **1896 in poetry** Death of Paul Verlaine

- **1895 in poetry** Birth of Robert Graves, Sergei Yesenin

- **1894 in poetry** Death of Charles Marie René Leconte de Lisle, Oliver Wendell Holmes, Sr.

- **1893 in poetry** Birth of Vladimir Mayakovsky

- **1892 in poetry** Emily Dickinson First collection published; Death of Walt Whitman James Russell Lowell, Alfred Lord Tennyson, Afanasy Fet; Birth of Marina Tsvetaeva, Hugh MacDiarmid

- **1891 in poetry** Death of Arthur Rimbaud, Herman Melville; Birth of Nelly Sachs, Osip Mandelstam

- **1890 in poetry** Birth of Boris Pasternak

5.3.2   1880s

- **1889 in poetry** Birth of Anna Akhmatova; death of Gerard Manley Hopkins

- **1888 in poetry** Birth of T. S. Eliot

- **1887 in poetry** *Lāčplēsis* by Andrejs Pumpurs; Birth of Marianne Moore, Joseph Plunkett, Edith Sitwell DBE

- **1886 in poetry** Death of Emily Dickinson; birth of H.D.

- **1885 in poetry** Birth of D. H. Lawrence, Ezra Pound; Death of Victor Hugo

- **1884 in poetry**

- **1883 in poetry** Birth of William Carlos Williams

- **1882 in poetry** Death of Ralph Waldo Emerson, Henry Wadsworth Longfellow; Birth of James Joyce, A. A. Milne

- **1881 in poetry**

- **1880 in poetry** Birth of Guillaume Apollinaire, Andrei Bely, Tom Kettle, Alfred Noyes, Alexander Blok

5.3.3   1870s

- **1879 in poetry** Birth of Patrick Pearse, Wallace Stevens

- **1878 in poetry** Birth of Oliver St. John Gogarty, Carl Sandburg, John Edward Masefield, Adelaide Crapsey

- **1877 in poetry** Jacint Verdaguer's *L'Atlàntida*

- **1876 in poetry**

- **1875 in poetry** French translation of Edgar Allan Poe's "The Raven", by Stéphane Mallarmé with drawings by Édouard Manet; - Birth of Rainer Maria Rilke, important pre-modernist 20th-century poet in German.

- **1874 in poetry** Arthur Rimbaud's *Illuminations*First collection of George Eliot's poetry; - Birth of Gertrude Stein, Robert Frost, important American poet

- **1873 in poetry** Arthur Rimbaud's *Une Saison en Enfer (A Season in Hell)*; Publication of *Daredevils of Sassoun*; Death of Fyodor Tyutchev

- **1872 in poetry** Christina Rossetti's *In the Bleak Midwinter* (Christmas carol); José Hernández's *Martín Fierro*; Michel Rodange's *Rénert the Fox*

- **1871 in poetry** Lewis Carroll published, *Through the Looking-Glass*, including the complete *Jabberwocky*. Arthur Rimbaud wrote "Letters of the Seer." Birth of Lesya Ukrainka, important Ukrainian poet

- **1870 in poetry**

5.3.4   1860s

- **1869 in poetry** George Eliot sonnet **Brother & Sister**; Birth of Zinaida Gippius, important Russian poet

- **1868 in poetry**

- **1867 in poetry** Death of Charles Baudelaire, French poet and art critic; Birth of Shiki the haiku poet, Konstantin Balmont, Russian symbolist poet

- **1866 in poetry**

- **1865 in poetry** Birth of William Butler Yeats, Rudyard Kipling

- **1864 in poetry** Death of John Clare, Walter Savage Landor

- **1863 in poetry**

- **1862 in poetry** Christina Rossetti *Goblin Market*, George Meredith's *Modern Love*

- **1861 in poetry** Death of Taras Shevchenko

- **1860 in poetry**

5.3.5   1850s

- **1859 in poetry** Death of Leigh Hunt

- **1858 in poetry** Henry Wadsworth Longfellow, *The Courtship of Miles Standish*

- **1857 in poetry** Charles Baudelaire's *Les Fleurs du mal*

- **1856 in poetry** Death of Heinrich Heine; - *Aurora Leigh* by Elizabeth Barrett Browning

- **1855 in poetry** Walt Whitman's *Leaves of Grass*, a first stanza of Lewis Carroll's *Jabberwocky*, Henry Wadsworth Longfellow's *Song of Hiawatha*; - Death of Adam Mickiewicz

- **1854 in poetry** Birth of Arthur Rimbaud

- **1853 in poetry** First and unprinted version of Friedrich Reinhold Kreutzwals's *Kalevipoeg*

- **1852 in poetry** Death of Thomas Moore

- **1851 in poetry**

- **1850 in poetry** Elizabeth Barrett Browning, *Sonnets from the Portuguese*; Robert Browning *Christmas-Eve and Easter-Day*; - Death of William Wordsworth

5.3.6   1840s

- **1849 in poetry** Death of Edgar Allan Poe, Edgar Allan Poe's *Annabel Lee*, Birth of Sarah Orne Jewett (Martha's Lady)

- **1848 in poetry** Founding of Pre-Raphaelite Brotherhood

- **1847 in poetry** Henry Wadsworth Longfellow's *Evangeline*; Petar II Petrović-Njegoš's *The Mountain Wreath*

- **1846 in poetry**

- **1845 in poetry** Edgar Allan Poe's *The Raven*

- **1844 in poetry** Birth of Paul Verlaine

- **1843 in poetry** William Wordsworth becomes Poet Laureate

- **1842 in poetry** Birth of Stéphane Mallarmé

- **1841 in poetry** Death of Mikhail Lermontov

- **1840 in poetry** Birth of Thomas Hardy

5.3.7 1830s

- **1839 in poetry**

- **1838 in poetry** *Florante at Laura* by Francisco Balagtas

- **1837 in poetry** Death of Aleksandr Pushkin

- **1836 in poetry**

- **1835 in poetry** *The Kalevala* by Elias Lönnrot; The *Baptism on the Savica* by France Prešeren

- **1834 in poetry** *Pan Tadeusz* by Adam Mickiewicz; Death of Samuel Taylor Coleridge

- **1833 in poetry**

- **1832 in poetry** Birth of Lewis Carroll; - Death of Sir Walter Scott, Johann Wolfgang von Goethe

- **1831 in poetry** Birth of Emily Dickinson

- **1830 in poetry** Birth of Christina Rossetti in London

5.3.8 1820s

- **1829 in poetry** Alfred Lord Tennyson is awarded the Chancellor's Gold Medal for an English Poem

- **1828 in poetry** Birth of Dante Gabriel Rossetti

- **1827 in poetry** Death of William Blake

- **1826 in poetry** Death of Issa the haiku poet

- **1825 in poetry** Alexander Pushkin begins publishing *Eugene Onegin* in serial form

- **1824 in poetry** Death of Lord Byron, important English Romantic poet

- **1823 in poetry** Birth of Sándor Petőfi, Hungarian national poet; Winthrop Mackworth Praed is awarded the Chancellor's Gold Medal for an English Poem

- **1822 in poetry** Lord Byron *The Vision of Judgment*; Death of Percy Bysshe Shelley, important English Romantic poet

- **1821 in poetry** Death of John Keats, important English Romantic poet; - Birth of Charles Baudelaire, French poet and art critic

- **1820 in poetry**

5.3.9   1810s

- **1819 in poetry** Scholars described - *The Great Year* for John Keats, who publishes his famous *Odes*; *Don Juan (Byron)* - Lord Byron; - Birth of George Eliot, Walt Whitman, important American poet, Herman Melville, American poet, novelist, James Russell Lowell, American poet, Julia Ward Howe, American poet

- **1818 in poetry** Lord Byron's *Childe Harold's Pilgrimage, Book IV*, published; - Birth of Charles Marie René Leconte de Lisle; - Mary Shelley (*née* Mary Wollstonecraft Godwin publishes *Frankenstein; or, The Modern Prometheus* anonymously; Percy Bysshe Shelley's *Ozymandias*

- **1817 in poetry** Percy Bysshe Shelley, *Laon and Cythna*

- **1816 in poetry** Shelley marries Mary Woolstonecraft Godwin, Lord Byron's *Childe Harold's Pilgrimage, Book III*, published; Samuel Coleridge's *Kubla Khan*

- **1815 in poetry**

- **1814 in poetry** *West-östlicher Diwan* - Johann Wolfgang von Goethe; *She Walks in Beauty* - Lord Byron; Percy Bysshe Shelley and Mary Wollstonecraft Godwin elope to war-ravaged France, accompanied by Godwin's stepsister, Mary Jane. Birth of Mikhail Lermontov, important Russian poet; Birth of Taras Shevchenko, important Ukrainian poet

- **1813 in poetry** The Chancellor's Gold Medal for an English Poem is awarded for the first time. Recipient is George Waddington.

- **1812 in poetry** *Childe Harold's Pilgrimage* - Lord Byron; Birth of Afanasy Fet, important Russian poet

- **1811 in poetry**

- **1810 in poetry** *Milton: a Poem*, epic poem by William Blake, written and illustrated between 1804 and 1810

5.3.10   1800s

- **1809 in poetry** Birth of Edgar Allan Poe, Alfred Lord Tennyson, Oliver Wendell Holmes, Sr. American poet, physician, and essayist

- **1808 in poetry** Johann Wolfgang von Goethe - *Faust, Part One*

- **1807 in poetry** Birth of Henry Wadsworth Longfellow, John Greenleaf Whittier

- **1806 in poetry** Birth of Elizabeth Barrett Browning

- **1805 in poetry** *Jerusalem* poem by William Blake; - Death of Friedrich Schiller, German poet

- **1804 in poetry**

- **1803 in poetry** Birth of Fyodor Tyutchev, important Russian poet

- **1802 in poetry** Birth of Victor Hugo

- **1801 in poetry**

- **1800 in poetry** Death of William Cowper

5.4 18th century in poetry

5.4.1 1790s

- **1799 in poetry** Birth of Aleksandr Pushkin, important Russian poet

- **1798 in poetry** William Wordsworth and Samuel Taylor Coleridge publish *Lyrical Ballads*. Birth of Adam Mickiewicz, important Polish poet

- **1797 in poetry** Birth of Mary Wollstonecraft Godwin, Heinrich Heine

- **1796 in poetry** Death of Robert Burns, James Macpherson

- **1795 in poetry** Birth of John Keats, important English poet; - William Blake, *The Book of Los*, *The Book of Ahania*, *The Song of Los*

- **1794 in poetry** *Songs of Innocence and of Experience: Shewing the Two Contrary States of the Human Soul* two books of poetry and *The Book of Urizen* by English poet and painter William Blake

- **1793 in poetry** William Blake, *Visions of the Daughters of Albion* and *America, A Prophecy*; - Birth of John Clare

- **1792 in poetry** Birth of Percy Bysshe Shelley, important English poet; - William Blake *Song of Liberty*

- **1791 in poetry** William Blake, *The French Revolution*

- **1790 in poetry** William Blake, *The Marriage of Heaven and Hell*

5.4.2 1780s

- **1789 in poetry** William Blake publishes *Songs of Innocence* and *The Book of Thel*

- **1788 in poetry** Birth of Lord Byron, (English)

- **1787 in poetry**

- **1786 in poetry** Robert Burns publishes *Poems Chiefly in the Scottish Dialect*

- **1785 in poetry** William Cowper publishes *The Task*

- **1784 in poetry** Birth of Leigh Hunt; Death of Samuel Johnson English author, wrote Lives of the Most Eminent English Poets, (1779–81)

- **1783 in poetry** Death of Buson the haiku poet

- **1782 in poetry**

- **1781 in poetry**

- **1780 in poetry**

5.4.3 1770s

- **1779 in poetry** Birth of Irish poet Thomas Moore

- **1778 in poetry**

- **1777 in poetry**

- **1776 in poetry**

- **1775 in poetry** Birth of Charles Lamb, Walter Savage Landor

- **1774 in poetry** Birth of Robert Southey; Death of Oliver Goldsmith

- **1773 in poetry** - Eibhlín Dubh Ní Chonaill composes "Caoineadh Airt Uí Laoghaire"

- **1772 in poetry** "Prometheus" - Johann Wolfgang von Goethe; Birth of Samuel Taylor Coleridge

- **1771 in poetry** Death of Thomas Gray, English poet, (born 1716); - Birth of Sir Walter Scott

- **1770 in poetry** Birth of William Wordsworth, important English poet (died 1850); - Death of Thomas Chatterton, 17-year-old English poet and forger of pseudo-medieval poetry born 1752

5.4.4   1760s

- **1769 in poetry**

- **1768 in poetry**

- **1767 in poetry**

- **1766 in poetry**

- **1765 in poetry** Thomas Percy, *Reliques of Ancient English Poetry*; Kristijonas Donelaitis, *The Seasons*

- **1764 in poetry** Oliver Goldsmith, *The Traveller*

- **1763 in poetry** Birth of Samuel Rogers

- **1762 in poetry** Birth of Issa the haiku poet

- **1761 in poetry**

- **1760 in poetry**

5.4.5   1750s

- **1759 in poetry** Birth of Robert Burns, Friedrich Schiller, German poet philosopher, and dramatist (died 1805)

- **1758 in poetry**

- **1757 in poetry**

- **1756 in poetry**

- **1755 in poetry**

- **1754 in poetry**

- **1753 in poetry**

- **1752 in poetry**

- **1751 in poetry**

- **1750 in poetry**

5.4.6 1740s

- **1749 in poetry** Birth of Johann Wolfgang von Goethe, German poet and author
- **1748 in poetry** Death of James Thomson
- **1747 in poetry**
- **1746 in poetry**
- **1745 in poetry** Death of Jonathan Swift, Anglo-Irish satirist, essayist, political pamphleteer, poet
- **1744 in poetry** Death of Alexander Pope, English poet; - Anonymous, *Tommy Thumb's Pretty Song Book*, the first extant collection of nursery rhymes
- **1743 in poetry** Death of Richard Savage, English poet
- **1742 in poetry**
- **1741 in poetry**
- **1740 in poetry**

5.4.7 1730s

- **1739 in poetry**
- **1738 in poetry**
- **1737 in poetry**
- **1736 in poetry** Birth of James Macpherson, Scottish poet
- **1735 in poetry**
- **1734 in poetry**
- **1733 in poetry**
- **1732 in poetry**
- **1731 in poetry**
- **1730 in poetry**

5.4.8 1720s

- **1729 in poetry**
- **1728 in poetry**
- **1727 in poetry**
- **1726 in poetry**
- **1725 in poetry**
- **1724 in poetry**
- **1723 in poetry**
- **1722 in poetry**
- **1721 in poetry**
- **1720 in poetry**

5.4.9   1710s

- **1719 in poetry** Death of Joseph Addison, English essayist and poet

- **1718 in poetry**

- **1717 in poetry**

- **1716 in poetry** First printed version of the *Epic of King Gesar*; First printed version of *The Jangar Epic*; Birth of Thomas Gray, English poet, (died 1771)

- **1715 in poetry** Birth of Buson the haiku poet

- **1714 in poetry** First printed version of *Popol Vuh*

- **1713 in poetry**

- **1712 in poetry**

- **1711 in poetry**

- **1710 in poetry**

5.4.10   1700s

- **1709 in poetry** Birth of Samuel Johnson, English author, biographer

- **1708 in poetry**

- **1707 in poetry**

- **1706 in poetry**

- **1705 in poetry** Death of Michael Wigglesworth (born 1631), English poet, colonist in America called "the most popular of early New England poets"

- **1704 in poetry**

- **1703 in poetry**

- **1702 in poetry**

- **1701 in poetry**

- **1700 in poetry** *Hikayat Hang Tuah*; Death of John Dryden, influential English poet, literary critic, translator and playwright; - Birth of James Thomson, English poet

5.5   17th century in poetry

5.5.1   1690s

- **1699 in poetry**

- **1698 in poetry**

- **1697 in poetry** Birth of Richard Savage, English poet

- **1696 in poetry**

- **1695 in poetry**

- **1694 in poetry** Death of the haiku poet Matsuo Bashō

- **1693 in poetry**

- **1692 in poetry**

- **1691 in poetry**

- **1690 in poetry**

5.5.2 1680s

- **1689 in poetry** - *Oku no Hosomichi* by Matsuo Basho

- **1688 in poetry** Birth of Alexander Pope, English poet

- **1687 in poetry**

- **1686 in poetry**

- **1685 in poetry**

- **1684 in poetry**

- **1683 in poetry**

- **1682 in poetry**

- **1681 in poetry**

- **1680 in poetry**

5.5.3 1670s

- **1679 in poetry**

- **1678 in poetry**

- **1677 in poetry**

- **1676 in poetry**

- **1675 in poetry**

- **1674 in poetry** Death of John Milton, important English poet

- **1673 in poetry**

- **1672 in poetry** Birth of Joseph Addison, English essayist and poet

- **1671 in poetry**

- **1670 in poetry**

5.5.4   1660s

- **1669 in poetry**

- **1668 in poetry**

- **1667 in poetry** Birth of Jonathan Swift, Anglo-Irish satirist, essayist, political pamphleteer, poet

- **1666 in poetry**

- **1665 in poetry**

- **1664 in poetry** Anne Bradstreet, *Meditations Divine and Moral*[3]

- **1663 in poetry**

- **1662 in poetry**

- **1661 in poetry**

- **1660 in poetry**

5.5.5   1650s

- **1659 in poetry**

- **1658 in poetry**

- **1657 in poetry**

- **1656 in poetry**

- **1655 in poetry**

- **1654 in poetry**

- **1653 in poetry**

- **1652 in poetry**

- **1651 in poetry**

- **1650 in poetry**

5.5.6   1640s

- **1649 in poetry**

- **1648 in poetry**

- **1647 in poetry** *The Siege of Sziget* by Miklós Zrínyi; April 1 — birth of John Wilmot, Earl of Rochester (died 1680)

- **1646 in poetry**

- **1645 in poetry**

- **1644 in poetry** Birth of Matsuo Bashō the haiku poet

- **1643 in poetry**

- **1642 in poetry**

- **1641 in poetry**

- **1640 in poetry** - *Biag ni Lam-ang* first transcribed by Pedro Bucaneg

5.5.7 1630s

- **1639 in poetry**

- **1638 in poetry**

- **1637 in poetry** Death of Ben Jonson, important English poet, playwright, actor

- **1636 in poetry**

- **1635 in poetry**

- **1634 in poetry**

- **1633 in poetry**

- **1632 in poetry**

- **1631 in poetry** Death of John Donne, important English poet, essayist, author, preacher; - Birth of John Dryden influential English poet, literary critic, translator and playwright; - Birth of Michael Wigglesworth (died 1705), English poet, colonist in America called "the most popular of early New England poets"[4]

- **1630 in poetry**

5.5.8 1620s

- **1629 in poetry**

- **1628 in poetry**

- **1627 in poetry**

- **1626 in poetry**

- **1625 in poetry**

- **1624 in poetry**

- **1623 in poetry**

- **1622 in poetry**

- **1621 in poetry**

- **1620 in poetry**

5.5.9 1610s

- **1619 in poetry**

- **1618 in poetry** Death of Sir Walter Raleigh

- **1617 in poetry**

- **1616 in poetry** Death of William Shakespeare English poet, playwright and genius

- **1615 in poetry**

- **1614 in poetry** *A Wife,* poem by Sir Thomas Overbury published posthumously

- **1613 in poetry** Death of Thomas Overbury English poet

- **1612 in poetry**

- **1611 in poetry**

- **1610 in poetry**

5.5.10   1600s

- **1609 in poetry** Publication of William Shakespeare's *Sonnets*

- **1608 in poetry** Birth of John Milton, important English poet

- **1607 in poetry**

- **1606 in poetry**

- **1605 in poetry**

- **1604 in poetry**

- **1603 in poetry**

- **1602 in poetry**

- **1601 in poetry**

- **1600 in poetry**

5.6   16th century in poetry

5.6.1   1590s

- **1599 in poetry** Death of Edmund Spenser English poet

- **1598 in poetry**

- **1597 in poetry**

- **1596 in poetry**

- **1595 in poetry**

- **1594 in poetry**

- **1593 in poetry** Birth of George Herbert Welsh poet; - Death of Christopher Marlowe English poet

- **1592 in poetry**

- **1591 in poetry**

- **1590 in poetry**

5.6.2 1580s

- **1589 in poetry**

- **1588 in poetry**

- **1587 in poetry**

- **1586 in poetry** Birth of John Ford English poet and playwright (d. c.1640)

- **1585 in poetry** Death of Pierre de Ronsard

- **1584 in poetry**

- **1583 in poetry**

- **1582 in poetry**

- **1581 in poetry** *Jerusalem Delivered* by Torquato Tasso; Birth of Thomas Overbury English poet (d.1613)

- **1580 in poetry**

5.6.3 1570s

- **1579 in poetry**

- **1578 in poetry**

- **1577 in poetry** Illustrated manuscript of the *Hamzanama*

- **1576 in poetry**

- **1575 in poetry**

- **1574 in poetry**

- **1573 in poetry**

- **1572 in poetry** Luís Vaz de Comões – *Os Lusíadas*; Birth of John Donne, important English poet, essayist, author, preacher; - Birth of Ben Jonson, important English poet, playwright, actor

- **1571 in poetry**

- **1570 in poetry**

5.6.4 1560s

- **1569 in poetry**

- **1568 in poetry**

- **1567 in poetry**

- **1566 in poetry**

- **1565 in poetry**

- **1564 in poetry** Birth of William Shakespeare English poet, playwright, and genius, Christopher Marlowe English poet

- **1563 in poetry**

- **1562 in poetry**

- **1561 in poetry**

- **1560 in poetry**

5.6.5   1550s

- **1559 in poetry**

- **1558 in poetry**

- **1557 in poetry**

- **1556 in poetry**

- **1555 in poetry**

- **1554 in poetry** Miles Huggarde, *The Assault of the Sacrament of the Altar*; Henry Howard, *The Fourth Boke of Virgill, Intreating of the Love Betweene Aeneas & Dido*; Sir David Lindsay, *The Monarche*[5]

- **1553 in poetry** Anonymous, *Pierce the Ploughmans Crede*; Gavin Douglas, translator, *Aeneid*, *The Palis of Honoure*, second, revised edition (publication year conjectural)[5]

- **1552 in poetry** Birth of Edmund Spenser, Walter Raleigh; Works: Thomas Churchyard, *A Myrrour for Man*[5]

- **1551 in poetry** Robert Crowley, published anonymously, *Philargyrie of Greate Britayne; or, The Fable of the Great Giant*[5]

- **1550 in poetry** Charles Bansley, *The Pride of Women*; Robert Crowley, One and Thyrtye Epigrammes; *John Heywood,* An Hundred Epigrammes; *William Langland (attributed),* Piers Plowman, the B text[5]

5.6.6   1540s

- **1549 in poetry**

- **1548 in poetry**

- **1547 in poetry**

- **1546 in poetry**

- **1545 in poetry**

- **1544 in poetry**

- **1543 in poetry**

- **1542 in poetry**

- **1541 in poetry**

- **1540 in poetry**

5.6.7 1530s

- **1539 in poetry**
- **1538 in poetry**
- **1537 in poetry**
- **1536 in poetry**
- **1535 in poetry**
- **1534 in poetry**
- **1533 in poetry**
- **1532 in poetry**
- **1531 in poetry**
- **1530 in poetry**

5.6.8 1520s

- **1529 in poetry**
- **1528 in poetry**
- **1527 in poetry**
- **1526 in poetry**
- **1525 in poetry**
- **1524 in poetry** Birth of Pierre de Ronsard
- **1523 in poetry**
- **1522 in poetry**
- **1521 in poetry**
- **1520 in poetry**

5.6.9 1510s

- **1519 in poetry**
- **1518 in poetry**
- **1517 in poetry**
- **1516 in poetry**
- **1515 in poetry**
- **1514 in poetry**
- **1513 in poetry**
- **1512 in poetry**
- **1511 in poetry**
- **1510 in poetry**

5.6.10   1500s

- **1509 in poetry**

- **1508 in poetry**

- **1507 in poetry**

- **1506 in poetry**

- **1505 in poetry**

- **1504 in poetry**

- **1503 in poetry**

- **1502 in poetry**

- **1501 in poetry** - *Judita* - Marko Marulić

- **1500 in poetry** - *La Araucana* - Alonso de Ercilla

5.7   15th century in poetry

5.7.1   1490s

- **1499 in poetry** *La Celestina* by Fernando de Rojas

- **1498 in poetry**

- **1497 in poetry**

- **1496 in poetry**

- **1495 in poetry**

- **1494 in poetry**

- **1493 in poetry**

- **1492 in poetry**

- **1491 in poetry**

- **1490 in poetry**

5.7.2   1480s

- **1489 in poetry**

- **1488 in poetry**

- **1487 in poetry**

- **1486 in poetry**

- **1485 in poetry**

- **1484 in poetry**

- **1483 in poetry**

- **1482 in poetry**

- **1481 in poetry**

- **1480 in poetry**

5.7.3   1470s

- **1479 in poetry**

- **1478 in poetry**

- **1477 in poetry**

- **1476 in poetry**

- **1475 in poetry**

- **1474 in poetry**

- **1473 in poetry**

- **1472 in poetry**

- **1471 in poetry**

- **1470 in poetry**

5.7.4   1460s

- **1469 in poetry**

- **1468 in poetry**

- **1467 in poetry**

- **1466 in poetry**

- **1465 in poetry**

- **1464 in poetry**

- **1463 in poetry** Death of François Villon (circa)

- **1462 in poetry**

- **1461 in poetry**

- **1460 in poetry**

5.7.5 1450s

- **1459 in poetry**
- **1458 in poetry**
- **1457 in poetry**
- **1456 in poetry**
- **1455 in poetry**
- **1454 in poetry**
- **1453 in poetry**
- **1452 in poetry**
- **1451 in poetry**
- **1450 in poetry**

5.7.6 1440s

- **1449 in poetry**
- **1448 in poetry**
- **1447 in poetry**
- **1446 in poetry**
- **1445 in poetry**
- **1444 in poetry**
- **1443 in poetry**
- **1442 in poetry**
- **1441 in poetry**
- **1440 in poetry**

5.7.7 1430s

- **1439 in poetry**
- **1438 in poetry**
- **1437 in poetry**
- **1436 in poetry**
- **1435 in poetry**
- **1434 in poetry**
- **1433 in poetry**
- **1432 in poetry**
- **1431 in poetry** Birth of François Villon (circa)
- **1430 in poetry**

5.7.8   1420s

- **1429 in poetry**
- **1428 in poetry**
- **1427 in poetry**
- **1426 in poetry**
- **1425 in poetry**
- **1424 in poetry**
- **1423 in poetry**
- **1422 in poetry**
- **1421 in poetry**
- **1420 in poetry**

5.7.9   1410s

- **1419 in poetry**
- **1418 in poetry**
- **1417 in poetry**
- **1416 in poetry**
- **1415 in poetry**
- **1414 in poetry**
- **1413 in poetry**
- **1412 in poetry**
- **1411 in poetry**
- **1410 in poetry**

5.7.10   1400s

- **1409 in poetry**
- **1408 in poetry**
- **1407 in poetry**
- **1406 in poetry**
- **1405 in poetry**
- **1404 in poetry**
- **1403 in poetry**
- **1402 in poetry**
- **1401 in poetry**
- **1400 in poetry** Death of Geoffrey Chaucer

5.8 14th century in poetry

5.8.1 1390s

- **1399 in poetry**
- **1398 in poetry**
- **1397 in poetry**
- **1396 in poetry**
- **1395 in poetry**
- **1394 in poetry**
- **1393 in poetry**
- **1392 in poetry**
- **1391 in poetry**
- **1390 in poetry**

5.8.2 1380s

- **1389 in poetry** Death of Hafez
- **1388 in poetry**
- **1387 in poetry**
- **1386 in poetry**
- **1385 in poetry**
- **1384 in poetry**
- **1383 in poetry**
- **1382 in poetry**
- **1381 in poetry**
- **1380 in poetry**

5.8.3 1370s

- **1379 in poetry**
- **1378 in poetry**
- **1377 in poetry**
- **1376 in poetry**
- **1375 in poetry** John Barbour's *The Brus*
- **1374 in poetry**
- **1373 in poetry**

- **1372 in poetry**

- **1371 in poetry**

- **1370 in poetry**

5.8.4   1360s

- **1369 in poetry**

- **1368 in poetry**

- **1367 in poetry**

- **1366 in poetry**

- **1365 in poetry**

- **1364 in poetry**

- **1363 in poetry**

- **1362 in poetry**

- **1361 in poetry**

- **1360 in poetry** Approximate date of the *Mocedades de Rodrigo*

5.8.5   1350s

- **1359 in poetry**

- **1358 in poetry**

- **1357 in poetry**

- **1356 in poetry**

- **1355 in poetry**

- **1354 in poetry**

- **1353 in poetry**

- **1352 in poetry**

- **1351 in poetry**

- **1350 in poetry**

5.8.6   1340s

- **1349 in poetry**

- **1348 in poetry**

- **1347 in poetry**

- **1346 in poetry**

- **1345 in poetry**

- **1344 in poetry**

- **1343 in poetry** (circa) Birth of Geoffrey Chaucer, known as father of English poetry (died 1400)

- **1342 in poetry**

- **1341 in poetry**

- **1340 in poetry**

5.8.7   1330s

- **1339 in poetry**

- **1338 in poetry**

- **1337 in poetry**

- **1336 in poetry**

- **1335 in poetry**

- **1334 in poetry**

- **1333 in poetry**

- **1332 in poetry**

- **1331 in poetry**

- **1330 in poetry**

5.8.8   1320s

- **1329 in poetry**

- **1328 in poetry**

- **1327 in poetry**

- **1326 in poetry**

- **1325 in poetry** Birth of Hafez,Persian poet

- **1324 in poetry**

- **1323 in poetry**

- **1322 in poetry**

- **1321 in poetry**

- **1320 in poetry**

5.8.9 1310s

- **1319 in poetry**
- **1318 in poetry**
- **1317 in poetry**
- **1316 in poetry**
- **1315 in poetry**
- **1314 in poetry**
- **1313 in poetry**
- **1312 in poetry**
- **1311 in poetry**
- **1310 in poetry**

5.8.10 1300s

- **1309 in poetry**
- **1308 in poetry**
- **1307 in poetry**
- **1306 in poetry**
- **1305 in poetry**
- **1304 in poetry**
- **1303 in poetry**
- **1302 in poetry**
- **1301 in poetry**
- **1300 in poetry** - *Kebra Nagast, Sundiata Keita* in oral form

5.9 13th century in poetry

5.9.1 1290s

- **1299 in poetry**
- **1298 in poetry**
- **1297 in poetry**
- **1296 in poetry**
- **1295 in poetry**
- **1294 in poetry**

- **1293 in poetry**

- **1292 in poetry**

- **1291 in poetry** Death of Saadi

- **1290 in poetry**

5.9.2   1280s

- **1289 in poetry**

- **1288 in poetry**

- **1287 in poetry** - The *Jewang Un'gi* by Yi Seung-hyu

- **1286 in poetry**

- **1285 in poetry**

- **1284 in poetry**

- **1283 in poetry**

- **1282 in poetry**

- **1281 in poetry**

- **1280 in poetry**

5.9.3   1270s

- **1279 in poetry**

- **1278 in poetry**

- **1277 in poetry**

- **1276 in poetry**

- **1275 in poetry**

- **1274 in poetry**

- **1273 in poetry**

- **1272 in poetry**

- **1271 in poetry**

- **1270 in poetry**

5.9.4   1260s

- **1269 in poetry**
- **1268 in poetry**
- **1267 in poetry**
- **1266 in poetry**
- **1265 in poetry**
- **1264 in poetry**
- **1263 in poetry**
- **1262 in poetry**
- **1261 in poetry**
- **1260 in poetry**

5.9.5   1250s

- **1259 in poetry**
- **1258 in poetry**
- **1257 in poetry**
- **1256 in poetry**
- **1255 in poetry**
- **1254 in poetry**
- **1253 in poetry**
- **1252 in poetry**
- **1251 in poetry**
- **1250 in poetry**

5.9.6   1240s

- **1249 in poetry**
- **1248 in poetry**
- **1247 in poetry**
- **1246 in poetry**
- **1245 in poetry**
- **1244 in poetry**
- **1243 in poetry**
- **1242 in poetry**
- **1241 in poetry**
- **1240 in poetry**

5.9.7   1230s

- **1239 in poetry**
- **1238 in poetry**
- **1237 in poetry**
- **1236 in poetry**
- **1235 in poetry**
- **1234 in poetry**
- **1233 in poetry**
- **1232 in poetry**
- **1231 in poetry**
- **1230 in poetry**

5.9.8   1220s

- **1229 in poetry**
- **1228 in poetry**
- **1227 in poetry**
- **1226 in poetry**
- **1225 in poetry**
- **1224 in poetry**
- **1223 in poetry**
- **1222 in poetry**
- **1221 in poetry**
- **1220 in poetry**

5.9.9   1210s

- **1219 in poetry**
- **1218 in poetry**
- **1217 in poetry**
- **1216 in poetry**
- **1215 in poetry**
- **1214 in poetry**
- **1213 in poetry**
- **1212 in poetry**
- **1211 in poetry**
- **1210 in poetry** Birth of Saadi,Persian poet

5.9.10   1200s

- **1209 in poetry**

- **1208 in poetry** Estimated date of the *Gesta Danorum*

- **1207 in poetry**

- **1206 in poetry**

- **1205 in poetry**

- **1204 in poetry**

- **1203 in poetry**

- **1202 in poetry**

- **1201 in poetry**

- **1200 in poetry**

5.10   12th century in poetry

5.10.1   1190s

- **1199 in poetry**

- **1198 in poetry**

- **1197 in poetry**

- **1196 in poetry**

- **1195 in poetry** Approximate date of *El Cantar de mio Cid*

- **1194 in poetry**

- **1193 in poetry**

- **1192 in poetry**

- **1191 in poetry**

- **1190 in poetry** Approximate date of *The Tale of Igor's Campaign*

5.10.2   1180s

- **1189 in poetry**

- **1188 in poetry**

- **1187 in poetry**

- **1186 in poetry**

- **1185 in poetry**

- **1184 in poetry**

- 1183 in poetry

- 1182 in poetry

- 1181 in poetry

- 1180 in poetry

5.10.3   1170s

- 1179 in poetry

- 1178 in poetry

- 1177 in poetry

- 1176 in poetry

- 1175 in poetry

- 1174 in poetry

- 1173 in poetry

- 1172 in poetry

- 1171 in poetry

- 1170 in poetry

5.10.4   1160s

- 1169 in poetry

- 1168 in poetry

- 1167 in poetry

- 1166 in poetry

- 1165 in poetry

- 1164 in poetry

- 1163 in poetry

- 1162 in poetry

- 1161 in poetry

- 1160 in poetry

5.10.5 1150s

- 1159 in poetry
- 1158 in poetry
- 1157 in poetry
- 1156 in poetry
- 1155 in poetry
- 1154 in poetry
- 1153 in poetry
- 1152 in poetry
- 1151 in poetry
- 1150 in poetry

5.10.6 1140s

- 1149 in poetry
- 1148 in poetry
- 1147 in poetry
- 1146 in poetry
- 1145 in poetry
- 1144 in poetry
- 1143 in poetry
- 1142 in poetry
- 1141 in poetry
- 1140 in poetry

5.10.7 1130s

- 1139 in poetry
- 1138 in poetry
- 1137 in poetry
- 1136 in poetry
- 1135 in poetry
- 1134 in poetry
- 1133 in poetry
- 1132 in poetry
- 1131 in poetry
- 1130 in poetry

5.10.8   1120s

- **1129 in poetry**
- **1128 in poetry**
- **1127 in poetry**
- **1126 in poetry**
- **1125 in poetry**
- **1124 in poetry**
- **1123 in poetry**
- **1122 in poetry**
- **1121 in poetry**
- **1120 in poetry**

5.10.9   1110s

- **1119 in poetry**
- **1118 in poetry**
- **1117 in poetry**
- **1116 in poetry**
- **1115 in poetry**
- **1114 in poetry**
- **1113 in poetry**
- **1112 in poetry**
- **1111 in poetry**
- **1110 in poetry**

5.10.10   1100s

- **1109 in poetry**
- **1108 in poetry**
- **1107 in poetry**
- **1106 in poetry**
- **1105 in poetry**
- **1104 in poetry**
- **1103 in poetry**
- **1102 in poetry**
- **1101 in poetry**
- **1100 in poetry** *The Knight in the Panther's Skin* by Shota Rustaveli

5.11 11th century in poetry

5.11.1 1090s

- 1099 in poetry
- 1098 in poetry
- 1097 in poetry
- 1096 in poetry
- 1095 in poetry
- 1094 in poetry
- 1093 in poetry
- 1092 in poetry
- 1091 in poetry
- 1090 in poetry

5.11.2 1080s

- 1089 in poetry
- 1088 in poetry
- 1087 in poetry
- 1086 in poetry
- 1085 in poetry
- 1084 in poetry
- 1083 in poetry
- 1082 in poetry
- 1081 in poetry
- 1080 in poetry

5.11.3 1070s

- 1079 in poetry
- 1078 in poetry
- 1077 in poetry
- 1076 in poetry
- 1075 in poetry
- 1074 in poetry
- 1073 in poetry

- **1072 in poetry**

- **1071 in poetry**

- **1070 in poetry**

5.11.4   1060s

- **1069 in poetry**

- **1068 in poetry**

- **1067 in poetry**

- **1066 in poetry**

- **1065 in poetry**

- **1064 in poetry**

- **1063 in poetry**

- **1062 in poetry**

- **1061 in poetry**

- **1060 in poetry**

5.11.5   1050s

- **1059 in poetry**

- **1058 in poetry**

- **1057 in poetry**

- **1056 in poetry**

- **1055 in poetry**

- **1054 in poetry**

- **1053 in poetry**

- **1052 in poetry**

- **1051 in poetry**

- **1050 in poetry**

5.11.6 1040s

- **1049 in poetry**
- **1048 in poetry**
- **1047 in poetry**
- **1046 in poetry**
- **1045 in poetry**
- **1044 in poetry**
- **1043 in poetry**
- **1042 in poetry**
- **1041 in poetry**
- **1040 in poetry**

5.11.7 1030s

- **1039 in poetry**
- **1038 in poetry**
- **1037 in poetry**
- **1036 in poetry**
- **1035 in poetry**
- **1034 in poetry**
- **1033 in poetry**
- **1032 in poetry**
- **1031 in poetry**
- **1030 in poetry**

5.11.8 1020s

- **1029 in poetry**
- **1028 in poetry**
- **1027 in poetry**
- **1026 in poetry**
- **1025 in poetry**
- **1024 in poetry**
- **1023 in poetry**
- **1022 in poetry**
- **1021 in poetry**
- **1020 in poetry**

5.11.9   1010s

- 1019 in poetry

- 1018 in poetry

- 1017 in poetry

- 1016 in poetry

- 1015 in poetry

- 1014 in poetry

- 1013 in poetry

- 1012 in poetry

- 1011 in poetry

- 1010 in poetry

5.11.10   1000s

- 1009 in poetry

- 1008 in poetry

- 1007 in poetry

- 1006 in poetry

- 1005 in poetry

- 1004 in poetry

- 1003 in poetry

- 1002 in poetry

- 1001 in poetry

- 1000 in poetry

5.12   10th century in poetry

5.12.1   990s

- 999 in poetry

- 998 in poetry

- 997 in poetry

- 996 in poetry

- 995 in poetry

- 994 in poetry

- **993 in poetry**

- **992 in poetry**

- **991 in poetry**

- **990 in poetry**

5.12.2 980s

- **989 in poetry**

- **988 in poetry**

- **987 in poetry**

- **986 in poetry**

- **985 in poetry**

- **984 in poetry**

- **983 in poetry**

- **982 in poetry**

- **981 in poetry**

- **980 in poetry**

5.12.3 970s

- **979 in poetry**

- **978 in poetry**

- **977 in poetry** - The *Shahnameh* by Ferdowsi

- **976 in poetry**

- **975 in poetry**

- **974 in poetry**

- **973 in poetry**

- **972 in poetry**

- **971 in poetry**

- **970 in poetry**

5.12.4 960s

- **969** in poetry
- **968** in poetry
- **967** in poetry
- **966** in poetry
- **965** in poetry
- **964** in poetry
- **963** in poetry
- **962** in poetry
- **961** in poetry
- **960** in poetry

5.12.5 950s

- **959** in poetry
- **958** in poetry
- **957** in poetry
- **956** in poetry
- **955** in poetry
- **954** in poetry
- **953** in poetry
- **952** in poetry
- **951** in poetry
- **950** in poetry

5.12.6 940s

- **949** in poetry
- **948** in poetry
- **947** in poetry
- **946** in poetry
- **945** in poetry
- **944** in poetry
- **943** in poetry
- **942** in poetry
- **941** in poetry
- **940** in poetry

5.12.7   930s

- **939 in poetry**
- **938 in poetry**
- **937 in poetry**
- **936 in poetry**
- **935 in poetry**
- **934 in poetry**
- **933 in poetry**
- **932 in poetry**
- **931 in poetry**
- **930 in poetry**

5.12.8   920s

- **929 in poetry**
- **928 in poetry**
- **927 in poetry**
- **926 in poetry**
- **925 in poetry**
- **924 in poetry**
- **923 in poetry**
- **922 in poetry**
- **921 in poetry**
- **920 in poetry**

5.12.9   910s

- **919 in poetry**
- **918 in poetry**
- **917 in poetry**
- **916 in poetry**
- **915 in poetry**
- **914 in poetry**
- **913 in poetry**
- **912 in poetry**
- **911 in poetry**
- **910 in poetry**

5.12.10   900s

- **909** in poetry
- **908** in poetry
- **907** in poetry
- **906** in poetry
- **905** in poetry
- **904** in poetry
- **903** in poetry
- **902** in poetry
- **901** in poetry
- **900** in poetry Earliest possible date of *Lebor Gabála Érenn*

5.13   5th century in poetry-9th century in poetry

5.13.1   890s

- **899** in poetry
- **898** in poetry
- **897** in poetry
- **896** in poetry
- **895** in poetry
- **894** in poetry
- **893** in poetry
- **892** in poetry
- **891** in poetry
- **890** in poetry

5.13.2   880s

- **889** in poetry
- **888** in poetry
- **887** in poetry
- **886** in poetry
- **885** in poetry
- **884** in poetry

- **883 in poetry**

- **882 in poetry**

- **881 in poetry**

- **880 in poetry**

5.13.3 870s

- **879 in poetry**

- **878 in poetry**

- **877 in poetry**

- **876 in poetry**

- **875 in poetry**

- **874 in poetry**

- **873 in poetry**

- **872 in poetry**

- **871 in poetry**

- **870 in poetry**

5.13.4 860s

- **869 in poetry**

- **868 in poetry**

- **867 in poetry**

- **866 in poetry**

- **865 in poetry**

- **864 in poetry**

- **863 in poetry**

- **862 in poetry**

- **861 in poetry**

- **860 in poetry**

5.13.5   850s

- 859 in poetry

- 858 in poetry

- 857 in poetry

- 856 in poetry

- 855 in poetry

- 854 in poetry

- 853 in poetry

- 852 in poetry

- 851 in poetry

- 850 in poetry

5.13.6   840s

- 849 in poetry

- 848 in poetry

- 847 in poetry

- 846 in poetry

- 845 in poetry

- 844 in poetry

- 843 in poetry

- 842 in poetry

- 841 in poetry

- 840 in poetry

5.13.7   830s

- 839 in poetry

- 838 in poetry

- 837 in poetry

- 836 in poetry

- 835 in poetry

- 834 in poetry

- 833 in poetry

- 832 in poetry

- 831 in poetry

- 830 in poetry

5.13.8   820s

- **829 in poetry**
- **828 in poetry**
- **827 in poetry**
- **826 in poetry**
- **825 in poetry**
- **824 in poetry**
- **823 in poetry**
- **822 in poetry**
- **821 in poetry**
- **820 in poetry**

5.13.9   810s

- **819 in poetry**
- **818 in poetry**
- **817 in poetry**
- **816 in poetry**
- **815 in poetry**
- **814 in poetry**
- **813 in poetry**
- **812 in poetry**
- **811 in poetry**
- **810 in poetry**

5.13.10   800s

- **809 in poetry**
- **808 in poetry**
- **807 in poetry**
- **806 in poetry**
- **805 in poetry**
- **804 in poetry**
- **803 in poetry**
- **802 in poetry**
- **801 in poetry**
- **800 in poetry**

5.13.11 700s

5.13.12 600s

- 600 – Venantius Fortunatus born (c. 530 – c. 600), Latin poet and hymnodist from Northern Italy

- 615 – Saint Columbanus (born 543), Hiberno-Latin poet and writer

- 625 – Maymun Ibn Qays Al-a'sha born (died 625)

- 661 – Labīd died this year (born 560); Arabic poet

5.13.13 500s

- 500 – Procopius born about this year (died 565)

- 505 – Blossius Aemilius Dracontius born about this year (born 455) of Carthage, a Latin poet

- 521

    - July 17 – Magnus Felix Ennodius died (born 474 – July 17, 521), Bishop of Pavia and poet, writing in Latin
    - November – Jacob of Serugh died (born 451), writing in Syriac

- 530 – Venantius Fortunatus born (c. 530 – c. 600), Latin poet and hymnodist from Northern Italy

- 534 – Taliesin born about this year (died c. 599), the earliest identified Welsh poet

- 536 – Agathias born about this year (died 582/594); Ancient Greek poet and historian

- 539 – Chilperic I born (died September 584) Frankish king of Neustria and a Latin poet

- 543 – Saint Columbanus (died 615), Hiberno-Latin poet and writer

- 544 – Arator declaims his poem *De Actibus Apostolorum* in the Church of San Pietro-in-Vinculi

- 554 – 'Abid ibn al-Abris died about this year; Arabic poet

- 560:

    - Samaw'al ibn 'Adiya died about this year; Jewish poet writing in Arabic
    - Labīd born this year (died 661); Arabic poet

- 565 – Procopius died (born about 500)

- 570 – Maymun Ibn Qays Al-a'sha born (died 625)

- 580 – Antara Ibn Shaddad died about this year; Arabic poet

- 584

    - (September) – Chilperic I died (born 539) Frankish king of Neustria and a Latin poet
    - Amr ibn Kulthum died about this year; Arabic poet

- 599 – Taliesin died about this year (born c. 534), the earliest identified Welsh poet

5.13.14 400s

- Unknown – Compilation of the *Mahavamsa* by Buddhist monks

- 451 – Jacob of Serugh born (died November 521), writing in Syriac

- 455 – Blossius Aemilius Dracontius born about this year (died c. 505) of Carthage, a Latin poet

- 474 – Magnus Felix Ennodius (died July 17, 521), Bishop of Pavia and poet, writing in Latin

5.14 Poetry before the 5th century

- 4th century in poetry

- 3rd century in poetry

- 2nd century in poetry

- 1st century in poetry

- 1st century BC in poetry

- 2nd century BC in poetry

- 3rd century BC in poetry

- 4th century BC in poetry

- 5th century BC in poetry

- 6th century BC in poetry

- 7th century BC in poetry

5.15 Before 1000 BC in poetry

- 1500 BC – The *Vedas*

- 2500 BC – The *Tale of the Shipwrecked Sailor*

5.16 See also

- History of poetry

5.17 References

[1] Retrieved November 10, 2010

[2] Ackroyd, Peter, *Ezra Pound*, Thames and Hudson Ltd., London, 1980, "Chronology" chapter, p 118

[3] Davis, Cynthia J., and Kathryn West, *Women Writers in the United States: A Timeline of Literary, Cultural, and Social History*, Oxford University Press US, 1996 ISBN 978-0-19-509053-6, retrieved via Google Books on February 7, 2009

[4] Trent, William P. and Wells, Benjamin W., *Colonial Prose and Poetry: The Beginnings of Americanism 1650-1710*, New York: Thomas Y. Crowell Co., 1903 edition, page 41

[5] Cox, Michael, editor, *The Concise Oxford Chronology of English Literature*, Oxford University Press, 2004, ISBN 0-19-860634-6

Chapter 6

Bengali poetry

Bengali poetry is a form that originated in Pāli and other Prakrit socio-cultural traditions. It is antagonistic towards Vedic rituals and laws as opposed to the shramanic traditions such as Buddhism and Jainism. However the modern Bengali owes much to Sanskrit.

6.1   Early history

The history of Bengali poetry underwent three successive stages of development: poetry of the early age (like *Charyapad*), the Medieval period and the age of modern poetry. Modernity was introduced into Bengali poetry in the 1930s.

6.1.1   Origins

Bengali poetry probably began during the 10th century. It is known for the mystic poems called *Charyacharyavinishchaya*, and sometimes called *Charyapad* or *Charyagiti*. These poems were discovered in Nepal's Royal Library by Bengali scholar Mahamahopadhyay Haraprasad Shastri.

Medieval Age

Translation of Epics into Vernacular

- Krittibas Ojha

- Kashiram Das

The Medieval period of Bengali poetry was between 1350 and 1800. It was known as the period of Jayadeva, the renowned 12th-century poet from neighboring Odisha who was famous for his poem *Gitagovinda*.

Other noted poets from this period include 13th century Vidyapati, known for his love lyrics and Badu, Chandidas, writer of *Sri Krishna Kirtan*. *Sri Krishna Kirtan* is considered to be the most important philosophical and erotic work of the period.

The period from 1500 to 1800 is known as the Late Middle Bengali Period. During this period, there was a marked influence of Chaitanya, leading to the development of Vaishnava literature. Vaishnava poets include Govinddas and Gyandas.

Beside Vaishnava poetry, the most significant work of the 16th century was Mukunda Chakravarti's *Chandimangal*. Other Mangal-Kāvyas or religious texts are Manasamangal, Dharmamangal and Phullaketu.

Two of Bengal's most well known Muslim poets, Daulat Qazi and Alaol, lived in the 15th century (1607–1680) in Myanmar.

6.2 Birth of modern poetry

Bharat Chandra marks the transition between Precolonial theocentric poetry and modern poetry. Iswar Gupta, Michael Madhusudan Dutta (1834–1873), Biharilal Chakravarti (1834–94), Rabindranath Tagore(1861–1941) are noteworthy poets of this period.

6.3 Modern Bengali poetry

With Rabindranath Tagore founding a firm basis for modern Bengali poetry, the new poets of the early 1920s consciously moved for transcending the frontiers of traditional verses to establishing a realm of truly modern poetry. It was a successful movement that brought permanent change to the structure and theme of poetry. Kazi Nazrul Islam (1899-1976) first built the foundation of modern Bengali poetry by introducing modern concept of revolt against all autocracy, hypocrisy, superstition and inhumanity in Bengali. One notable sect of modernists included pro-socialism poets like Sukanta Bhattacharya and Samar Sen.

Modern Bengali poetry has also witnessed feminist intellect Kabita Singha, mallika Sengupta, Krishna Basu and Sriparna Bandyopadhyay being some of the most prominent names.

6.4 See also

- List of Bengali poets
- List of national poetries
- Kavita of Buddhadeva Bose
- Hungry generation
- List of Bangladeshi poets
- New Age Bengali Literature

6.5 References

6.6 External links

- Bangla Poetry in English Translation
- Poets of Bangladesh in English Translation
- Indian Story Tellers in English

Nobel Laurate Rabindranath Tagore is the most famous Bengali poet of modern era

Chapter 7

Biblical poetry

The ancient Hebrews perceived that there were poetical portions in their sacred texts, as shown by their entitling as songs or chants passages such as Exodus 15:1-19 and Numbers 21:17-20; a song or chant (*shir*) is, according to the primary meaning of the term, poetry. The question as to whether the poetical passages of the Old Testament show signs of regular rhythm or meter is yet unsolved.[1]

7.1 Characteristics of Ancient Hebrew poetry

7.1.1 Rhyme

It is often stated that ancient Hebrew poetry contains almost no rhyme. This assertion is understandable because the ancient texts preserved in the Hebrew Bible were written over a period of at least a millennium. Over that length of time, the pronunciation of every language changes. Words that were rhyming pairs at the beginning of that period may no longer rhyme at the end of that period. Further, different tribal groups or other groups of Hebrew speakers undoubtedly pronounced words differently in one and the same era. Using English as an example, we would be hard-pressed to find rhyme or even meter in the opening verses of Chaucer's Canterbury Tales, written in Middle English, if we were to pronounce the words of that poem as we pronounce their direct descendants in Modern English. Even within contemporary English, some speakers rhyme "again" with "rain" while others (northern English accents especially) rhyme "again" with "pen."

The phonological phenomena that obscure the rhymes of Chaucer only 600 years after his death, are also to be found in Biblical Hebrew texts which spanned a millennium. One fine example of rhyme and meter in ancient Hebrew texts is found in the Book of Proverbs, 6:9, 10. As Hebraist Seth Ben-Mordecai (author, *The Exodus Haggadah*) points out, these two verses, split into four lines of poetry, demonstrate both internal rhyme (common to Biblical Hebrew texts) and end-of-line rhyme (less common in Hebrew but the norm in English rhyming poetry), as well as noticeable meter. Thus, the last word of the first line ('AD maTAI 'aTZEL tishKAV) rhymes with the last word of the last line (me'AT khibBUQ yaDAYM lishKAV). In the third line, the second and fourth words create an internal rhyme with each other (me'AT sheNOT, me'AT tenuMOT). Finally, the first word of the second line (maTAI taQUM mishshenaTEksgha) is identical to the first word of the first line, linking those two lines even without obvious rhyme. Similar rhyming verses within the Hebrew Bible ought to put to rest the [question]. It is sometimes stated that ancient Hebrew texts demonstrate assonance more often than rhyme. Indeed, assonance is prominent in ancient Hebrew texts - as are other forms of "sound matching." An example of assonance is found in the first song mentioned above (Exodus 15:1-19), where assonance occurs at the ends of the lines, as in "anwehu" and "aromemenhu" (15:2). It is, of course, true that consonance of "hu" (= "him") can occur frequently in the Hebrew, because the language allows speakers to affix object-case as suffixes to verbs. What is notable when comparing ancient Hebrew poetry to contemporary English poetry is the playfulness of the authors, and their evident willingness to use multiple sound-matching schemes, rather than limiting themselves to simple rhymes at the end of verses, as in English.

7.1.2   Unusual forms

The employment of unusual forms of language cannot be considered as a sign of ancient Hebrew poetry. In the sentences of Noah[2] the form "lamo" occurs. But this form, which represents partly "lahem" and partly "lo", has many counterparts in Hebrew grammar, as, for example, "kemo" instead of "ke-";[3] or "-emo" = "them";[4] or "-emo" = "their";[5] or "clemo" = "to them"[6]—forms found in passages for which no claim to poetical expressions is made. Then there are found "ḥayeto" = "beast",[7] "osri" = "tying",[8] and "yeshu'atah" = "salvation"[9]—three forms that probably retain remnants of the old endings of the nominative, genitive, and accusative: "u(n)," "i(n)," "a(n)."

Again, in Lamech's words, "Adah and Zillah, hear my voice; ye wives of Lamech, harken unto my speech",[10] the two words "he'ezin" and "imrah" attract attention, because they occur for the first time in this passage, although there had been an earlier opportunity of using them: in Genesis 3:8 and 3:10, "He'ezin" = "to harken" could have been used just as well as its synonym "shama'" = "to hear".[11]

Furthermore, "imrah" = "speech" might have been used instead of the essentially identical "dabar" in Genesis 9:1 and following, but its earliest use is, as stated above, in Genesis 4:23.[12] In place of "adam" = "man"[13] "enosh" is employed.[14] (compare the Aramaic "enash"[15]).

A systematic review of similar unusual forms of Hebrew grammar and Hebrew words occurring in certain portions of the Old Testament.[16] Such forms have been called "dialectus poetica" since the publication of Robert Lowth's "Prælectiones de Sacra Poesi Hebræorum" iii. (1753); but this designation is ambiguous and can be accepted only in agreement with the rule *a parte potiori fit denominatio* for some of these unusual forms and words are found elsewhere than in the "songs" of the Old Testament.

These unusual forms and expressions do not occur in all songs, and there are several Psalms that have none of these peculiarities.

7.1.3   Parallelism

Main article: Parallelism (rhetoric)

Not even the *parallelismus membrorum* is an absolutely certain indication of ancient Hebrew poetry. This "parallelism" is a phenomenon noticed in the portions of the Old Testament that are at the same time marked frequently by the so-called *dialectus poetica*; it consists in a remarkable correspondence in the ideas expressed in two successive units (hemistiches, verses, strophes, or larger units); for example, the above-cited words of Lamech, "Adah and Zillah, hear my voice; ye wives of Lamech, harken unto my speech",[17] in which are found "he'ezin" and "imrah," show a remarkable repetition of the same thought.

But this ideal corythmy is not always present in the songs of the Old Testament or in the Psalter, as the following passages will show:

- "The Lord is my strength and song, and he is become my salvation" (Exodus 15:2).

- "Saul and Jonathan, the beloved and the lovely, in life and in death they were not divided".[18]

- "Ye daughters of Israel, weep over Saul, who clothed you in scarlet, and fine linen".[19]

- "And he shall be like a tree planted by the rivers of water, that bringeth forth his fruit in his season";[20]

- "I laid me down and slept; I awaked; for the Lord sustained me. I will not be afraid of ten thousands of people, that have set themselves against me round about".[21]

Julius Ley[22] says therefore correctly that

> "the poets did not consider themselves bound by parallelism to such an extent as not to set it aside when the thought required it."

Though this restriction must be made to James Robertson's view, it remains the case that:[23] "The distinguishing feature of the Hebrew poetry ... is the rhythmical balancing of parts, or parallelism of thought."

Various rhetorical forms are found in the parallelisms of Biblical poetry. These include:

- Synonymous parallelism; in this form, the second unit (hemistich or half line of verse, verse, strophe, or larger unit) says much the same thing as the first one, with variations. An example is found in Amos 5:24:

    But let judgment run down as waters,

    > *and righteousness as a mighty stream.*

Another example of synonymous parallelism is found in Isaiah 2:4 or Micah 4:3:

    "They will beat their swords into plowshares

    > *and their spears into pruning hooks.*

- Antithesis is also found; here, the second unit directly contrasts with the first, often making the same point from the opposite perspective. From Proverbs 10:1:

    A wise son maketh a glad father,

    > *but a foolish son* is *the heaviness of his mother.*

- Emblematic parallelism occurs where one unit renders figuratively the literal meaning of another.

- Synthetic parallelism occurs where the units balance, clause for clause, with one unit building upon or adding to the first. From Psalm 14:2:

    The LORD looked down from heaven upon the children of men,

    > *to see if there were any that did understand* and *seek God.*

- Climactic parallelism occurs where the second unit partially balances the first, but also adds a summative thought or completes the series. From Psalm 29:1:

    Give unto the LORD, O ye mighty,

    > *give unto the LORD glory and strength.*

- External parallelism occurs when the syntactic units balance one another across multiple verses. Here, some of the permitted sorts of parallelisms are added not only within a single line of verse, but also between lines. From Isaiah 1:27-28:

    Zion shall be redeemed with judgment,

    > *and her converts with righteousness.*

    And the destruction of the transgressors and the sinners shall be *together,*

    > *and they that forsake the LORD shall be consumed.*

It should also be noted that external parallelism can also "accumulate" in a chiastic or "ring" structure that may include many verses. For example Psalm 1 utilizes synonymous, synthetic, and emblematic parallelism before "turning" antithetically back to emblematic, synthetic, and then synonymous parallels.

7.1.4 Quantitative Rhythm

The poetry of the ancient Hebrews is not distinguished from the other parts of the Old Testament by rhythm based on quantity, though in view of Greek and Roman poetry it was natural to seek such a rhythm in the songs and Psalms of the Old Testament. William Jones, for example,[24] attempted to prove that there was a definite sequence of long and short syllables in the ancient Hebrew poems; but he could support this thesis only by changing the punctuation in many ways, and by allowing great license to the Hebrew poets. However, on reading the portions of the Old Testament marked by the so-called *dialectus poetica* or by parallelism (e.g., Genesis 4:23 and following) no such sequence of long and short syllables can be discovered; and Sievers[25] says: "Hebrew prosody is not based on quantity as classical prosody is."

7.1.5 Accentual rhythm

Many scholars hold that the Hebrew poet considered only the syllables receiving the main accent, and did not count the intervening ones. Examples contrary to this are not found in passages where forms of the so-called *dialectus poetica* are used, as Ley holds;[26] and Israel Davidson has proved[27] that the choice of "lamo" instead of "lahem" favors in only a few passages the opinion that the poet intended to cause an accented syllable to be followed by an unaccented one.

The rhythm of Hebrew poetry may be similar to that of the German *Nibelungenlied* — a view that is strongly supported by the nature of the songs sung by the populace of Palestine in the early 20th century. These songs have been described by L. Schneller[28] in the following words:

> "The rhythms are manifold; there may be eight accents in one line, and three syllables are often inserted between two accents, the symmetry and variation being determined by emotion and sentiment."

Also in Palestine, Gustaf Hermann Dalman observed:

n:"Lines with two, three, four, and five accented syllables may be distinguished, between which one to three, and even four, unaccented syllables may be inserted, the poet being bound by no definite number in his poem. Occasionally two accented syllables are joined" ("Palästinischer Diwan", 1901, p23).

Such free rhythms are, in Davidson's opinion, found also in the poetry of the Old Testament. Under the stress of their thoughts and feelings the poets of Israel sought to achieve merely the material, not the formal symmetry of corresponding lines. This may be observed, for example, in the following lines of Psalm 2: "Serve the LORD with fear" ("'Ibdu et-Yhwh be-yir'ah", 2:11), "rejoice with trembling" ("we-gilu bi-re'adah"). This is shown more in detail by König;[29] and Carl Heinrich Cornill has confirmed this view[30] by saying:

> "Equal length of the several stichoi was not the basic formal law of Jeremiah's metric construction."

Sievers is inclined to restrict Hebrew rhythm by various rules, as he attacks[31] Karl Budde's view, that

> "a foot which is lacking in one-half of a verse may find a substitute in the more ample thought of this shorter line".[32]

Furthermore, the verse of the Old Testament poetry is naturally iambic or anapestic, as the words are accented on one of the final syllables.

7.1.6 The Dirges

A special kind of rhythm may be observed in the dirges, called by the Hebrews "kinot". A whole book of these elegies is contained in the Hebrew Bible, the first of them beginning thus: "How does the city sit solitary—that was full of people—how is she become as a widow—she that was great among the nations—and princess among the provinces—how is she become tributary!" (Lamentations 1:1).

The rhythm of such lines lies in the fact that a longer line is always followed by a shorter one. As in the hexameter and pentameter of Greek poetry, this change was intended to symbolize the idea that a strenuous advance in life is followed by fatigue or reaction. This rhythm, which may be designated "elegiac measure," occurs also in Amos 5:2, expressly designated as a ḳinah. The sad import of his prophecies induced Jeremiah also to employ the rhythm of the dirges several times in his utterances (Jeremiah 9:20, 13:18 and following). He refers here expressly to the "meḳonenot" (the mourning women) who in the East still chant the death-song to the trembling tone of the pipe (48:36 and following). "Ḳinot" are found also in Ezekiel 19:1, 26:17, 27:2, 32:2 and following, 32:16, 32:19 and following.

This elegiac measure, being naturally a well-known one, was used also elsewhere, as, for example, in Psalm 19:8-10. The rhythm of the ḳinah has been analyzed especially by Budde (in Stade's "Zeitschrift", 1883, p299). Similar funeral songs of the modern Arabs are quoted by Wetzstein (in "Zeitschrift für Ethnologie", v. 298), as, e.g.: "O, if he only could be ransomed! truly, I would pay the ransom!" (see König, l.c. p315).

7.1.7 Anadiplosis

A special kind of rhythm was produced by the frequent employment of the so-called anadiplosis, a mode of speech in which the phrase at the end of one sentence is repeated at the beginning of the next, as, for instance, in the passages "they came not to the help of the Lord [i.e., to protect God's people], to the help of the Lord against the mighty" (Judges 5:23; compare "ẓidḳot" [5:11a] and "nilḥamu" [5:19a-20a, b]), and "From whence shall my help come? My help cometh from the Lord" (Psalm 121:1b-2a, R. V.).

Many similar passages occur in fifteen of the Psalms, 120-134, which also contain an unusual number of epanalepsis, or catch-words, for which Israel Davidson proposed the name "Leittöne." Thus there is the repetition of "shakan" in Psalm 120:5, 6; of "shalom" in verses 6 and 7 of the same psalm; and the catch-word "yishmor" in Psalm 121:7, 8 (all the cases are enumerated in König, l.c. p. 302).

As the employment of such repetitions is somewhat suggestive of the mounting of stairs, the superscription "shir ha-ma'alot," found at the beginning of these fifteen psalms, may have a double meaning: it may indicate not only the purpose of these songs, to be sung on the pilgrimages to the festivals at Jerusalem, but also the peculiar construction of the songs, by which the reciter is led from one step of the inner life to the next. Such graduated rhythm may be observed elsewhere; for the peasants in modern Syria accompany their national dance by a song the verses of which are connected like the links of a chain, each verse beginning with the final words of the preceding one (Wetzstein, l.c. v. 292).

7.1.8 Acrostics

Alphabetical acrostics are used as an external embellishment of a few poems. The letters of the alphabet, generally in their ordinary sequence, stand at the beginning of smaller or larger sections of Psalms 9-10 (probably), 15, 34, 37, 111, 112, 119, 145; Proverbs 31:10-31; Lamentations 1-4; and also of Sirach 51:13-29, as the newly discovered Hebrew text of this book has shown (see, on Psalms 25 and 34 especially, Hirsch in "Am. Jour. Semit. Lang." 1902, p167-173).

Alphabetical and other acrostics occur frequently in Neo-Hebraic poetry.[33] The existence of acrostics in Babylonian literature has been definitely proved;[34] and alphabetical poems are found also among the Samaritans, Syrians, and Arabs. Cicero says ("De Divinatione," II.54) that the verse of the sibyl was in acrostics; and the so-called *Oracula Sibyllina* contain an acrostic.[35]

A secondary phenomenon, which distinguishes a part of the poems of the Old Testament from the other parts, is the so-called "accentuatio poetica"; it has been much slighted (Sievers, l.c. § 248, p. 375). Although not all the poetical portions of the Old Testament are marked by a special accentuation, the Book of Job in 3:3-42:6 and the books of Psalms and Proverbs throughout have received unusual accents. This point will be further discussed later on.

7.2 Division of the poetical portions of the Hebrew Bible

7.2.1   Poems that deal with events

First may be mentioned poems that deal principally with events, being epic-lyric in character: the triumphal song of Israel delivered from Egypt, or the *song of the sea*;[36] the mocking song on the burning of Heshbon;[37] the so-called *song of Moses*;[38] the song of Deborah;[39] the derisive song of victory of the Israelite women;[40] Hannah's song of praise;[41] David's song of praise on being saved from his enemies;[42] Hezekiah's song of praise on his recovery;[43] Jonah's song of praise;[44] and many of the Psalms, e.g., those on the creation of the world,[45] and on the election of Israel.[46] A subdivision is formed by poems that deal more with description and praise: the so-called Well song;[47] the song of praise on the uniqueness of the god of Israel;[48] and those on his eternity;[49] his omnipresence and omniscience;[50] and his omnipotence.[51]

7.2.2   Didactic poems

Poems appealing more to reason, being essentially didactic in character. These include fables, like that of Jotham (Judges 9:7-15, although in prose); parables, like those of Nathan and others (2 Samuel 12:1-4, 14:4-9; 1 Kings 20:39 and following, all three in prose), or in the form of a song (Isaiah 5:1-6); riddles (Judges 14:14 and following; Proverbs 30:11 and following); maxims, as, for instance, in 1 Samuel 15:22, 24:14, and the greater part of Proverbs; the monologues and dialogues in Job 3:3 and following; compare also the reflections in monologue in Ecclesiastes. A number of the Psalms also are didactic in character. A series of them impresses the fact that God's law teaches one to abhor sin (Psalms 5, 58), and inculcates a true love for the Temple and the feasts of Yahweh (Psalms 15, 81, 92). Another series of Psalms shows that God is just, although it may at times not seem this way to a short-sighted observer of the world and of history ("theodicies": Psalms 49, 73; compare Psalms 16, 56, 60).

7.2.3   Lyrics

Poems that portray feelings based on individual experience. Many of these lyrics express joy, as, e.g., Lamech's so-called *Song of the sword*;[52] David's "last words";[53] the words of praise of liberated Israel;[54] songs of praise like Psalms 18, 24, 126, etc. Other lyrics express mourning. First among these are the dirges proper for the dead, as the ḳinah on the death of Saul and Jonathan;[55] that on Abner's death;[56] and all psalms of mourning, as, e.g., the expressions of sorrow of sufferers,[57] and the expressions of penitence of sinners.[58]

7.2.4   Poems that urge action

Finally, a large group of poems of the Old Testament that urge action and are exhortatory. These may be divided into two sections:

1. The poet wishes something for himself, as in the so-called "signal words" (Numbers 10:35 and following, "Arise, LORD" etc.); at the beginning of the Well song (21:17 and following, "ali be'er"); in the daring request, "Sun, stand thou still" (Joshua 10:12); in Habakkuk's prayer ("tefillah"; Habakkuk 3:1-19); or in psalms of request for help in time of war (44, 60, etc.) or for liberation from prison (122, 137, etc.).

2. The poet pronounces blessings upon others, endeavoring to move God to grant these wishes. To this group belong the blessing of Noah (Genesis 9:25-27), of Isaac (27:28-29 and 39-40), and of Jacob (49:3-27); Jethro's congratulation of Israel (Exodus 18:10); the blessing of Aaron (Numbers 6:24-26) and of Balaam (23:7-10, 18-24, 24:5-9, 24:17-24); Moses' farewell (Deuteronomy 33:1 and following); the psalms that begin with "Ashre" = "Blessed is," etc., or contain this phrase, as Psalms 1, 41, 84:5 and following, 84:13, 112, 119, 128.

It was natural that in the drama, which is intended to portray a whole series of external and internal events, several of the foregoing kinds of poems should be combined. This combination occurs in Canticles, which, in Davidson's opinion, is most correctly characterized as a kind of drama.

The peculiar sublimity of the poems of the Old Testament is due partly to the high development of monotheism which finds expression therein and partly to the beauty of the moral ideals which they exalt. This subject has been discussed by

J. D. Michaelis in the preface to his Arabic grammar, second edition, p29, and by Emil Kautzsch in "Die Poesie und die Poetischen Bücher des A. T." (1902) although this all may be true he Hebrew poetry follows a totally different rhyming scheme and as it has been translated into English we cannot comprehend this.

7.3 See also

- Poetry
- Hebrew Bible
- List of national poetries

7.4 References

[1] Joseph Jacobs, W. H. Cobb. "METER IN THE BIBLE". JewishEncyclopedia.com. Retrieved December 7, 2011.

[2] Such as Genesis 9:25-27.

[3] Exodus 15:5, 15:8.

[4] 15:9, 15:15.

[5] Psalm 2:3.

[6] 2:5.

[7] Genesis 1:24.

[8] 49:11.

[9] Psalm 3:3.

[10] Genesis 4:23.

[11] It occurs also in Exodus 15:26; Numbers 23:18 (a sentence of Balaam); Deuteronomy 1:45, 32:1; Judges 5:3; Isaiah 1:2, 1:10, 8:9, 28:23, 32:9, 42:23, 51:4, 44:3; Book of Jeremiah 13:15; Hosea 5:1; Joel 1:2; Nehemiah 9:30 (in a prayer); and in 2 Chronicles 24:19 (probably an imitation of Isaiah 44:3).

[12] It is found also in Deuteronomy 32:2, 33:9; 2 Samuel 22:31; Isaiah 5:24, 28:23, 39:4, 32:9; Psalm 12:7, etc.; Proverbs 30:5; and Lamentations 2:17.

[13] Genesis 1:26 and following.

[14] In Deuteronomy 32:26; Isaiah 8:1, 13:7, 13:12; 24:6, 33:8; 51:7, 51:12; 56:2; Jeremiah 20:10; Psalm 8:5, 9:20, 10:18, 55:14, 56:2, 66:12, 73:5, 90:3, 103:15, 104:15, 154:3; Job 4:17, 5:17, 7:1, 7:17, 9:2, 10:4; 13:9, 14:19, 15:14, 25:4, 25:6, 28:4, 28:13, 32:8; 33:12, 33:26, 36:25; 2 Chronicles 14:10.

[15] In Daniel 2:10; Ezra 4:11, 6:11.

[16] See E. König, "Stilistik", etc., p. 277-283.

[17] Genesis 4:23

[18] H. P. Smith, in "International Commentary," on 2 Samuel 1:23.

[19] 2 Samuel 1:24/

[20] Psalm 1:3; compare 2:12.

[21] Psalm 3:6-7 [A. V. 5-6]; see also 4:7 and following, 9:4 and following.

[22] "Leitfaden der Hebräischen Metrik," 1887, p. 10.

[23] "The Poetry of the Psalms", 1898, p. 160.

[24] "Poeseos Asiaticæ Commentarii", chapter 2, London, 1774

[25] "Metrische Untersuchungen," 1901, § 53.

[26] In his "Grundzüge des Rhythmus, des Vers- und Strophenbaues in der Hebräischen Poesie", p. 99, p. 116.

[27] In his "Stilistik", p. 333, for example.

[28] In his "Kennst Du das Land?" (section "Musik").

[29] l.c. p. 334.

[30] "Die Metrischen Stücke des Buches Jeremia", 1901, p. 8.

[31] l.c. §§ 52, 88.

[32] "Handkommentar zu Hiob", p.47.

[33] Winter and Wünsche, "Die Jüdische Literatur seit Abschluss des Kanons," 1894-1896, iii. 10.

[34] H. Zimmern, in "Zeitschrift für Keilschriftforschung," 1895, p. 15.

[35] In book 8, lines 217-250.

[36] Exodus 15:1-18.

[37] Numbers 21:27-30.

[38] Deuteronomy 32:1-43.

[39] Judges 5.

[40] "Saul hath slain," etc.; 1 Samuel 18:7

[41] 2:1-10.

[42] 2 Samuel 22.

[43] Isaiah 38:9-20.

[44] Jonah 2:3-10.

[45] 8, 104).

[46] 99, 100, 105.

[47] Numbers 21:17 and following.

[48] Psalms 95, 97.

[49] 90.

[50] 139.

[51] 115.

[52] Beginning at Genesis 4:23.

[53] 2 Samuel 23:1-7.

[54] Isaiah 12:1-6.

[55] 2 Samuel 1:19-27.

[56] 3:33 and following.

[57] Psalms 16, 22, 27, 39.

[58] 6, 32, 38, 51, 106, 130, 143.

7.5 Further reading

- Alter, Robert (2011-09-06). *The Art of Biblical Poetry* (Second ed.). Basic Books. ISBN 0-465-02256-1.

- Alter, Robert (2009-10-19). *The Book of Psalms: A Translation with Commentary.* W. W. Norton & Company. ISBN 0-393-33704-9.

- Tod Linafelt, "Private Poetry and Public Rhetoric: Hearing and Overhearing David's Lament for Saul and Jonathan in 2 Samuel 1," in the *Journal of Religion* 88:4 (2008), 497-526.

7.6 External links

- Biblical Hebrew Poetry - Reconstructing the Original Oral, Aural and Visual Experience

- Jewish Encyclopedia - Poetry - Biblical

- "Hebrew Poetry of the Old Testament". *Catholic Encyclopedia.* New York: Robert Appleton Company. 1913.

Chapter 8

Biker poetry

Biker poetry [1][2] is a movement of poetry that grew out of the predominantly American lifestyle of the Biker and Motorcycle clubs following World War II.[3]

8.1 Background

Poets such as Hunter S. Thompson are credited with writing biker poetry, playing no small part in the genus by popularizing a literary movement that focused on the biker lifestyle when he released *Hell's Angels: The Strange and Terrible Saga of the Outlaw Motorcycle Gangs*.

8.2 Overview

Biker poetry often embraces form. Fixed verse, free verse, folk song, Concrete poetry, Poetry slam and even "Baiku" a form of Haiku.[4] Notable biker poets include Diane Wakoski, who authored a collection known as *The motorcycle betrayal poems*. Writers such as Colorado T. Sky and K Peddlar Bridges work with experimental poetry, however the biker genre tends to work with form, especially rhyming verse. Groups such as The Highway Poets Motorcycle Club [5] have an international membership. The genre is a regular feature in many motorcycle magazines and motorcycle rallies.

Biker poets often use pseudonyms.[6] These include "The Holy Ranger" (Dr. Martin Jack Rosenblum),[7] "Wild Bill, the Alaskan Biker Poet" (William B Rogers), "Ironhorse Writer" (Laurence P. Scerri), "Gypsypashn" (Betsy Lister),[8] "Biker Jer" (Jerry Sawinski) and "Joe Go" (Jose Gouveia).[9]

8.3 Themes

Falling in love with a mustache
is like saying
you can fall in love with
the way a man polishes his shoes
which,
of course,
is one of the things that turns on
my tuned-up engine

"

"

From "Uneasy Rider"
The Motorcycle Betrayal Poems
By Diane Wakoski, 1971

Biker Poetry is similar to cowboy poetry in that it can reflect a romantic American lifestyle.[10][11] Verse will often focus on the loneliness or camaraderie associated with motorcycling, the day-to-day affairs of maintenance on the motorcycle, personal problems within a family that lives a biker lifestyle as well as substance abuse and its relation to bikers.[12] Other popular themes include "the freedom of the road", outlaw clubs,[13][14] interactions with cars and trucks also referred to as 'cages', biker values and practices and the conflicts and tragedies associated with highway incidents.[1]

8.4   References

[1]   "Rubber Side Down": The Biker Poet Anthology, published by Archer Books, CA ISBN 978-1-931122-19-1

[2]   "Some Biker Bitches Poetry" by Kimberly Manning-Keller Authors Choice Press ISBN 0-595-15258-9

[3]   Guggenheim Museum: Freedom and Post War Mobility: 1946-1958

[4]   *The Boston Globe* "The rhythms of the road", Emma Brown, Globe Correspondent October 21, 2008

[5]   The Highway Poets Motorcycle Club

[6]   *The Rebels* p75) By Daniel R. Wolf, University of Toronto Press ISBN 0-8020-7363-8,

[7]   Milwaukee professor riffs on poetry's history, evolution. The UMW Post by Graham Marlowe September 26, 2011

[8]   "A biker who runs her own business, writes poetry, and works for social causes makes it all look simple", *The Boston Globe* by Bill Griffith June 26, 2011

[9]   WGBH Boston interview with author José Gouveia on One Guest

[10]   The American Interest Online "High on the Hog" by Thomas M. Rickers December 2008

[11]   Biker Poetry & the Highway Poets Motorcycle Club By MJ Reynolds, editor Bikeweek.com

[12]   *Amphetamine Misuse: International Perspectives on Current Trends*, Edited by Hilary Klee p 116 Harwood Academic Press

[13]   *Austin Chronicle* "The "One Percenters", Jordon Smith May 19, 2006

[14]   Statement by the Blue Knights Law Enforcement M.C. on "The Motorcycle Brotherhood"

8.5   External links

- Highway Poets Motorcycle Club

- Biker Poets and Writers Association

- Road Poets of New York

- "Motorcycles and the art of poetic utterance", *The Guardian* 16 November 2007

Chapter 9

Cowboy poetry

Cowboy poetry is a form of poetry which grew out of a tradition of extemporaneous composition carried on by workers on cattle drives and ranches. After a day of work, cowboys would gather around a campfire and entertain one another with tall tales and folk songs. Illiteracy was common, so poetic forms were employed to aid memory.

9.1 Authorship

Contrary to common belief, cowboy poetry does not actually have to be written by cowboys, though adherents would claim that authors should have some connection to the cowboy life such that they can write poetry with an "insider's perspective". One example of a popular "cowboy poem" written by a non-cowboy is "The Ride of Paul Venarez" by Eben E. Rexford, a 19th-Century freelance author.

9.2 Style

Newcomers are surprised to hear cowboy poetry that is contemporary. Many people tend to focus on the historic cowboy lifestyle, but the work that cowboys do continues. The cowboy lifestyle is a living tradition that exists in western North America and other areas, thus, contemporary cowboy poetry is still being created, still being recited, and still entertaining many camp visitors around campfires and convention halls. Much of what is known as "old time" country music originates from the rhyming couplet style often seen in cowboy poetry along with guitar music.

9.3 Themes

Typical themes of cowboy poetry include:

- Ranch work and those who perform it
- Western lifestyle
- Landscape of the American and Canadian West
- Cowboy values and practices
- Humorous anecdotes
- Memories of times and people long gone
- Sarcasm regarding modern *contraptions* and/or *ways*

The following is a verse from LaVerna Johnson's poem "Homestead", which exhibits traditional cowboy poetry features:

> We hear calls of cattle lowing, voices carry on the breeze
>
> As it wanders down the canyon, then meanders through the trees.
>
> While we stop to smell the sage, light shimmers "quakie's" golden leaves,
>
> And it sure feels good to be back home again.

(Note the use of cowboy vernacular such as *quakie* (Populus tremuloides, trembling poplar or aspen known as a "quakie tree").

Though it deals with those who work with livestock and nature, it would be incorrect to categorize cowboy poetry as pastoral. Cowboy poetry is noted for its romantic imagery, but at no time does it sacrifice realism in favor of it.

Few examples of experimental verse are known in cowboy poetry. One argument is that cowboy poetry is meant to be recited and should "sound like poetry." The counter-argument runs that imposing a particular structure on cowboy poetry would move the focus away from the subject matter. Regardless, most cowboy poets stay within more classical guidelines, especially rhyming verse. So-called *free verse* poetry is uncommon in cowboy poetry.

9.4 Poetry weeks

Cowboy poetry continues to be written and celebrated today. Baxter Black is probably the most famous, and possibly the most prolific, contemporary cowboy poet. Many cities in the United States and Canada have annual "roundups" dedicated to cowboy poetry. Cowboy Poetry week is celebrated each April in the United States and Canada.[1]

9.5 Prominent cowboy poets

- S. Omar Barker
- Baxter Black
- Arthur Chapman
- Badger Clark
- Curley Fletcher
- Bruce Kiskaddon
- Wally McRae
- Joel Nelson
- Georgie Sicking
- Red Steagall
- Steven Fromholz
- Waddie Mitchell
- Paul Zarzyski
- Dan Hess
- Dalton Wilcox, "Poet Laureate of the West"

In addition, Robert W. Service is sometimes classified as a cowboy poet.

Famed spoken-word artist Bingo Gazingo has done at least one cowboy poem, "Everything's OK at the OK Corral."

9.6 See also

- Bush ballads
- Cowboy
- Rodeo

9.7 Notes

[1] http://www.cowboypoetry.com/week.htm

9.8 External links

- National Cowboy Poetry Gathering, Elko, Nevada
- Cowboy Poetry Gathering, Heber City, Utah
- Pincher Creek, Alberta, Cowboy Gathering
- Cowboy and Western Poetry at the Bar-D Ranch
- Jim Janke's Old West Cowboy Poetry
- Texas Cowboy Poetry Gathering
- Video from Texas Cowboy Poetry Gathering
- cowboy poetry gathering in Cartersville, GA
- Website of the Alberta Cowboy Poetry Association
- "Cowboy Poets" film at folkstreams.net
- Western & Cowboy Poetry by Clark Crouch
- Waddie Mitchell web page
- KPOV-FM Community Radio features Cowboy Poetry on the "Calling All Cowboys" online radio program. Live broadcast on 88.9 KPOV, on Wednesdays at 6PM and Sundays at 4PM (Pacific time) through the "Listen Live" link. It can also be streamed on demand at the following link: http://kpov-od.streamguys.us/calling_all_cowboys_new_56k.mp3

Chapter 10

English poetry

The Seeds and Fruits of English Poetry, *Ford Madox Brown.*

This article focuses on poetry written in English from the United Kingdom: England, Scotland, Wales, and Northern Ireland (and Ireland before 1922). However, though the whole of Ireland was politically part of the United Kingdom between January 1801 and December 1922, it is controversial to describe Irish literature as British. For some this includes works by authors from Northern Ireland. The article does not include poetry from other countries where the English language is spoken.

The earliest surviving **English poetry**, written in Anglo-Saxon, the direct predecessor of modern English, may have been composed as early as the 7th century.

10.1   The earliest English poetry

Main article: Old English poetry

The earliest known English poem is a hymn on the creation; Bede attributes this to Cædmon (fl. 658–680), who was, according to legend, an illiterate herdsman who produced extemporaneous poetry at a monastery at Whitby.[1] This is generally taken as marking the beginning of Anglo-Saxon poetry.

Much of the poetry of the period is difficult to date, or even to arrange chronologically; for example, estimates for the date of the great epic *Beowulf* range from AD 608 right through to AD 1000, and there has never been anything even approaching a consensus.[2] It is possible to identify certain key moments, however. *The Dream of the Rood* was written before circa AD 700, when excerpts were carved in runes on the Ruthwell Cross.[3] Some poems on historical events, such as *The Battle of Brunanburh* (937) and *The Battle of Maldon* (991), appear to have been composed shortly after the events in question, and can be dated reasonably precisely in consequence.

By and large, however, Anglo-Saxon poetry is categorised by the manuscripts in which it survives, rather than its date of composition. The most important manuscripts are the four great poetical codices of the late 10th and early 11th centuries, known as the Cædmon manuscript, the Vercelli Book, the Exeter Book, and the Beowulf manuscript.

While the poetry that has survived is limited in volume, it is wide in breadth. *Beowulf* is the only heroic epic to have survived in its entirety, but fragments of others such as Waldere and the Finnesburg Fragment show that it was not unique in its time. Other genres include much religious verse, from devotional works to biblical paraphrase; elegies such as *The Wanderer*, *The Seafarer*, and *The Ruin* (often taken to be a description of the ruins of Bath); and numerous proverbs, riddles, and charms.

With one notable exception (Rhyming Poem), Anglo-Saxon poetry depends on alliterative verse for its structure and any rhyme included is merely ornamental.

10.2   The Anglo-Norman period and the Later Middle Ages

See also: Anglo-Norman literature

With the Norman conquest of England, beginning in 1111 the Anglo-Saxon language rapidly diminished as a written literary language. The new aristocracy spoke predominantly Norman, and this became the standard language of courts, parliament, and polite society. As the invaders integrated, their language and literature mingled with that of the natives: the Oïl dialect of the upper classes became Anglo-Norman, and Anglo-Saxon underwent a gradual transition into Middle English.

While Anglo-Norman or Latin was preferred for high culture, English literature by no means died out, and a number of important works illustrate the development of the language. Around the turn of the 13th century, Layamon wrote his *Brut*, based on Wace's 12th century Anglo-Norman epic of the same name; Layamon's language is recognisably Middle English, though his prosody shows a strong Anglo-Saxon influence remaining. Other transitional works were preserved as popular entertainment, including a variety of romances and lyrics. With time, the English language regained prestige, and in 1362 it replaced French and Latin in Parliament and courts of law.

It was with the 14th century that major works of English literature began once again to appear; these include the so-called Pearl Poet's *Pearl*, *Patience*, *Cleanness*, and *Sir Gawain and the Green Knight*; Langland's political and religious allegory *Piers Plowman*; Gower's *Confessio Amantis*; and the works of Chaucer, the most highly regarded English poet of the Middle Ages, who was seen by his contemporaries as a successor to the great tradition of Virgil and Dante.

The reputation of Chaucer's successors in the 15th century has suffered in comparison with him, though Lydgate and Skelton are widely studied. A group of Scottish writers arose who were formerly believed to be influenced by Chaucer. The rise of Scottish poetry began with the writing of *The Kingis Quair* by James I of Scotland. The main poets of this Scottish group were Robert Henryson, William Dunbar and Gavin Douglas. Henryson and Douglas introduced a note of almost savage satire, which may have owed something to the Gaelic bards, while Douglas' *Eneados*, a translation into Middle Scots of Virgil's *Aeneid*, was the first complete translation of any major work of classical antiquity into an English or Anglic language.

10.3 The Renaissance in England

The Renaissance was slow in coming to England, with the generally accepted start date being around 1509. It is also generally accepted that the English Renaissance extended until the Restoration in 1660. However, a number of factors had prepared the way for the introduction of the new learning long before this start date. A number of medieval poets had, as already noted, shown an interest in the ideas of Aristotle and the writings of European Renaissance precursors such as Dante.

The introduction of movable-block printing by Caxton in 1474 provided the means for the more rapid dissemination of new or recently rediscovered writers and thinkers. Caxton also printed the works of Chaucer and Gower and these books helped establish the idea of a native poetic tradition that was linked to its European counterparts. In addition, the writings of English humanists like Thomas More and Thomas Elyot helped bring the ideas and attitudes associated with the new learning to an English audience.

Three other factors in the establishment of the English Renaissance were the Reformation, Counter Reformation, and the opening of the era of English naval power and overseas exploration and expansion. The establishment of the Church of England in 1535 accelerated the process of questioning the Catholic world-view that had previously dominated intellectual and artistic life. At the same time, long-distance sea voyages helped provide the stimulus and information that underpinned a new understanding of the nature of the universe which resulted in the theories of Nicolaus Copernicus and Johannes Kepler.

10.3.1 Early Renaissance poetry

With a small number of exceptions, the early years of the 16th century are not particularly notable. The Douglas *Aeneid* was completed in 1513 and John Skelton wrote poems that were transitional between the late Medieval and Renaissance styles. The new king, Henry VIII, was something of a poet himself. The most significant English poet of this period was Thomas Wyatt, who was among the first poets to write sonnets in English.

10.3.2 The Elizabethans

The Elizabethan period (1558 to 1603) in poetry is characterized by a number of frequently overlapping developments. The introduction and adaptation of themes, models and verse forms from other European traditions and classical literature, the Elizabethan song tradition, the emergence of a courtly poetry often centred around the figure of the monarch and the growth of a verse-based drama are among the most important of these developments.

Elizabethan Song

A wide range of Elizabethan poets wrote songs, including Nicholas Grimald, Thomas Nashe and Robert Southwell. There are also a large number of extant anonymous songs from the period. Perhaps the greatest of all the songwriters was Thomas Campion. Campion is also notable because of his experiments with metres based on counting syllables rather than stresses. These quantitative metres were based on classical models and should be viewed as part of the wider Renaissance revival of Greek and Roman artistic methods.

The songs were generally printed either in miscellanies or anthologies such as Richard Tottel's 1557 *Songs and Sonnets* or in songbooks that included printed music to enable performance. These performances formed an integral part of both public and private entertainment. By the end of the 16th century, a new generation of composers, including John Dowland, William Byrd, Orlando Gibbons, Thomas Weelkes and Thomas Morley were helping to bring the art of Elizabethan song to an extremely high musical level.

Elizabethan poems and plays were often written in iambic meters, based on a metrical foot of two syllables, one unstressed and one stressed. However, much metrical experimentation took place during the period, and many of the songs, in particular, departed widely from the iambic norm.

Courtly poetry

With the consolidation of Elizabeth's power, a genuine court sympathetic to poetry and the arts in general emerged. This encouraged the emergence of a poetry aimed at, and often set in, an idealised version of the courtly world.

Among the best known examples of this are Edmund Spenser's *The Faerie Queene*, which is effectively an extended hymn of praise to the queen, and Philip Sidney's *Arcadia*. This courtly trend can also be seen in Spenser's *Shepheardes Calender*. This poem marks the introduction into an English context of the classical pastoral, a mode of poetry that assumes an aristocratic audience with a certain kind of attitude to the land and peasants. The explorations of love found in the sonnets of William Shakespeare and the poetry of Walter Raleigh and others also implies a courtly audience.

Classicism

Virgil's *Aeneid*, Thomas Campion's metrical experiments, and Spenser's *Shepheardes Calender* and plays like Shakespeare's *Antony and Cleopatra* are all examples of the influence of classicism on Elizabethan poetry. It remained common for poets of the period to write on themes from classical mythology; Shakespeare's *Venus and Adonis* and the Christopher Marlowe/George Chapman *Hero and Leander* are examples of this kind of work.

Translations of classical poetry also became more widespread, with the versions of Ovid's *Metamorphoses* by Arthur Golding (1565–67) and George Sandys (1626), and Chapman's translations of Homer's *Iliad* (1611) and *Odyssey* (c.1615), among the outstanding examples.

10.3.3   Jacobean and Caroline poetry

English Renaissance poetry after the Elizabethan poetry can be seen as belonging to one of three strains; the Metaphysical poets, the Cavalier poets and the school of Spenser. However, the boundaries between these three groups are not always clear and an individual poet could write in more than one manner.

The Metaphysical poets

Main article: Metaphysical poets

The early 17th century saw the emergence of this group of poets who wrote in a witty, complicated style. The most famous of the Metaphysicals is probably John Donne. Others include George Herbert, Thomas Traherne, Henry Vaughan, Andrew Marvell, and Richard Crashaw. John Milton in his *Comus* falls into this group. The Metaphysical poets went out of favour in the 18th century but began to be read again in the Victorian era. Donne's reputation was finally fully restored by the approbation of T. S. Eliot in the early 20th century.

The Cavalier poets

The Cavalier poets wrote in a lighter, more elegant and artificial style than the Metaphysical poets. Leading members of the group include Ben Jonson, Richard Lovelace, Robert Herrick, Edmund Waller, Thomas Carew and John Denham. The Cavalier poets can be seen as the forerunners of the major poets of the Augustan era, who admired them greatly.

10.4   The Restoration and 18th century

It is perhaps ironic that *Paradise Lost*, a story of fallen pride, was the first major poem to appear in England after the Restoration. The court of Charles II had, in its years in France, learned a worldliness and sophistication that marked it as distinctively different from the monarchies that preceded the Republic. Even if Charles had wanted to reassert the divine right of kingship, the Protestantism and taste for power of the intervening years would have rendered it impossible.

10.4.1 Satire

It is hardly surprising that the world of fashion and scepticism that emerged encouraged the art of satire. All the major poets of the period, Samuel Butler, John Dryden, Alexander Pope and Samuel Johnson, and the Irish poet Jonathan Swift, wrote satirical verse. What is perhaps more surprising is that their satire was often written in defence of public order and the established church and government. However, writers such as Pope used their gift for satire to create scathing works responding to their detractors or to criticise what they saw as social atrocities perpetrated by the government. Pope's "The Dunciad" is a satirical slaying of two of his literary adversaries (Lewis Theobald, and Colley Cibber in a later version), expressing the view that British society was falling apart morally, culturally, and intellectually.

10.4.2 18th century classicism

The 18th century is sometimes called the Augustan age, and contemporary admiration for the classical world extended to the poetry of the time. Not only did the poets aim for a polished high style in emulation of the Roman ideal, they also translated and imitated Greek and Latin verse resulting in measured rationalised elegant verse. Dryden translated all the known works of Virgil, and Pope produced versions of the two Homeric epics. Horace and Juvenal were also widely translated and imitated, Horace most famously by John Wilmot, Earl of Rochester and Juvenal by Samuel Johnson's *Vanity of Human Wishes*.

10.4.3 Women poets in the 18th century

A number of women poets of note emerged during the period of the Restoration, including Aphra Behn, Margaret Cavendish, Mary Chudleigh, Anne Finch, Anne Killigrew, and Katherine Philips. Nevertheless, print publication by women poets was still relatively scarce when compared to that of men, though manuscript evidence indicates that many more women poets were practicing than was previously thought. Disapproval of feminine "forwardness", however, kept many out of print in the early part of the period, and even as the century progressed women authors still felt the need to justify their incursions into the public sphere by claiming economic necessity or the pressure of friends. Women writers were increasingly active in all genres throughout the 18th century, and by the 1790s women's poetry was flourishing. Notable poets later in the period include Anna Laetitia Barbauld, Joanna Baillie, Susanna Blamire, Felicia Hemans, Mary Leapor, Lady Mary Wortley Montagu, Hannah More, and Mary Robinson. In the past decades there has been substantial scholarly and critical work done on women poets of the long 18th century: first, to reclaim them and make them available in contemporary editions in print or online, and second, to assess them and position them within a literary tradition.

10.4.4 The late 18th century

Towards the end of the 18th century, poetry began to move away from the strict Augustan ideals and a new emphasis on sentiment and the feelings of the poet. This trend can perhaps be most clearly seen in the handling of nature, with a move away from poems about formal gardens and landscapes by urban poets and towards poems about nature as lived in. The leading exponents of this new trend include Thomas Gray, George Crabbe, Christopher Smart and Robert Burns as well as the Irish poet Oliver Goldsmith. These poets can be seen as paving the way for the Romantic movement.

10.5 The Romantic movement

The last quarter of the 18th century was a time of social and political turbulence, with revolutions in the United States, France, Ireland and elsewhere. In Great Britain, movement for social change and a more inclusive sharing of power was also growing. This was the backdrop against which the Romantic movement in English poetry emerged.

The main poets of this movement were William Blake, William Wordsworth, Samuel Taylor Coleridge, Percy Bysshe Shelley, Lord Byron, and John Keats. The birth of English Romanticism is often dated to the publication in 1798 of Wordsworth and Coleridge's *Lyrical Ballads*. However, Blake had been publishing since the early 1780s. Much of the focus on Blake only came about during the last century when Northrop Frye discussed his work in his book "The Anatomy of

Criticism." Shelley is most famous for such classic anthology verse works as *Ozymandias*, and long visionary poems which include *Prometheus Unbound*. Shelley's groundbreaking poem *The Masque of Anarchy* calls for nonviolence in protest and political action. It is perhaps the first modern statement of the principle of nonviolent protest.[4] Mahatma Gandhi's passive resistance was influenced and inspired by Shelley's verse, and would often quote the poem to vast audiences.[4][5]

In poetry, the Romantic movement emphasised the creative expression of the individual and the need to find and formulate new forms of expression. The Romantics, with the partial exception of Byron, rejected the poetic ideals of the 18th century, and each of them returned to Milton for inspiration, though each drew something different from Milton. They also put a good deal of stress on their own originality.

To the Romantics, the moment of creation was the most important in poetic expression and could not be repeated once it passed. Because of this new emphasis, poems that were not complete were nonetheless included in a poet's body of work (such as Coleridge's "Kubla Khan" and "Christabel").

Additionally, the Romantic movement marked a shift in the use of language. Attempting to express the "language of the common man", Wordsworth and his fellow Romantic poets focused on employing poetic language for a wider audience, countering the mimetic, tightly constrained Neo-Classic poems (although it's important to note that the poet wrote first and foremost for his/her own creative, expression). In Shelley's "Defense of Poetry", he contends that poets are the "creators of language" and that the poet's job is to refresh language for their society.

The Romantics were not the only poets of note at this time. In the work of John Clare the late Augustan voice is blended with a peasant's first-hand knowledge to produce arguably some of the finest nature poetry in the English language. Another contemporary poet who does not fit into the Romantic group was Walter Savage Landor. Landor was a classicist whose poetry forms a link between the Augustans and Robert Browning, who much admired it.

10.6 Victorian poetry

The Victorian era was a period of great political change, social and economic change. The Empire recovered from the loss of the American colonies and entered a period of rapid expansion. This expansion, combined with increasing industrialisation and mechanisation, led to a prolonged period of economic growth. The Reform Act 1832 was the beginning of a process that would eventually lead to universal suffrage.

10.6.1 High Victorian poetry

The major High Victorian poets were John Clare, Alfred, Lord Tennyson, Robert Browning, Elizabeth Barrett Browning, Matthew Arnold and Gerard Manley Hopkins, though Hopkins was not published until 1918.

John Clare came to be known for his celebratory representations of the English countryside and his lamentation of its disruption. His biographer Jonathan Bate states that Clare was "the greatest labouring-class poet that England has ever produced. No one has ever written more powerfully of nature, of a rural childhood, and of the alienated and unstable self".

Tennyson was, to some degree, the Spenser of the new age and his *Idylls of the Kings* can be read as a Victorian version of *The Faerie Queen*, that is as a poem that sets out to provide a mythic foundation to the idea of empire.

The Brownings spent much of their time out of England and explored European models and matter in much of their poetry. Robert Browning's great innovation was the dramatic monologue, which he used to its full extent in his long novel in verse, *The Ring and the Book*. Elizabeth Barrett Browning is perhaps best remembered for *Sonnets from the Portuguese* but her long poem *Aurora Leigh* is one of the classics of 19th century feminist literature.

Matthew Arnold was much influenced by Wordsworth, though his poem *Dover Beach* is often considered a precursor of the modernist revolution. Hopkins wrote in relative obscurity and his work was not published until after his death. His unusual style (involving what he called "sprung rhythm" and heavy reliance on rhyme and alliteration) had a considerable influence on many of the poets of the 1940s.

10.6.2 Pre-Raphaelites, arts and crafts, Aestheticism, and the "Yellow" 1890s

The Pre-Raphaelite Brotherhood was a mid-19th century arts movement dedicated to the reform of what they considered the sloppy Mannerist painting of the day. Although primarily concerned with the visual arts, two members, the brother and sister Dante Gabriel Rossetti and Christina Rossetti, were also poets of some ability. Their poetry shares many of the concerns of the painters; an interest in Medieval models, an almost obsessive attention to visual detail and an occasional tendency to lapse into whimsy.

Dante Rossetti worked with, and had some influence on, the leading arts and crafts painter and poet William Morris. Morris shared the Pre-Raphaelite interest in the poetry of the European Middle Ages, to the point of producing some illuminated manuscript volumes of his work.

Towards the end of the century, English poets began to take an interest in French symbolism and Victorian poetry entered a decadent *fin-de-siecle* phase. Two groups of poets emerged, the *Yellow Book* poets who adhered to the tenets of Aestheticism, including Algernon Charles Swinburne, Oscar Wilde and Arthur Symons and the Rhymers' Club group that included Ernest Dowson, Lionel Johnson and William Butler Yeats.

10.6.3 Comic verse

Comic verse abounded in the Victorian era. Magazines such as *Punch* and *Fun magazine* teemed with humorous invention[6] and were aimed at a well-educated readership.[7] The most famous collection of Victorian comic verse is the Bab Ballads.[8]

10.7 The 20th century

10.7.1 The first three decades

The Victorian era continued into the early years of the 20th century and two figures emerged as the leading representative of the poetry of the old era to act as a bridge into the new. These were Yeats and Thomas Hardy. Yeats, although not a modernist, was to learn a lot from the new poetic movements that sprang up around him and adapted his writing to the new circumstances. Hardy was, in terms of technique at least, a more traditional figure and was to be a reference point for various anti-modernist reactions, especially from the 1950s onwards.

A. E. Housman (1859 – 1936) was poet who was born in the Victorian era and who first published in the 1890s, but who only really became known in the 20th century. Housman is best known for his cycle of poems *A Shropshire Lad* (1896). This collection was turned down by several publishers so that Housman published it himself, and the work only became popular when "the advent of war, first in the Boer War and then in World War I, gave the book widespread appeal due to its nostalgic depiction of brave English soldiers".[9] The poems' wistful evocation of doomed youth in the English countryside, in spare language and distinctive imagery, appealed strongly to late Victorian and Edwardian taste, and the fact that several early 20th-century composers set it to music helped its popularity. Housman published a further highly successful collection *Last Poems* in 1922 while a third volume, *More Poems*, was published posthumously in 1936.[10]

The Georgian poets and World War I

The Georgian poets were the first major grouping of the post-Victorian era. Their work appeared in a series of five anthologies called *Georgian Poetry* which were published by Harold Monro and edited by Edward Marsh. The poets featured included Edmund Blunden, Rupert Brooke, Robert Graves, D. H. Lawrence, Walter de la Mare and Siegfried Sassoon. Their poetry represented something of a reaction to the decadence of the 1890s and tended towards the sentimental.

Brooke and Sassoon were to go on to win reputations as war poets and Lawrence quickly distanced himself from the group and was associated with the modernist movement. Graves distanced himself from the group as well and wrote poetry in accordance with a belief in a prehistoric Muse he described as The White Goddess. Other notable poets who wrote about the war include Isaac Rosenberg, Edward Thomas, Wilfred Owen, May Cannan and, from the home front, Hardy and

Rudyard Kipling, whose inspirational poem *If—* is a national favourite. Like William Ernest Henley's poem *Invictus* that has inspired such people as Nelson Mandela when he was incarcerated,[13] *If—* is a memorable evocation of Victorian stoicism, regarded as a traditional British virtue. Although many of these poets wrote socially-aware criticism of the war, most remained technically conservative and traditionalist.

Modernism

Among the foremost *avant-garde* writers were the American-born poets Gertrude Stein, T. S. Eliot, H.D. and Ezra Pound, each of whom spent an important part of their writing lives in England, France and Italy.

Pound's involvement with the Imagists marked the beginning of a revolution in the way poetry was written. English poets involved with this group included D. H. Lawrence, Richard Aldington, T. E. Hulme, F. S. Flint, Ford Madox Ford, Allen Upward and John Cournos. Eliot, particularly after the publication of *The Waste Land*, became a major figure and influence on other English poets.

In addition to these poets, other English modernists began to emerge. These included the London-Welsh poet and painter David Jones, whose first book, *In Parenthesis*, was one of the very few experimental poems to come out of World War I, the Scot Hugh MacDiarmid, Mina Loy and Basil Bunting.

10.7.2   The Thirties

The poets who began to emerge in the 1930s had two things in common; they had all been born too late to have any real experience of the pre-World War I world and they grew up in a period of social, economic and political turmoil. Perhaps as a consequence of these facts, themes of community, social (in)justice and war seem to dominate the poetry of the decade.

The poetic space of the decade was dominated by four poets; W. H. Auden, Stephen Spender, Cecil Day-Lewis and Louis MacNeice, although the last of these belongs at least as much to the history of Irish poetry. These poets were all, in their early days at least, politically active on the Left. Although they admired Eliot, they also represented a move away from the technical innovations of their modernist predecessors. A number of other, less enduring, poets also worked in the same vein. One of these was Michael Roberts, whose *New Country* anthology both introduced the group to a wider audience and gave them their name.

The 1930s also saw the emergence of a home-grown English surrealist poetry whose main exponents were David Gascoyne, Hugh Sykes Davies, George Barker, and Philip O'Connor. These poets turned to French models rather than either the *New Country* poets or English-language modernism, and their work was to prove of importance to later English experimental poets as it broadened the scope of the English *avant-garde* tradition.

John Betjeman and Stevie Smith, who were two of the most significant poets of this period, stood outside all schools and groups. Betjeman was a quietly ironic poet of Middle England with a fine command of a wide range of verse techniques. Smith was an entirely unclassifiable one-off voice.

10.7.3   The Forties

The 1940s opened with the United Kingdom at war and a new generation of war poets emerged in response. These included Keith Douglas, Alun Lewis, Henry Reed and F. T. Prince. As with the poets of the First World War, the work of these writers can be seen as something of an interlude in the history of 20th century poetry. Technically, many of these war poets owed something to the 1930s poets, but their work grew out of the particular circumstances in which they found themselves living and fighting.

The main movement in post-war 1940s poetry was the New Romantic group that included Dylan Thomas, George Barker, W. S. Graham, Kathleen Raine, Henry Treece and J. F. Hendry. These writers saw themselves as in revolt against the classicism of the *New Country* poets. They turned to such models as Gerard Manley Hopkins, Arthur Rimbaud and Hart Crane and the word play of James Joyce. Thomas, in particular, helped Anglo-Welsh poetry to emerge as a recognisable force.

Other significant poets to emerge in the 1940s include Lawrence Durrell, Bernard Spencer, Roy Fuller, Norman Nicholson, Vernon Watkins, R. S. Thomas and Norman MacCaig. These last four poets represent a trend towards regionalism and poets writing about their native areas; Watkins and Thomas in Wales, Nicholson in Cumberland and MacCaig in Scotland.

10.7.4 The Fifties

The 1950s were dominated by three groups of poets, The Movement, The Group and a number of poets that gathered around the label Extremist Art.

The Movement poets as a group came to public notice in Robert Conquest's 1955 anthology *New Lines*. The core of the group consisted of Philip Larkin, Elizabeth Jennings, D. J. Enright, Kingsley Amis, Thom Gunn and Donald Davie. They were identified with a hostility to modernism and internationalism, and looked to Hardy as a model. However, both Davie and Gunn later moved away from this position.

As befits their name, the Group were much more formally a group of poets, meeting for weekly discussions under the chairmanship of Philip Hobsbaum and Edward Lucie-Smith. Other Group poets included Martin Bell, Peter Porter, Peter Redgrove, George MacBeth and David Wevill. Hobsbaum spent some time teaching in Belfast, where he was a formative influence on the emerging Northern Ireland poets including Seamus Heaney.

The term Extremist Art was first used by the poet A. Alvarez to describe the work of the American poet Sylvia Plath. Other poets associated with this group included Plath's one-time husband Ted Hughes, Francis Berry and Jon Silkin. These poets are sometimes compared with the Expressionist German school.

A number of young poets working in what might be termed a modernist vein also started publishing during this decade. These included Charles Tomlinson, Gael Turnbull, Roy Fisher and Bob Cobbing. These poets can now be seen as fore-runners of some of the major developments during the following two decades.

10.7.5 The 1960s and 1970s

In the early part of the 1960s, the centre of gravity of mainstream poetry moved to Northern Ireland, with the emergence of Seamus Heaney, Tom Paulin, Paul Muldoon and others. In England, the most cohesive groupings can, in retrospect, be seen to cluster around what might loosely be called the modernist tradition and draw on American as well as indigenous models.

The British Poetry Revival was a wide-reaching collection of groupings and subgroupings that embraces performance, sound and concrete poetry as well as the legacy of Pound, Jones, MacDiarmid, Loy and Bunting, the Objectivist poets, the Beats and the Black Mountain poets, among others. Leading poets associated with this movement include J. H. Prynne, Eric Mottram, Tom Raworth, Denise Riley and Lee Harwood.

The Mersey Beat poets were Adrian Henri, Brian Patten and Roger McGough. Their work was a self-conscious attempt at creating an English equivalent to the Beats. Many of their poems were written in protest against the established social order and, particularly, the threat of nuclear war. Although not actually a Mersey Beat poet, Adrian Mitchell is often associated with the group in critical discussion. Contemporary poet Steve Turner has also been compared with them.

About half-way from the Beats and the Angry Young Men stands Keith Barnes whose themes are WWII, love, social criticism and death. His Collected Poems were published in France.

10.8 English poetry now

Many consider Geoffrey Hill to be the finest English poet writing today.[14] Mark Ford is an English poet who writes in the tradition of the New York School. The last three decades of the 20th century saw a number of short-lived poetic groupings, including the Martians, along with a general trend towards what has been termed 'Poeclectics',[15] namely an intensification within individual poets' oeuvres of "all kinds of style, subject, voice, register and form". There has also been a growth in interest in women's writing, and in poetry from England's minorities, especially the West Indian community. Performance poetry has gained popularity, fuelled by the poetry slam movement. Poets who emerged in this period include Carol Ann Duffy, Andrew Motion, Craig Raine, Wendy Cope, James Fenton, Blake Morrison, Liz Lochhead, Linton Kwesi Johnson and Benjamin Zephaniah.

Even more recent activity focused around poets in Bloodaxe Books' The New Poetry, including Simon Armitage, Kathleen Jamie, Glyn Maxwell, Selima Hill, Maggie Hannan, Michael Hofmann and Peter Reading. The New Generation movement flowered in the 1990s and early 2000s, producing poets such as Don Paterson, Julia Copus, John Stammers, Jacob Polley, K M Warwick, David Morley and Alice Oswald. A new generation of innovative poets has also sprung up in the wake of the Revival grouping, notably Caroline Bergvall, Tony Lopez, Allen Fisher and Denise Riley.[16] There has been, too, a remarkable upsurge in independent and experimental poetry pamphlet publishers such as Barque, Flarestack, Knives, Forks and Spoons Press, Penned in the Margins, Heaventree (founded in 2002 but no longer publishing) and Perdika Press. Throughout this period, and to the present, independent poetry presses such as Enitharmon have continued to promote original work from (among others) Dannie Abse, Martyn Crucefix and Jane Duran.

10.9 Notes

[1] Bede, Historia ecclesiastica gentis Anglorum.

[2] *See, for example, Beowulf: a Dual-Language Edition*, Doubleday, New York, NY, 1977; Newton, S., 1993. *The Origins of Beowulf and the Pre-Viking Kingdom of East Anglia.* Cambridge.

[3] Brendan Cassidy (ed.), *The Ruthwell Cross*, Princeton University Press (1992).

[4] http://www.morrissociety.org/JWMS/SP94.10.4.Nichols.pdf

[5] Thomas Weber, "Gandhi as Disciple and Mentor," Cambridge University Press, 2004, pp. 28–29.

[6] Spielmann, M. H. *The History of "Punch"*, from Project Gutenberg

[7] Vann, J. Don. "Comic Periodicals", *Victorian Periodicals & Victorian Society* (Aldershot: Scholar Press, 1994)

[8] Stedman, Jane W. (1996). *W. S. Gilbert, A Classic Victorian & His Theatre*, pp. 26–29. Oxford University Press. ISBN 0-19-816174-3

[9] Poetry.org

[10]

[11] Emma Jones (2004) The Literary Companion Robson, 2004.

[12] Mike Robinson (2004) Literature and tourism

[13] Elleke Boehmer (2008). Nelson Mandela: a very short introduction. p.157. Oxford University Press, 2008. "'Invictus', taken on its own, Mandela clearly found his Victorian ethic of self-mastery given compelling expression within the frame of a controlled rhyme scheme supported by strong, monosyllabic nouns. It was only a small step from espousing this poem to assuming a Victorian persona, as he could do in letters to his children. In ways they predictably found alienating, he liked to exhort them to ever-greater effort, reiterating that ambition and drive were the only means of escaping an 'inferior position' in life".

[14] William Logan, The New Criterion, "Stouthearted Men," June 2004.

[15] Making Voices: Identity, Poeclectics and the Contemporary British Poet; *New Writing*, The International Journal for the Practice and Theory of Creative Writing; Volume 3 (1); pp 66–77

[16] Don Paterson, The Dark Art of Poetry: T.S. Eliot Lecture, 9 November 2004: "Geniune talents such as, say, Tony Lopez and Denise Riley, working recognisably within the English and European lyric traditions, are drowned by the chorus of articulate but fundamentally talentless poet-commentators".

10.10 See also

- English literature
- British literature
- Imagism
- Irish poetry
- List of years in poetry
- Modernist poetry
- New Oxford Book of English Verse 1250–1950
- Poets' Corner
- Scottish literature
- Welsh literature in English

10.11 References

Print

- Hamilton, Ian. *The Oxford Companion to Twentieth-Century Poetry in English*

Online

- A Time-line of English poetry

10.12 External links

- Poets perform their own work

HWÆT WE GARDE
na in geardagum. þeod cyninga
þrym gefrunon huða æþelingas elle
fremedon. oft scyld scefing sceaþe
þreatum monegu mægþum meodo setla
ofteah egsode eorl syððan ærest wear
feasceaft funden he þæs frofre geba
weox under wolcnum weorð myndum þah
oð þ him æghpylc þara ymb sittendra
ofer hron rade hyran scolde. gomban
gyldan þ wæs god cyning. ðæm eafera wæs
æfter cenned geong ingeardum þone god
sende folce tofrofre fyren ðearfe on
geat þ hie ær drugon aldor ease. lange
hpile him þæs lif frea wuldres wealder
worold are forgeaf. beowulf wæs bren
blæd wide sprang. scyldes eafera scede
landum in. ...
ge hpylcum gmonnum ...

Edmund Spenser

John Donne

Aphra Behn

William Wordsworth

Lord Byron

John Clare

Elizabeth Barrett Browning

Dante Gabriel Rossetti: selfportrait

Rudyard Kipling's If— *(1895), often voted Britain's favourite poem.*[11][12]

Chapter 11

Hebrew poetry

Hebrew poetry is poetry written in the Hebrew language. It encompasses such things as:

- Biblical poetry, the poetry found in the poetic books of the Hebrew Bible
- Piyyut, religious Jewish liturgical poetry in Hebrew or Aramaic
- Medieval Hebrew poetry written in Hebrew
- Modern Hebrew poetry, poetry written after the revival of the Hebrew language

See also:

- List of Hebrew language poets
- Hebrew literature
- Israeli literature
- Jewish literature

Chapter 12

Indian poetry

Indian poetry and Indian literature in general, has a long history dating back to Vedic times. They were written in various Indian languages such as Vedic Sanskrit, Classical Sanskrit, Oriya, Tamil, Kannada, Bengali and Urdu. Poetry in foreign languages such as Persian and English also has a strong influence on Indian poetry. The poetry reflects diverse spiritual traditions within India. In particular, many Indian poets have been inspired by mystical experiences.Poetry is the oldest form of literature and has a rich written and oral tradition.

12.1   Forms of Indian poetry

- Assamese poetry

- Bengali poetry

- Doha

- English Poetry in India

- Epic Poetry in India

- Ghazal

- Gujarati poetry

- Hindi poetry

- Kannada poetry

- Kashmiri poetry

- Konkani poetry

- haeieoriroer

- Malayalam poetry

- Manipuri Bishnupriya poetry

- Marathi poetry

- Meitei poetry

- Nepali poetry

- Oriya poetry

- Punjabi poetry

- Rajasthani poetry

- Sanskrit Classical poetry

- Sindhi poetry

- Tamil poetry

- Telugu poetry

- Urdu poetry

12.2   Indian Poetry Awards

There are very few literary awards in India for poetry alone. The prestigious awards like Jnanapeeth, Sahitya Akademi and Kalidas Samman etc. are given away to writers of both prose and poetry. Most of the awards have gone to novelists. Few outstanding poets have received these prestigious awards.

12.2.1   Jnanpith Award

The following poets have won the prestigious Jnanpith award for their poetry :- Firaq Gorakhpuri for his *Gul-e-Naghma* (1969), Amrita Pritam for her *Kagaz te Kanvas* (1981), Qurratulain Hyder for her *Akhire Sab ke Humsafar* (1989) and O. N. V. Kurup for his contribution to Malayalam poetry (2007).

12.2.2   Ananda Puraskar and Rabindra Puraskar

Ananda Bazar Patrika have instituted the prestigious annual Ananda Puraskar for Bengali literature. There is also prestigious Rabindra Puraskar. But these awards have usually gone to novelists. The rare poets to have won these awards include Premendra Mitra for *Sagar theke phera* (1957), Buddhadeb Basu for *Swagato Biday* (1974), Aruna Mitra for *Suddhu Rater Shabda* (1979), Joy Goswami for *Ghumeichho* (1990), Srijato for *Uranto Sab Joker* (2004) and Pinaki Thakur for *Chumbaner Kshato* (2012).

12.2.3   Sahitya Akademi Awards

Sahitya Akademi gives away annual prizes for both original works of poetry in the recognised Indian languages, as well as outstanding works of translation of Indian poetry. The award winners for English poetry include Jayanta Mahapatra for *Relationship* (1981), Nissim Ezekiel for *Latter-Day Psalms* (1983), Keki N. Daruwalla for *The Keeper of the Dead* (1984), Kamala Das for *Collected Poems* (1985), Shiv K. Kumar for *Trapfalls in the Sky* (1987), Dom Moraes for *Serendip* (1994), A. K. Ramanujan for *Collected Poems* (1999) and Jeet Thayil for *These Errors are Correct* (1912).[1] Recent Akademi awardees for poetry in other Indian languages include H. S. Shivaprakash (Kannada) and K. Satchidanandan (Malayalam).[2] Other eminent Sahitya Akademi award winning poets include Amrita Pritam (Punjabi) for *Sunehe* (1956), V. K. Gokak (Kannada) for *Divya Prithvi* (1960), G. Sankara Kurup (Malayalam) for *Viswadarshanam* (1963), Kusumagraj (Marathi) for *Natsamrat* (1974), Kaifi Azmi (Urdu) for *Awara Sajde* (1975), Sunil Gangopadhyay (Bengali) for *Sei Somoy* (1984), Kanhaiyalal Sethia (Rajasthani) for *Lilatamsa* (1984), Hiren Bhattacharyya (Assamese) for *Saichor Pathar Manuh* (1992), Gunturu Seshendra Sarma (Telugu) for *Kaala Rekha* (1994), Srinivas Rath (Sanskrit) for *Tadaiva Gaganam Shaivadhara* (1999) and Pratibha Satpathy (Oriya) for *Tanmaya Dhuli* (2001).

12.2.4 Indian Literature Golden Jubilee Poetry Awards

On the occasion of its Golden Jubilee, Sahitya Akademi awarded the following prizes for outstanding works of poetry in translation from Indian languages.

- Rana Nayar for his translation of the verses of the Sikh saint Baba Farid from Punjabi.

- Dr Tapan Kumar Pradhan for English translation of his own Oriya poem collection Kalahandi.

- Paromita Das for English translation of Parvati Prasad Baruwa's poems in Assamese.

The Golden Jubilee Prize for Life Time Achievement was won by Namdeo Dhasal, Ranjit Hoskote, Abdul Rashid, Neelakshi Singh and Sithara S.

12.2.5 All India Poetry Champions

The Poetry Society (India) gives annual awards solely for poetry. Following poets have won the prestigious annual prizes instituted by the Poetry Society (India) in collaboration with British Council and Ministry of Human Resource Development (India) ;-

- 1988 : Vijay Nambisan for *"Madras Central"*

- 1990 : Rukmini Bhaya Nair for *"Kali"*

- 1991 : Rajlukshmee Debee Bhattacharya for *"Punarnava"*

- 1993 : Shampa Sinha for *"Siesta"*, and Tarun Cherian for *"A Writer's Prayer"*

- 1994 : Anju Makhija for *"A Farmer's Ghost"*, and Smita Agarwal for *"Our Foster Nurse of Nature is Repose"*

- 1995 : Tabish Khair for *"Birds of North Europe"*, and Gopi Krishnan Kottoor for *"The Coffin Maker"*

- 1997 : Ranjit Hoskote for *"Portrait of a Lady"*, and Gopi Krishnan Kottoor for *"Digging"*

- 1998 : K. Sri Lata for *"In Santa Cruz, Diagnosed Home Sick"*

- 2000 : Shahnaz Habib for *"Of Hypocrisy and Cheekbones"*, and Revathy Gopal for *"I Would Know You Anywhere"*

- 2013 : Mathew John for *"Another Letter from Another Father to Another Son"*.

12.3 Western thinkers and poets interested in Indian poetry

In the 19th century, American Transcendentalist writers and many German Romantic writers became interested in Indian poetry, literature and thought. In the 20th century, few Western poets became interested in Indian thought and literature, and the interest of many of those was minor: T. S. Eliot studied Sanskrit at Harvard, but later lost interest. Buddhism brought Allen Ginsberg and Gary Snyder to India, but they became more interested in Tibetan and Japanese forms of the religion. Mexican poet and writer Octavio Paz developed a strong, lasting interest in Indian poetry after living in the country as part of the Mexican diplomatic mission (and as ambassador in the 1960s). Paz married an Indian woman, translated Sanskrit *kavyas*, and wrote extensively about India.[3] The Australian poet Colin Dean as listed in the Australian Literature Resource database shows interested in Indian thought and literature and as such has written many poems on Indian themes: Indian mythology;classical Sanskrit plays; Indian philosophy;Indian folktales and translated Sanskrit poetry. Some of these works are:The Caurapâñcâśikâ (The Love-Thief) Of Bilhana ;The Amarusataka of Amaru;Shakuntala;The Subhashitasringar;The-Travels-Of-Pandit-Ganja-Deen-The-Sadhaka;The-Twenty-Fifth-Tale-Of-The-Vetala;Rishyasringa;Gitavesya.

12.4 See also

- List of Indian poets

- The Poetry Society (India)

- Indian literature

- Journal : *Indian Literature*

- Sahitya Akademi Award

12.5 References

[1] List of Sahitya Akademi Award winners for English

[2] "Sahitya Akademi Award 2012" (PDF).

[3] Weinberger, Eliot, "Introduction", *A Tale of Two Gardens: Poems from India, 1952-1995* by Octavio Paz, translated by Eliot Weinberger, New Directions Publishing, 1997, ISBN 978-0-8112-1349-3, retrieved via Google Books on January 19, 2009

12.6 External links

- The National Academy of Letters

Chapter 13

Javanese poetry

Javanese poetry (poetry in the Javanese or especially the Kawi language; Low Javanese: *tembang*; High Javanese: *sekar*) is traditionally recited in song form. The standard forms are divided into three types, **sekar ageng**, **sekar madya**, and **tembang macapat**. All three types follow strict rules of poetic construction. These forms are highly influential in Javanese gamelan.

13.1 Sekar ageng

The most sacred are the *sekar ageng* (Low Javanese: *tembang gedhé*; "great songs"). These were traditionally held to be the most ancient of the forms, but Jaap Kunst believed that the indigenous forms represented an older tradition. The ancient forms of these, known as kakawin, use meters from Indian poetry, specifying the number of syllables in each line, their vowel length, and the location of caesurae. Exactly how this ancient form sounded when sung is hard to know, as the modern form has been influenced by gamelan structures. It may have resembled modern Indian or Balinese chant.

The modern form of sekar ageng are always in stanzas of four lines, and the number of syllables in each (*lampah*) is fixed and divided into parts (*pedhotan*) by caesurae. (Vowel length is no longer distinguished.) These indications are ordinarily indicated with the form; for example, sekar ageng *Bongsa patra*, lampah 17, pedhotan 4,6,7. According to Padmasasustra, there are 44 types of sekar ageng used in Surakarta.[1]

A sekar ageng is sometimes used as a type of buka (song introduction) known as a *bawa*. It is sung solo, or may be supported by the gendér. Only the first line is used in the introduction, and the rest may follow in the actual gendhing. Martopangrawit believes that this began only in the late 19th century, at the time of Paku Buwana IX (r. 1861-93).[2]

13.2 Sekar madya and tembang macapat

Sekar madya (Low Javanese: *Tembang tengahan*; "middle songs") are supposed to lie between the other two genres, but there is no agreement about which genres are considered sekar madya and which are *tembang macapat* (old orthography: *machapat*). Both of these, in contrast to sekar ageng, use varying number of lines of varying length, but always in a specific form. Furthermore, the vowel sound of the final syllable must match a specific pattern (note that this is different from syllable rime, as consonants that follow, if any, do not have to match). The pattern of the length of lines is known as *guru wilangan*, *guru pètungan*, or *guru wichalan*, while the pattern of vowels is known as *dhongdhing* or *guru lagu*. In the schemes below, the number represents the guru wilangan, while the letter is the guru lagu of the corresponding line.

In addition to these formal structures, each of these forms has a specific mood. The typical use is indicated after the form for many of the structures below.

Padmasoesastra listed 11 types of sekar madya forms used in Surakarta.[3] Many of them, however, are no longer used. The ones in modern use are:

- **Juru demung**: 8A, 8U, 8U, 8A, 8U, 8A, 8U

- **Wirangrong**: 8I, 8O, 10U, 6I, 7A, 8A

- **Balabah**: 12A, 3É, 12A, 3Á, 12A, 3Á

Two meters were classified as macapat forms in the past, but are now considered sekar madya:

- **Megatruh** (or **Duduk wuluh**): 12U, 8I, 8U, 8I, 8O

- **Gambuh**: 7U, 10U, 12I, 8U, 8O (there are a number of variants of this form)

The common macapat forms are:

- **Dhangdhang gula**: 10I, 10A, 8É(O), 7U, 9I, 7A, 6U, 8A, 12I, 7A; neutral character, used especially for introducing another poem

- **Sinom**: 8A, 8I, 8A, 8I, 7I, 8U, 7A, 8I, 12A; didactic poems

- **Asmarandana**: 8I, 8A, 8O(É), 8A, 7A, 8U, 8A; love poems

- **Kinanthi**: 8U, 8I, 8A, 8I, 8A, 8I; love poems

- **Pangkur**: 8A, 11I, 8U, 7A, 12U, 8A, 8I; violent passions or fighting

- **Durma**: 12A, 7I, 6A, 7A, 8I, 5A, 7I; violent passions or fighting

- **Mijil**: 10I, 6O, 10É, 10I, 6I, 6U; love poems

- **Mas kumambang**: 12I, 6A, 8I, 8A; longing or homesickness

- **Puchung**: 12U, 6A, 8I, 12A; neutral character, used for riddles

As an example, consider the following Kinanthi verse, a stanza from the Serat Centhini:

> Ki Jayèngraga agupuh
> anggamel rebab respati
> rebabé langkung prayoga
> watangan pinonthang gadhing
> kosok pinatra pinrada
> batok jamangan balenggin[4]

These forms are the basis of kidung poetry.

The text for these songs is frequently used in works for the gamelan, frequently sung by the gerong. Indeed, many modern gendhing share common macapat texts, especially Kinanthi, fit into their individual melodic pattern. Sumarsam believes that the singing of these forms led to the development of the early gendhing gerong, in the mid-19th century.[5] Wayang performances make use of the Mahabharata and Ramayana in macapat form, created in the 18th and 19th centuries.[6]

13.3 Notes

[1] Padmasoesastra, *Tatatjara*; publication no. 2 of *Volkslectuur*, 1891, page 249 et seq. Cited in Kunst, 123.

[2] Sumarsam, page 97.

[3] Padmasoesastra, *Tatatjara*; publication no. 2 of *Volkslectuur*, 1891, page 251. Cited in Kunst, 123.

[4] Serat Centhini, Canto 276, stanza 5; cited in Kunst, 224.

[5] Sumarsam, page 98-99.

[6] Sumarsam, page 96.

13.4 References

- Kunst, Jaap. *Music in Java: Its History, Its Theory and Its Technique*. The Hague: Martinus Nijhoff, 1949. Pages 122-125 discuss the forms, and is the source for the article except when noted above.

- Sumarsam. *Gamelan: Cultural Interaction and Musical Development in Central Java*. Chicago: University of Chicago Press, 1995.

Chapter 14

Kannada poetry

Kannada poetry is poetry written in the Kannada language spoken in Karnataka. Karnataka is the land that gave birth to eight Jnanapeeth award winners, the highest honour bestowed for Indian literature. From the period of Adikavi Pampa, who proclaimed his wish to be reborn as a little bee in the land of Kannada, Kannada poetry has come a long way to Kuvempu and Dattatreya Ramachandra Bendre.

14.1   Pre-history

Kannada poetry has been traced back to around 5th century A.D, though none of those early works have been found. The earliest extant poetry in *tripadi* meter are the Kappe Arabhatta records of 700 C.E. The first well known Kannada poet was Adikavi Pampa who wrote in an archaic style of Kannada called Halegannada (literally "Old Kannada"). His Vikramarjuna Vijaya is hailed as a classic even to this day. With this and his other important work Adipurana he set a trend of poetic excellence for the Kannada poets of the future.

Kannada poetry called vachanas, were pithy comments on that period's social, religious and economic conditions. More importantly, they hold a mirror to the seed of a social revolution, which caused a radical re-examination of the ideas of caste, creed and religion. One of the important ideas coming out of this revolution was the view that Work is worship and a path to spirituality.

14.2   Bhakti

Kannada poets have the unique distinction of sowing the seeds of one of the richest forms of classical music: South Indian Carnatic music. The Dasas or saints, around 15th century, sang the glory of God through poems. These poems called Padas were usually of 10 to 20 lines. They expressed the desire of the Bhakta or devotee to be one with God. This form of poetry was highly amenable to musical composition and exposition. This music evolved into the highly sophisticated and codified Carnatic music.

The Haridasas spread the message of peace, love and bhakti in their Dasa Sahitya, which are also popularly known as Devaranamas.

14.3   Navodaya (New birth)

Navodaya literally means a *new birth*. This indeed was the reincarnation of Kannada poetry which was dormant for quite a few centuries in the face of British occupation of India. This period saw greats like Srikanthaiah, Kuvempu, Bendre, Shivaram Karanth writing poetry. This genre was highly influenced by Romantic English poetry. It was B. M. Srikanthaiah who started this movement of sorts with his translation of a few critically acclaimed English poems of the

Romantic period. Many educated Kannadigas, especially those were in the teaching profession, realised that they need to express themselves in their mother tongue and started writing poetry in Kannada. Kuvempu is a case in point who was convinced by his professor (of British origin) that he should write in his mother tongue. Kuvempu went on to become a "Rashtrakavi" (national poet). His love of nature, realisation of the greatness of man's spirit and the vision to see the blend of nature and God made him more than Kannada's Wordsworth. Another interesting case is that of Shivaram Karanth who was a man of great intellect, rock-solid convictions and a profound social sense. He was the Leonardo da Vinci of Karnataka.123

14.4 Navya (New)

Indian Independence in 1947 brought with it the promises of freedom and a new genre sprouted in Kannada poetry. The torch-bearer of this tradition was Gopalakrishna Adiga. The Navya poets wrote for and liked disillusioned intellectuals. The sophistication in the use of language and the importance of technique to poetry reached new heights in this genre.

14.5 Other genres

Kannada poetry in the last 50 years has been closely related to social aspects. The caste system gave rise to the Bandaya and Dalita genres of poetry. The atrocities against women and the general ill-treatment meted out to them in Indian society gave rise to the Stri (Woman) genre of poetry.

14.6 Awards

Kannada poetry has won eight Jnanapeeth awards, the second highest for any other Indian language after hindi.

14.7 Reaching people

The popularity of poetry is gauged in terms of the response that the educated and interested elite give. But the real popularity of poetry is when common people sing it. Popular appeal is not very easy to achieve for any form of poetry; especially when audiences are not kept in mind. Kannada poetry has a few instances of such mass popularity. Kumaravyasa's retelling of the Mahabharata is recited in homes even today. Bhavageete (literally "emotion poetry") has popularized many Kannada poems and has people humming them.

14.8 See also

- List of Kannada language poets

- Kannada Poets

- Kannada literature

- Kannada meter (poetry)

- Kannada language

- Karnataka

14.9   References

Dr. Suryanath U. Kamat, Concise History of Karnataka, 2001, MCC, Bangalore, Reprinted 2002

14.10   External links

- Some Vachans by Basavanna, Akkamahadevi, Allamaprabhu, Sarvajna, and selected poems by Dr. Siddalingaiah.

- Kavanas from Upcoming Poets Some Kannada Poems by Upcoming Poets. Encourage people to write more kavanas.

Chapter 15

Kashmiri language

Kashmiri (/kæʃˈmɪəri/)[5] (कॉशुर, کأشیر), or **Koshur**, is a language from the Dardic subgroup[6] of the Indo-Aryan languages and it is spoken primarily in the Kashmir Valley, in Jammu and Kashmir.[7][8][9] There are approximately 5,527,698 speakers throughout India, according to the Census of 2001.[10] Most of the 105,000 speakers in Pakistan are emigrants from the Kashmir Valley after the partition of India.[1][11] They include a few speakers residing in border villages in Neelam District.

Kashmiri is close to other dardic languages spoken in Gilgit, Pakistan and in northern regions of Kargil, India. Outside the Dardic group, tonal aspects and loanwords of Arabic, Persian and Sanskrit, especially its northern dialects.[12][13]

The Kashmiri language is one of the 22 scheduled languages of India,[14] and is a part of the *eighth Schedule* in the constitution of the Jammu and Kashmir. Along with other regional languages mentioned in the *Sixth Schedule*, as well as Hindi and Urdu, the Kashmiri language is to be developed in the state.[15] Most Kashmiri speakers use Urdu or English as a second language.[1] Since November 2008, the Kashmiri language has been made a compulsory subject in all schools in the Valley up to the secondary level.[16]

15.1 Literature

In 1919 George Abraham Grierson wrote that "Kashmiri is the only one of the Dardic languages that has a literature". Kashmiri literature dates back to over 750 years, this is, more-or-less, the age of many a modern literature including modern English.

See also: Kashmiri literature § Kashmiri_language_literature

15.2 Writing system

There are three orthographical systems used to write the Kashmiri language: the Sharada script, the Devanagari script and the Perso-Arabic script. The Roman script is also sometimes informally used to write Kashmiri, especially online.[3]

The Kashmiri language is traditionally written in the Sharada script after the 8th Century A.D.[17] This script however, is not in common use today, except for religious ceremonies of the Kashmiri Pandits.[18]

Today it is written in Devanagari script and Perso-Arabic script (with some modifications).[19] Among languages written in the Perso-Arabic script, Kashmiri is one of the very few which regularly indicates all vowel sounds.[20] This script has been in vogue since the Muslim conquest in India and has been used by the people for centuries, in the Kashmir Valley.[21] However, today, the Kashmiri Perso-Arabic script has come to be associated with Kashmiri Muslims, while the Kashmiri Devanagari script has come to be associated with the Kashmiri Hindu community.[21][22]

117

15.3 Phonology

Kashmiri has the following vowel phonemes:[23]

15.3.1 Vowels

15.3.2 Consonants

15.4 Grammar

Kashmiri, like German and Old English and unlike other Indo-Aryan languages, has V2 word order.[24]

There are four cases in Kashmiri: nominative, genitive, and two oblique cases: the ergative and the dative case.[25]

15.5 Vocabulary

Though Kashmiri has thousands of loan words (mainly from Persian and Arabic) due to the arrival of Islam in the Valley, however, it remains basically an Indo-Aryan language close to Rigvedic Sanskrit. There is a minor difference between the Kashmiri spoken by a Hindu and a Muslim. For 'fire', a traditional Hindu will use the word *agun* while a Muslim more often will use the Arabic word *nar*. [12][13] Shashishekhar Toshkhani, a scholar on Kashmir's heritage,[9][26] provides a detailed analysis where he shows extensive linguistic relationship between the Sanskrit language and the Kashmiri language, and presents detailed arguments contesting George Grierson's classification of the Kashmiri language as a member of the Dardic sub-group (of the Indo-Aryan group of languages). Kashmiri has strong links to Rigvedic Sanskrit. For example, 'cloud' is *obur*, 'rain' is *ruud* (from the Rigvedic Aryan god Rudra).

15.5.1 Preservation of old Indo-Aryan vocabulary

Kashmiri retains several features of Old Indo-Aryan that have been lost in other modern Indo-Aryan languages such as Hindi-Urdu, Punjabi and Sindhi.[27] For instance, it preserves the *dvi-* form for prefixes in numbers which is found in Sanskrit, but has been replaced entirely by *ba-/bi-* in other Indo-Aryan languages. *Seventy-two* is *dusatath* in Kashmiri and *dvisaptati* in Sanskrit, but *bahattar* in Hindi-Urdu and Punjabi.[27] Some vocabulary features that Kashmiri preserves clearly date from the Vedic Sanskrit era and had already been lost even in Classical Sanskrit. This includes the word-form *yodvai* (meaning *if*), which is mainly found in Vedic Sanskrit texts. Classical Sanskrit and modern Indo-Aryan render the word as *yadi*.[27] Certain words in Kashmiri even appear to stem from Indo-Aryan even predating the Vedic period. For instance, there was an /s/ → /h/ consonant shift in some words that had already occurred with Vedic Sanskrit (this tendency is even stronger in the Iranian branch of Indo-Iranian), yet is lacking in Kashmiri equivalents. The word *rahit* in Vedic Sanskrit and modern Hindi-Urdu (meaning *excluding* or *without*) corresponds to *rost* in Kashmiri. Similarly, *sahit* (meaning *including* or *with*) corresponds to *sost* in Kashmiri.[27]

15.5.2 First person pronoun

Both the Indo-Aryan and Iranian branches of the Indo-Iranian family have demonstrated a strong tendency to eliminate the distinctive first person pronoun ("I") used in the nominative (subject) case. The Indo-European root for this is reconstructed as *egHom, which is preserved in Sanskrit as *aham* and in Avestan Persian as *azam*. This contrasts with the *m*-form ("me", "my") that is used for the accusative, genitive, dative, ablative cases. Sanskrit and Avestan both used forms such as *ma(-m)*. However, in languages such as Modern Persian, Baluchi, Hindi and Punjabi, the distinct nominative form has been entirely lost and replaced with *m-* in words such as *ma-n* and *mai*. However, Kashmiri belongs to a relatively small set that preserves the distinction. 'I' is *bi/ba/boh* in various Kashmiri dialects, distinct from the other *me* terms. 'Mine' is *myoon* in Kashmiri. Other Indo-Aryan languages that preserve this feature include Dogri (*aun* vs *me-*), Gujarati (*hu-n* vs *ma-ri*), and Braj (*hau-M* vs *mai-M*). The Iranian Pashto preserves it too (*za* vs. *maa*).[28]

15.6 See also

- Shina language

- Dardic languages

- List of topics on the land and the people of "Jammu and Kashmir"

- List of Kashmiri poets

- States of India by Kashmiri speakers

- Kashmiri Wikipedia

- Kashmir Valley

15.7 References

[1] "Kashmiri: A language of India". Ethnologue. Retrieved 2007-06-02.

[2] Kashmiri at *Ethnologue* (18th ed., 2015)

[3] *Sociolinguistics*. Mouton de Gruyter. Retrieved 2009-08-30.

[4] Nordhoff, Sebastian; Hammarström, Harald; Forkel, Robert; Haspelmath, Martin, eds. (2013). "Kashmiri". *Glottolog*. Leipzig: Max Planck Institute for Evolutionary Anthropology.

[5] Laurie Bauer, 2007, *The Linguistics Student's Handbook*, Edinburgh

[6] "Kashmiri language". Encyclopædia Britannica. Retrieved 2007-06-02.

[7] "Koshur: An Introduction to Spoken Kashmiri". Kashmir News Network: Language Section (koshur.org). Retrieved 2007-06-02.

[8] "Kashmiri Literature". Kashmir Sabha, Kolkata. Retrieved 2007-06-02.

[9] S. S. Toshkhani. "Kashmiri Language: Roots, Evolution and Affinity". Kashmiri Overseas Association, Inc. (KOA). Retrieved 2007-06-02.

[10] Abstract of speakers' strength of languages and mother tongues – 2001, *Census of India* (retrieved 17 March 2008)

[11] "The Kashmir Dispute – a cause or a symptom?". Stockholm University. Retrieved 2009-07-07.

[12] Keith Brown, Sarah Ogilvie, *Concise encyclopedia of languages of the world*, Elsevier, 2008, ISBN 978-0-08-087774-7, ... *Kashmiri occupies a special position in the Dardic group, being probably the only dardic language that has a written literature dating back to the early 13th century ...*

[13] Krishna, Gopi (1967). *Kundalini: The Evolutionary Energy in Man*. Boston: Shambhala. p. 212. ISBN 978-1-57062-280-9.

[14] "Scheduled Languages of India". Central Institute of Indian Languages. Retrieved 2007-06-02.

[15] "The Constitution of Jammu and Kashmir (India)" (PDF). General Administrative Department of the Government of Jammu & Kashmir (India). Retrieved 2007-06-02.

[16] "Kashmiri made compulsory subject in schools". API News. Retrieved 2007-06-02.

[17] "Sarada". Lawrence. Retrieved 2007-06-02.

[18] "The Sharada Script: Origin and Development". Kashmiri Overseas Association. Retrieved 2009-07-07.

[19] "Kashmiri (कॉशुर / کأشرُ)". Omniglot. Retrieved 2009-07-07.

[20] Daniels & Bright (1996). *The World's Writing Systems*. pp. 753–754.

[21] "Valley divide impacts Kashmiri, Pandit youth switch to Devnagari". Indian Express. Retrieved 2009-07-07.

[22] "Devnagari Script for Kashmiri: A Study in its Necessity, Feasibility and Practicality". Kashmiri Overseas Association. Retrieved 2009-07-07.

[23] "Koshur: Spoken Kashmiri: A Language Course: Transcription". Retrieved 21 May 2014.

[24] Concerning V2 order in Kashmiri, see Hook (1976:133ff).

[25] Edelman (1983). *The Dardic and Nuristani Languages*.

[26] "Dr. Shashishekhar Toshkhani: The Literary Works". Kashmir News Network. Retrieved 2009-08-21.

[27] K.L. Kalla, *The Literary Heritage of Kashmir*, Mittal Publications, ... *Kashmiri alone of all the modern Indian languages preserves the dvi (Kashmiri du) of Sanskrit, in numbers such as dusatath (Sanskrit dvisaptati), dunamat (Sanskrit dvanavatih) ... the latter (Yodvai) is archaic and is to be come across mainly in the Vedas ...*

[28] John D. Bengtson, Harold Crane Fleming, *In hot pursuit of language in prehistory: essays in the four fields of anthropology*, John Benjamins Publishing Company, 2008, ISBN 978-90-272-3252-6, ... *However, Gujarati as well as a Dardic language like Kashmiri still preserve the root alternation between subject and non-subject forms (but they replaced the derivative of the Sanskrit subject form ahám by new forms) ...*

15.8   Further reading

- Chapter on Indo-Persian Literature in Kashmir in "The Rise, Growth And Decline Of Indo-Persian Literature" by R. M. Chopra, 2012, published by Iran Culture House, New Delhi. 2nd Edition 2013.

- Koul,Omkar N & Kashi Wali *Modern Kashmiri Grammar* Hyattsville, Dunwoody Press, 2006.

15.9   External links

- Modern Kashmiri Dictionary: Android based electronic Kashmiri Dictionary

- Grierson, George Abraham. A Dictionary of the Kashmiri Language. Calcutta: Asiatic Society of Bengal, 1932.

- Hook, Peter E.. 1976. Is Kashmiri an SVO language? Indian Linguistics 37: 133-142.

- *Lexical Borrowings in Kashmiri* by Ashok K Koul Delhi: Indian Institute of Language Studies,2008.

- Koul, Omkar. Kashmiri: A grammatical sketch

- Koshur: An Introduction to Spoken Kashmiri

- Dictionary of Kashmiri Proverbs

Chapter 16

Korean poetry

Korean poetry is poetry performed or written in the Korean language or by Korean people. Traditional Korean poetry is often sung in performance. Until the 20th century, much of Korean poetry was written in Hanja and later Hangul.

16.1 History

The performance of oral songs in the religious life of the ancient Korean people is vivildy recorded in Chinese dynastic histories. At state assemblies the chief ritualist would tell the story of the divine origin of the founder, as evinced by foundation myths, and his extraordinary deeds in war and peace. Recited narrative was interspersed with primal songs (*norae*) that not only welcomed, entertained, and sent off gods and spirits. Thus orality and performance were significant features of vernacular poetry in ancient Korea.[1]

A famous surviving example dates to 17 BC, Yuri's *Song of Yellow Birds* (Hwangjoga, 黄鳥歌/황조가). Some later Korean poetry followed the style of Tang lyric poetry such as the shi poetry form. Notable Korean poetry began to flourish during the Goryeo period (starting in 935). Collections were rarely printed.

Sijo, Korea's favorite poetic genre, is often traced to seonbi scholars of the 11th century, but its roots, too, are in those earlier forms. The earliest surviving poem of the sijo genre is from the 4th century. Its greatest flowering occurred in the 16th and 17th centuries under the Joseon Dynasty.

16.2 Hyangga

Hyangga poetry refers to vernacular Korean poetry which transcribed Korean sounds using Hanja (similar to the idu system, the hyangga style of transcription is called *hyangch'al*) and is characteristic of the literature of Unified Silla. It is one of the first uniquely Korean forms of poetry. The Goryeo period *Samguk Yusa* contains 14 poems that have been preserved to the present day. These are thought to have been taken by Ilyon (compiler of *Samguk Yusa*) from an anthology called the *Samdaemok*(三代目/삼대목) which was completed during the Shilla period, in 888 (according to *Samguk Sagi*), but is no longer extant today. This lost anthology is thought to have contained approximately 1,000 hyangga. Eleven poems from the later Goryeo Dynasty *Gyunyeojeon* (均如傳/균여전), characterized by the same style, have also been preserved.

Hyangga are characterized by a number of formal rules. The poems may consist of four, eight or ten lines. The ten-line poems are the most developed, structured into three sections with four, four, and two lines respectively. Many of the ten-line poems were written by Buddhist monks. The extent of the Shilla *hwarang's* role in the development and flourishing of the *hyangga* genre is a subject of much scholarly interest.

121

16.3   Goryeo songs

The Goryeo period was marked by a growing use of Hanja. Hyangga largely disappeared as a form of Korean literature, and "Goryeo songs" (*Goryeo gayo*) became more popular. Most of the Goryeo songs were transmitted orally and many survived into the Joseon period, when some of them were written down using hangul.

The poetic form of the Goryeo songs is known as *byeolgok*. There are two distinct forms: *dallyeonche* (☐☐☐) and *yeon-janche* (☐☐☐). The former is a short form, whereas the latter is a more extended form. The Goryeo songs are characterized by their lack of clear form, and by their increased length. Most are direct in their nature, and cover aspects of common life.

16.4   Sijo

During the Joseon dynasty, three-line poetry called sijo, became more popular and reached its apex in the late 18th century. Sijo is a modern term for what was then called *dan-ga* (literally, "short song").

The sijo having a strong foundation in nature in a short profound structure. Bucolic, metaphysical and astronomical themes are often explored. The lines average 14-16 syllables, for a total of 44-46. There is a pause in the middle of each line, so in English they are sometimes printed in six lines instead of three. Most poets follow these guidelines very closely although there are longer examples. The most famous example is possibly this piece by Yun Seondo:

> You ask how many friends I have? Water and stone, bamboo and pine.
>
> The moon rising over the eastern hill is a joyful comrade.
>
> Besides these five companions, what other pleasure should I ask?

Yun Seondo (1587–1671) also wrote a famous collection of forty sijo of the changing seasons through the eyes of a fisherman.

Either narrative or thematic, this lyric verse introduces a situation or problem in line 1, development (called a turn) in line 2, and a strong conclusion beginning with a surprise (a twist) in line 3, which resolves tensions or questions raised by the other lines and provides a memorable ending.

Sijo is, first and foremost, a song. This lyric pattern gained popularity in royal courts amongst the *yangban* as a vehicle for religious or philosophical expression, but a parallel tradition arose among the commoners. Sijo were sung or chanted with musical accompaniment, and this tradition survives. The word originally referred only to the music, but it has come to be identified with the lyrics.

16.5   Gasa

Gasa is a form of verse, although its content can include more than the expression of individual sentiment, such as moral admonitions. Gasa is a simple form of verse, with twinned feet of three or four syllables each. Some regard gasa a form of essay. Common themes in gasa were nature, the virtues of gentlemen, or love between man and woman.

The form had first emerged during the Goryeo period, and was popular during the Joseon Dynasty. They were commonly sung, and were popular among yangban women. Jeong Cheol, a poet of the 16th century, is regarded as having perfected the form, which consisted of parallel lines, each broken into two.

16.6   Modern poetry

See also South Korean literature, and List of Korean language poets (mainly 20th Century)

There were attempts at introducing imagist and modern poetry methods particularly in translations of early American moderns such as Ezra Pound and T. S. Eliot in the early 20th century. In the early Republic period (starting in 1953 after the Korean War), patriotic works were very successful.

Lyrical poetry dominated from the 1970s onwards. Poetry is quite popular in 21st century Korea, both in terms of number of works published and lay writing.

A corpus of modern Korean poetry is being compiled. The work provides linguistic information on 10,300 original Korean poems.[2]

16.7 See also

- List of Korea-related topics

- Korean culture

- Korean literature

- List of Korean language poets

16.8 References

[1] Lee, Peter H. (2002). *The Columbia Anthology of Traditional Korean Poetry*. New York: Columbia University Press. ISBN 0-231-11112-6.

[2] Kim Byong-sun (2002). "The Present Conditions and Tasks in Constructing the Database of Korean Literary Materials Centering on the Korean Poetry Corpus" (PDF). *The Review of Korean Studies* **8** (4): 105–140.

16.9 External links

- An outline history of Korean poetry

- "Traditional Korean Has Rich History"

- Korean poems in English translations

Chapter 17

Latin American poetry

Latin American poetry is the poetry of Latin America, mostly but not entirely written in Spanish or Portuguese. The unification of Indigenous and Spanish cultures produced a unique and extraordinary body of literature in Spanish America. Later with the introduction of African slaves to the new world, African traditions greatly influenced Spanish American poetry.[1]

17.1 Pre-Columbian poetry

We have multiple examples of Aztec poetry written in Nahuatl. Most of these were collected during the early period of the colonization of Mexico by Spanish clergy who involved themselves in an effort to collect firsthand knowledge of all things related to the indigenous civilizations of the newly conquered territory. One of these Spanish Clergy, fray Bernardino de Sahagún, enlisted the help of young Aztecs to interview and record stories, histories, poems and other information from older Aztecs who still remembered the pre-conquered times. Much of the information that was collected by these colonial anthropologists has been lost, but researchers find originals or copies of the original research in libraries around the world. Miguel León Portilla has published multiple books on Aztec poetry and *Ancient Nahuatl Poetry* by Daniel Garrison can be found online at gutenberg.org.

17.2 The colonial era

During the period of conquest and colonization many Hispanic Americans were educated in Spain. The poets of this historical period followed the European trends in literature but their subjects were always distinctly American.

The struggle for independence of the Spanish Colonies saw a literature of defiance of authority and a sense of social injustice that is ever present in Spanish American poetics. José Martí is an example of a poet-martyr who literally died fighting for the freedom of Cuba. His most famous poem, Yo soy un hombre sincero has entered into popular culture as it has been reproduced hundreds of times into the song "Guantanamera", most recently by Celia Cruz and even the Fugees.

17.3 The 19th century

Unsurprisingly, most of the early poetry written in the colonies and fledgling republic used contemporary Spanish models of poetic form, diction, and theme. However, in the 19th century, a distinctive Spanish-American tradition began to emerge with the creation of Modernismo (not to be confused with Modernism).

Modernismo: a literary movement that arose in Spanish America in the late 19th century and was subsequently transmitted to Spain. Introduced by Rubén Darío with the publication of "Azul" (1888), this new style of poetry was strongly influenced by the French symbolist and Parnassians. In rebellion against romanticism, the modernists attempted to renew

124

poetic language and to create a poetry characterized by formal perfection, musicality, and strongly evocative imagery. The wider use of the term applies to the various experimental and avant-garde trends of the early twentieth century.

17.4 The 20th century

Toward the end of the millennium, consideration of Spanish-American poetry has taken a multi-cultural approach, as scholars begin to emphasize poetry by women, Afro/a Hispanics, contemporary indigenous communities and other sub-cultural groupings. Poetry, and creative writing in general, also tended to become more professionalized with the growth of Creative Writing programs. After Modernismo and World War I, there were many new currents which influenced Spanish American poets — Cubism, Futurism, Dadaism, Surrealism, Ultraism — Argentinian poet Borges brings it to this continent. Creacionismo — Huidobro. All this (1910 and 1940). Many more movements and groups continue to write the history of Spanish American literature until the present. For instance the "Neo Baroco" movement with Néstor Perlongher, Emeterio Cerro...

The images found in Pre-Columbian culture appear again in poets like from across Latin America.

Nicolás Guillén from Cuba and Luis Palés-Matos from Puerto Rico incorporate the African roots in the rhythm of their poetry, making their song unique. Afro-Caribbean trends reappear in the poetry of Nuyorican poets such as Pedro Pietri, Miguel Algarin and Giannina Braschi who continue the tradition of poetry as performance art with anti-imperialist political punch.

In the late 20th century, Latin American poetry reached pre-eminent position in world literature with the emergence of Pablo Neruda, who was described by Gabriel García Márquez as *"the greatest poet of the twentieth century in any language"*.[2]

17.5 Contemporary poetry

- Elvia Ardalani (born 1963), Mexican poet

- Karina Galvez (1964–), Ecuadorian poet

- Juan Gelman (1930–2014), Buenos Aires argentinian poet

17.6 Notable Latin American poets

Pre-Columbian

Colonial period

- Juana Inés de la Cruz

19th century

- Andrés Bello

- José Martí

- Rubén Darío

20th century

- Jorge Luis Borges

- Giannina Braschi
- Nicolás Guillén
- Vicente Huidobro
- Vinicius de Moraes
- Carlos Drummond de Andrade
- Gabriela Mistral
- Pablo Neruda
- Nicanor Parra
- Benito Pastoriza Iyodo
- César Vallejo
- Emilio Adolfo Westphalen
- Raúl Zurita
- Andrés Morales
- Emeterio Cerro
- Eugenio Cruz Vargas
- Octavio Paz

17.7 See also

- Latin American literature
- Latino poetry
- Chicano poetry
- Caribbean poetry
- Décima

17.8 References

[1] Brotherston, Gordon (1975). *Latin American poetry: origins and presence*. CUP Archive. ISBN 0-521-09944-7.

[2] "Latin American poetry: origins and presence".

Chapter 18

Māori poetry

Traditional **Māori poetry** was always sung or chanted,[1] musical rhythms rather than linguistic devices served to distinguish it from prose. There is a large store of traditional chants and songs.[2] Rhyme or assonance were not devices used by the Māori; only when a given text is sung or chanted will the metre become apparent. The lines are indicated by features of the music. The language of poetry tends to differ stylistically from prose. Typical features of poetic diction are the use of synonyms or contrastive opposites, and the repetition of key words. As with poetry in other languages: "Archaic words are common, including many which have lost any specific meaning and acquired a religious mystique. Abbreviated, sometimes cryptic utterances and the use of certain grammatical constructions not found in prose are also common" (Biggs 1966:447–448).

18.1   Modern Māori poets

- Rowley Habib[3][4]

- Hone Tuwhare

18.2   References

[1] "Literary Forms", B.G. Biggs, Encyclopaedia of New Zealand (1966)

[2] "Chapter VIII. — The Poetry of the Maori", The Maori: Yesterday and To-day, James Cowan, 1930

[3]

[4]

- B.G. Biggs, 'Maori Myths and Traditions' in A.H. McLintock (editor), Encyclopaedia of New Zealand, 3 Volumes. (Government Printer: Wellington), 1966, II:447–454.

Chapter 19

Kantan Chamorrita

Kantan Chamorrita is an ancient style of improvised rhyming "debate" indigenous to the Chamoru natives of the Mariana Islands,[1] comparable to modern-day "battle rapping" or poetry slams.

19.1   See also

- Music of Guam

19.2   External links

- ChamorroWeb.com

- Kantan Chamorrita at Guampedia.com

19.3   References

[1] Souder, Laura (Summer 1993). "Kantan Chamorrita: Traditional Chamorro Poetry, Past and Future". *Manoa* (University of Hawai'i Press) **5** (1): 189–192. JSTOR 4228865.

Chapter 20

Modern Hebrew poetry

Modern Hebrew poetry is poetry written in the Hebrew language. It was pioneered by Rabbi Moshe Chaim Luzzatto,[1] and it was developed by the Haskalah movements, that saw poetry as the most quality genre for Hebrew writing. The first Haskalah poet, who heavily influenced the later poets, was Naphtali Hirz Wessely, at the end of the 18th Century, and after him came Shalom HaCohen,[2] Max Letteris, Abraham Dob Bär Lebensohn, his son Micah Joseph,[2] Judah Leib Gordon and others. Haskalah poetry was greatly influenced by the contemporary European poetry, as well as the poetry of the previous ages, especially Biblical poetry and pastoralism.[2] It was mostly a didactic form of poetry, and dealt with the world, the public, and contemporary trends, but not the individual. A secular Galician Jew, Naftali Herz Imber, wrote the lyrics to HaTikva in 1878; this later became the national anthem of Israel.

In the age after the Haskalah, many prominent poets were associated with Hovevei Zion. They included Shaul Tchernihovsky and Haim Nahman Bialik, who would later be considered Israel's national poet. They let go of the genre principles that were widely accepted at their time, and began writing personal poems, about the human being and the soul. In the Zionist national revival period, many arose as the literary heirs to Bialik, and the focal point of Hebrew poetry moved from Europe to the land of Israel. Women became prominent poets (Yokheved Bat Miryam, Esther Raab, Rachel and others). An expressionist genre also developed, as exemplified by Uri Zvi Greenberg and David Fogel.

In the 1930s and 1940s, a neo-symbolic style emerged as well, in Avraham Shlonsky, then Nathan Alterman, and then the Palmach age.

In the 1950s and 1960s, poets who had been raised in Israel or the British Mandate of Palestine were active. The poets Natan Zakh, David Avidan, Yehuda Amihai and Dalya Ravikovich rebelled against the style of Shlonsky and Alterman. At the same time a line of religious poets led by such figures as Yosef Zvi Rimon and Zelda emerged. These movements continue to be active to the present day.

20.1   References

[1] Stern, David (2004). *The Anthology in Jewish Literature*. Oxford University Press USA. p. 287. ISBN 0-19-513751-5. Retrieved 2009-03-11.

[2] Sharon, Moshe, ed. (1988). ""Here and "there" in modern Hebrew poetry (Glenda Abramson)". *The Holy Land in History and Thought: International Conference on the Relations Between the Holy Land and the World Outside It*. Bill Archive. pp. 141–149. ISBN 90-04-08855-5. Retrieved 2009-03-11.

20.2   Further reading

- Avidov Lipsker, *Red Poem\ Blue Poem: Seven Essays on Uri Zvi Grinberg and Two Essays on Else Lasker-Schüler*, Bar Ilan University Press, Ramat-Gan 2010.

20.3 External links

- Poems by Avot Yeshurun (1904–1992), one of the major figures in Twentieth century Hebrew poetry, translated by Lilach Lachman and Gabriel Levin. Featured in *Parnassus: Poetry in Review*--Parnassus (magazine)

Chapter 21

Old Norse poetry

Old Norse poetry encompasses a range of verse forms written in Old Norse, during the period from the 8th century (see Eggjum stone) to as late as the far end of the 13th century. Most of the Old Norse poetry that survives was preserved in Iceland, but there are also 122 preserved poems in Swedish rune inscriptions, 54 in Norwegian and 12 in Danish.[1]

Poetry played an important role in the social and religious world of the Vikings. In Norse mythology, *Skáldskaparmál* (1) tells the story of how Odin brought the mead of poetry to Asgard, which is an indicator of the significance of poetry within the contemporary Scandinavian culture.

Old Norse poetry is characterised by alliteration, a poetic vocabulary expanded by heiti, and use of kennings. An important source of information about poetic forms in Old Norse is the Prose Edda of Snorri Sturluson.

Old Norse poetry is conventionally, and somewhat arbitrarily, split into two types—Eddaic poetry (also sometimes known as *Eddic* poetry) and skaldic poetry. Eddaic poetry includes the poems of the Codex Regius and a few other similar ones. Skaldic poetry is usually defined as everything else not already mentioned.

21.1   Metrical forms

Old Norse poetry has many metrical forms. They range from the relatively simple fornyrðislag to the deeply complex dróttkvætt, the "courtly metre".

In Eddic poetry, the metric structures are generally simple, and are almost invariably ljóðaháttr or fornyrðislag. Ljóðaháttr, (known also as the "metre of chants"), because of its structure, which comprises broken stanzas, lends itself to dialogue and discourse. Fornyrðislag, "the metre of ancient words", is the more commonly used of the two, and is generally used where the poem is largely narrative. It is composed with four or more syllables per line. Other metrical forms include

- Málaháttr is similar to fornyrðislag, but with a fixed metrical length of five syllables.

- Hrynhenda, a variant of dróttkvætt, which uses all the rules of dróttkvætt, with the exception that the line comprises four metrical feet rather than three.

- Kviðuháttr, another variant of fornyrðislag with alternating lines of 3 and 4 syllables

- Galdralag, the "magic spell metre", which contains a fourth line which echoes and varies the third line

21.2   Eddaic poetry

Main article: Poetic Edda

The Eddaic poems have the following characteristics.

- The author is always anonymous.

- The meter is simple, fornyrðislag, málaháttr or ljóðaháttr.

- The word order is usually relatively straightforward.

- Kennings are used sparingly and opaque ones are rare.

21.3   Skaldic poetry

Main article: Skaldic poetry

The skaldic poems have the following characteristics.

- The author is usually known.

- The meter is ornate, usually dróttkvætt or a variation thereof.

- The syntax is ornate, with sentences commonly interwoven.

- Kennings are used frequently.

21.4   See also

- Skald

- Kennings

- List of kennings

- Alliterative verse

21.5   References

[1] "skaldic poetry project". Skaldic.arts.usyd.edu.au. Retrieved 2015-03-19.

- Den norsk-islandske skjaldedigtning ved Finnur Jónsson, 1912–1915

- Carmina Scaldica udvalg af norske og islandske skjaldekvad ved Finnur Jónsson, 1929

Chapter 22

Pakistani poetry

Pakistan has a rich and diverse tradition of poetry that includes Urdu poetry, English poetry, Sindhi poetry, Pashto poetry, Punjabi poetry, Saraiki poetry, Baluchi poetry, and Kashmiri poetry. Sufi poetry has a strong tradition in Pakistan and the poetry of popular Sufi poets is often recited and sung.

Persian poetry is still common in Pakistan as a literary vehicle because of the centuries of Persian influence on the region. Many Sufi poets wrote their Kalam in Persian. Pakistan's national poet Allama Mohammad Iqbal also wrote many volumes of poetry in Persian.

Poetry is widely read across Pakistan. Gatherings for the recitations of poetry known as Mushaira frequently take place. Verses of popular poets are also used as political slogans by political activists. The national poet of Pakistan is Muhammad Iqbal.

22.1 Poets by language

22.1.1 Urdu poetry

Main article: Urdu poetry

- Ahmad Faraz

- Ahmad Nadeem Qasmi

- Amjad Islam Amjad

- Faiz Ahmed Faiz

- Ehsan Sehgal

- Parveen Shakir

- Tanwir Phool

- Fehmida Riaz

- Habib Jalib

- Hafeez Jullundhri

- Hakim Ahmad Shuja

- Iftikhar Arif

- John Elia

- Josh Malihabadi

- Kishwar Naheed

- Majeed Amjad

- Mehmood Sham

- Mohsin Naqvi

- Mohsin Bhopali

- Munir Niazi

- Nasir Kazmi

- Qateel Shifai

- Shakeb Jalali

- Raees Warsi

22.1.2   Comical poetry

- Anwar Masood

- Dilawar Figar

- Zamir Jafri

22.1.3   English poetry

- Daud Kamal

- Alamgir Hashmi

- Zulfikar Ghose

- Shahid Suhrawardy

- Maki Kureishi

- Kaleem Omar

- Omer Tarin

22.1.4   Punjabi poetry

- Bulleh Shah

- Fariduddin Ganjshakar

- Mian Muhammad Bakhsh

- Waris Shah

- Sultan Bahu

- Shah Hussain

- Ustad Daman

22.1.5 Saraiki poetry

- Khawaja Farid
- Sachal Sarmast
- Bulleh Shah
- Sultan Bahu

22.1.6 Sindhi poetry

- Shah Abdul Latif
- Sachal Sarmast
- Lal Shahbaz Qalander
- Shah Inayatullah
- Shaikh Ayaz

22.1.7 Pashto poetry

- Khushal Khan Khattak
- Rahman Baba
- Ameer Hamza Shinwari
- Khan Abdul Ghani Khan
- Ajmal Khattak

22.1.8 Balochi poetry

Gul Khan Nasir

22.2 See also

- List of Pakistani writers

Chapter 23

Sanskrit literature

The oldest surviving manuscript of a text composed in Sanskrit, in an early Bhujimol script. The Devi Māhātmya on Palm-leaf, Bihar or Nepal, 11th century.

Literature in Sanskrit begins with the spoken or sung literature of the Vedas from the mid-2nd millennium BCE, and continues with the oral tradition of the Sanskrit epics of Iron Age India; the golden age of Classical Sanskrit literature dates to Late Antiquity (roughly the 3rd to 8th centuries CE). Indian literary production saw a late bloom in the 11th century before declining after 1100 CE, hastened by the Islamic conquest of India, due to the destruction of ancient seats of learning such as the universities at Taxila and Nalanda. There are contemporary efforts towards revival, with events like the *All-India Sanskrit Festival* (since 2002) holding composition contests.

Given its extensive use in religious literature, primarily in Hinduism, and the fact that most modern Indian languages have been directly derived from or strongly influenced by Sanskrit, the language and its literature is of great importance in Indian culture akin to that of Latin in European culture. Some Sanskrit literature such as the Yoga-Sutras of Patanjali and the Upanishads were translated into Arabic and Persian,[1] most significantly by the emperor Akbar. The Panchatantra was also translated into Persian.[2]

23.1 The Vedas

Main article: Vedas

Composed between approximately 1500 BCE and 600 BCE (the Late Bronze Age to Early Iron Age) in pre-classical Sanskrit, Vedic oral literature forms the basis for the further development of Hinduism. There are four Vedas - *Rig, Yajur, Sāma and Atharva*, each with a main Samhita and a number of circum-vedic genres, including Brahmanas, Aranyakas,

Grhyasutras and Shrautasutras. The main period of Vedic literary activity falls into ca. the 9th to 7th centuries when the various shakhas (schools) compiled and memorized their respective corpora. The oldest surviving manuscript of a text composed in Sanskrit is the Devi Māhātmya on Palm-leaf dating from the 11th century CE.[5]

The older Upanishads (BAU, ChU, JUB, KathU, MaitrU) belong to the Vedic period, but the larger part of the Muktika canon is post-Vedic. The Aranyakas form part of both the Brahmana and Upanishad corpus.

23.2 Sutra literature

Main article: Sutra
See also: Shulba Sutras, Kalpa (Vedanga), Dharma Sutras and Shastra

Continuing the tradition of the late Vedic Shrautasutra literature, Late Iron Age scholarship (ca. 500 to 100 BCE) organized knowledge into Sutra treatises, including the Vedanga and the religious or philosophical Brahma Sutras, Yoga Sutras, Nyaya Sutras.

In the Vedanga disciplines of grammar and phonetics, no author had greater influence than Pāṇini with his Aṣṭādhyāyī (ca. 5th century BC). In the tradition of Sutra literature exposing the full grammar of Sanskrit in extreme brevity, Panini's brilliance lies in the nature of his work of a prescriptive generative grammar, involving metarules, transformations and recursion. Being prescriptive for all later grammatical works, such as Patanjali's Mahābhāṣya, Pāṇini's grammar effectively fixed the grammar of Classical Sanskrit. The Backus-Naur Form or BNF grammars used to describe modern programming languages have significant similarities with Panini's grammar rules.

23.3 The epics

Main article: Indian epic poetry

The period between approximately the 6th and 1st centuries BC saw the composition and redaction of the two great epics, the *Ramayana* and the *Mahabharata*, with subsequent redaction progressing down to the 4th century CE. They are known as *itihasa*, or history.

23.3.1 The *Ramayana*

Main article: Ramayana

While not as long as the *Mahabharata*, the *Ramayana* is still twice as long as the *Iliad* and *Odyssey* put together. Traditionally, the authorship is attributed to the Hindu sage Valmiki, who is referred to as *Adikavi*, or "first poet". In the Ramayana, the *shloka* meter was introduced for the first time. Like the Mahabharata, the Ramayana was also handed down orally and evolved through several centuries before being transferred into writing. It includes tales that form the basis for modern Hindu festivals and even contains a description of the same marriage practice still observed in contemporary times by people of Hindu persuasion.

The story deals with Prince Rama, his exile and the abduction of his wife by the Rakshasa king Ravana, and the Lankan war. Similar to the Mahabharata, the Ramayana also has several full-fledged stories appearing as sub-plots.

The Ramayana has also played a similar and equally important role in the development of Indian and Southeast Asian culture as the Mahabharata.

The *Ramayana* is also extant in Southeast Asian versions.

The battle of Kurukshetra, folio from the Mahabharata.

23.3.2   The *Mahabharata*

Main article: Mahabharata

The *Mahabharata* (*Great Bharata*) is one of the longest poetic works in the world. While it is clearly a poetic epic, it contains large tracts of Hindu mythology, philosophy and religious tracts. Traditionally, authorship of the *Mahabharata* is attributed to the sage Vyasa. According to the Adi-parva of the Mahabharata (81, 101-102), the text was originally 8,800 verses when it was composed by Vyasa and was known as the *Jaya* (Victory), which later became 24,000 verses in the *Bharata Samhitha* recited by Vaisampayana.

The broad sweep of the story of the *Mahabharata* chronicles the story of the conflict between two families for control of Hastinapur, a city in ancient India.

The impact of the *Mahabharata* on India and Hinduism cannot be stressed enough. Having been molded by Indian culture, it has in turn molded the development of Indian culture. Thousands of later writers would draw freely from the story and sub-stories of the *Mahabharata*.

23.4   Buddhist and Jain works

Main article: Sanskrit Buddhist literature

Sanskrit also became a major language for Indian religions such as Buddhism and Jainism. Indian Buddhists began adopting Sanskrit during the rule of the Kushan empire (CE 30-375), at first in forms called Buddhist Hybrid Sanskrit

Sanskrit Buddhist manuscript.

which were influenced by the Prakrits. Asvaghosa wrote the Buddhacarita (acts of the Buddha) in classical Sanskrit and later Buddhists also adopted pure Sanskrit. One of the earliest Sanskrit dramas that survives (partially) is also from Asvaghosa, the Sariputra-Prakarana. Most Mahayana Buddhist texts such as the Diamond sutra were written in Sanskrit, as well as Tantric Buddhist texts. Sanskrit survives as a sacred language in the Newar Buddhism of Nepal. Jainism, though more varied in its use of local languages, also wrote many of its texts in Sanskrit.

23.5 Classical Sanskrit literature

The classical period of Sanskrit literature dates to the Gupta period and the successive pre-Islamic Middle kingdoms of India, spanning roughly the 3rd to 8th centuries CE.

23.5.1 Biography

The tradition of writing biographies in Sanskrit starts with the *Harshacharita* of Bāṇabhaṭṭa. Other biographical works include *Vikramankadevacharita* by Bilhana.[6]

23.5.2 Drama

Main article: Sanskrit drama

Drama as a distinct genre of Sanskrit literature emerges in the final centuries BC, influenced partly by Vedic mythology. It reaches its peak between the 4th and 7th centuries before declining together with Sanskrit literature as a whole.

Famous Sanskrit dramatists include Śhudraka, Bhasa, Asvaghosa and Kālidāsa. Though numerous plays written by these playwrights are still available, little is known about the authors themselves.

One of the earliest known Sanskrit plays is the Mrichakatika, thought to have been composed by Śhudraka in the 2nd century BC. The *Natya Shastra* (ca. 2nd century AD, literally "Scripture of Dance," though it sometimes translated as

"Science of Theatre'") is a keystone work in Sanskrit literature on the subject of stagecraft. Bhasa and Kālidāsa are major early authors of the first centuries AD, Kālidāsa qualifying easily as the greatest poet and playwright in Sanskrit. He deals primarily with famous Hindu legends and themes; three famous plays by Kālidāsa are *Vikramōrvaśīyam* (Vikrama and Urvashi), *Mālavikāgnimitram* (Malavika and Agnimitra), and the play that he is most known for: *Abhijñānaśākuntalam* (The Recognition of Shakuntala).

Late (post 6th century) dramatists include Dandin and Sriharsha. Nagananda, attributed to King Harsha, is an outstanding drama that outlines the story of King Jimutavahana, who sacrifices himself to save the tribe of serpents. It is also unique in that it invokes Lord Buddha in what is a predominantly Hindu drama.

The only surviving ancient Sanskrit drama theatre tradition is Koodiyattam, which is being preserved in Kerala by the Chakyar community.

23.5.3 Scholarly treatises

Main articles: Tantras, Shastra, Siddhanta and Jataka
Further information: Jyotihshastra

The earliest surviving treatise on astrology is the Jyotiṣa Vedānga as the science of observing the heavens in order to correctly perform Vedic sacrifice arises after the end of the Vedic period, during ca. the 6th to 4th centuries BCE. Classical Hindu astrology is based on early medieval compilations, notably the Bṛhat Parāśara Horāśāstra and Sārāvalī (7th to 8th century).[7] The astronomy of the classical Gupta period, the centuries following Indo-Greek contact, is documented in treatises known as Siddhantas (which means "established conclusions" [8]). Varahamihira in his *Pancha-Siddhantika* contrasts. five of these: The Surya Siddhanta besides the Paitamaha Siddhantas (which is more similar to the "classical" Vedanga Jyotisha), the Paulisha and Romaka Siddhantas (directly based on Hellenistic astronomy) and the Vasishtha Siddhanta.

The earliest extant treatise in Indian mathematics is the *Āryabhaṭīya* (written ca. 500 CE), a work on astronomy and mathematics. The mathematical portion of the *Āryabhaṭīya* was composed of 33 *sūtras* (in verse form) consisting of mathematical statements or rules, but without any proofs.[9] However, according to (Hayashi 2003, p. 123), "this does not necessarily mean that their authors did not prove them. It was probably a matter of style of exposition." From the time of Bhaskara I (600 CE onwards), prose commentaries increasingly began to include some derivations (*upapatti*).

"Tantra" is a general term for a scientific, magical or mystical treatise and mystical texts both Hindu and Buddhist said to concern themselves with five subjects, 1. the creation, 2. the destruction of the world, 3. the worship of the gods, 4. the attainment of all objects, 5. the four modes of union with the supreme spirit by meditation. These texts date to the entire lifespan of Classical Sanskrit literature.

23.5.4 Stories

Main articles: Panchatantra and Hitopadesha
Sanskrit fairy tales and fables are chiefly characterised by ethical reflections and proverbial philosophy. A peculiar style, marked by the insertion of a number of different stories within the framework of a single narrative, made its way to Persian and Arabic literatures, exerting a major influence on works such as *One Thousand and One Nights*.

The two most important collections are Panchatantra and Hitopadesha; originally intended as manuals for the instruction of kings in domestic and foreign policy, they belong to the class of literature which the Hindus call *nīti-śāstra*, or "Science of Political Ethics".

Other notable prose works include a collection of pretty and ingenious fairy tales, with a highly Oriental colouring, the *Vetāla-panchaviṃśati* or "Twenty-five Tales of the Vetāla" (a demon supposed to occupy corpses), the *Siṃhāsana-dvātriṃçikā* or "Thirty-two Stories of the Lion-seat" (i.e. throne), which also goes by the name of *Vikrama-charita*, or "Adventures of Vikrama" and the *Śuka-saptati*, or "Seventy Stories of a Parrot". These three collections of fairy tales are all written in prose and are comparatively short.

Somadeva's Kathā-sarit-sāgara or "Ocean of Rivers of Stories" is a work of special importance: composed in verse and of very considerable length, it contains more than 22,000 shlokas, equal to nearly one-fourth of the Mahābhārata. Like Kshemendra's *Brhatkathamanjari* and Budhasvamin's Br̥hatkathāślokasaṃgraha, it derives from Gunadhya's Brihatkatha.

Fable collections, originally serving as the handbooks of practical moral philosophy, provided an abundant reservoir of ethical maxims that become so popular that works consisting exclusively of poetical aphorisms started to appear. The most important are the two collections by the highly gifted Bhartr̥hari, entitled respectively *Nīti-śataka*, or "Century of Conduct," and *Vairāgya-śataka*, or "Century of Renunciation." The keynote prevailing in this new ethical poetry style is the doctrine of the vanity of human life, which was developed before the rise of Buddhism in the sixth century B.C., and has dominated Indian thought ever since.

23.5.5 Classical poetry

This refers to the poetry produced from the approximately the 3rd to 8th centuries. Kālidāsa is the foremost example of a classical poet. While Kalidasa's Sanskrit usage is simple but beautiful, later Sanskrit poetry shifted towards highly stylized literary accents: stanzas that read the same backwards and forwards, words that can be split in different ways to produce different meanings, sophisticated metaphors, and so on. A classic example is the poet Bharavi and his magnum opus, the *Kiratarjuniya* (6th-7th century).

The greatest works of poetry in this period are the five *Mahākāvyas*, or "great compositions":

- *Kumārasambhava* by Kālidāsa

- *Raghuvamsha* by Kālidāsa

- *Kiratarjuniya* by Bharavi

- *Shishupala Vadha* by Māgha

- *Naishadha Charita* by Sriharsha

Some scholars include the Bhattikavya as a sixth Mahākāvya.[10]

Other major literary works from this period are *Kadambari* by Banabhatta, the first Sanskrit novelist (6th-7th centuries), the *Kama Sutra* by Vatsyayana, and the three *shataka*s of Bhartr̥hari.

23.5.6 Puranas

Main article: Puranas

The corpus of the Hindu Puranas likewise falls into the classical period of Sanskrit literature, dating to between the 5th and 10th centuries, and marks the emergence of the Vaishnava and Shaiva denominations of classical Hinduism. The Puranas are classified into a *Mahā-* ("great") and a *Upa-* ("lower, additional") corpus. Traditionally[11] they are said to narrate five subjects, called *pañcalakṣaṇa* ("five distinguishing marks"):

Sargaśca pratisargasca vamśo manvantarāṇi ca I

Vamśānucaritam caiva Purāṇam pañcalakśaṇam II

They are:

1. Sarga — The creation of the universe.

2. Pratisarga — Secondary creations, mostly re-creations after dissolution.

3. Vaṃśa — Genealogy of royals and sages.

4. Manvantara — Various eras.

5. Vaṃśānucaritam — Dynastic histories.

A Purana usually gives prominence to a certain deity (Shiva, Vishnu or Krishna, Durga) and depicts the other gods as subservient.

23.6 Later Sanskrit literature

The *Avadhuta Gita*, an extreme nondual (Sanskrit: *advaita*) text, is held by Western scholarship to date in its present form from the 9th or 10th centuries.[12] Some important works from the 11th century include the *Katha-sarit-sagara* and the *Gita Govinda* of Jayadeva.

The *Katha-sarita-sagara* (An Ocean of Stories) by Somadeva was an 11th-century poetic adaptation in Sanskrit of *Brihat-katha*, written in the 5th century BC in the *Paishachi* dialect. One of the famous series of stories in this work is the *Vikrama and Vetāla* series (Sanskrit: वेतालपञ्चवशितिं), known across India today. On the other side of the spectrum, of the 'Bhana' style of drama, Ubhayabhisarika is a one-person drama of an endearing lecher who knows every courtesan and her family by name.

The *Gita Govinda* (The song of Govinda) by the Oriya composer Jayadeva is the story of Krishna's love for Radha, and is written in spectacularly lyrical and musical Sanskrit.

A central text for several Hindu sects in eastern India, the *Gita Govinda* is recited regularly at major Hindu pilgrimage sites such as Jagannath temple at Puri, Odisha. The *Ashtapadis* of the *Gita Govinda* also form a staple theme in Bharatanatyam and Odissi classical dance recitals.

Beyond the 11th century, the use of Sanskrit for general literature declined, most importantly because of the emergence of literature in vernacular Indian languages (notably Bengali, Hindi, Marathi, Telugu, and Kannada). Sanskrit literature fueled literature in vernacular languages, and the Sanskrit language itself continued to have a profound influence over the development of Indian literature in general.

Sanskrit continued to be learned by the Brahmans, and also patronized in the courts of many Muslim rulers (notably Akbar). Many translations of Sanskrit works in Persian and Arabic were created. Sanskrit also continued to be used for philosophical literature (the Dvaita school was founded in 13th century). Notable names in Sanskrit literature for this time period are Mallinatha and Bhattoji Dikshita.

23.7 Modern Sanskrit literature

See also: Sahitya Akademi Award for Sanskrit

Literature in Sanskrit continues to be produced. These works, however, have a very small readership. In the introduction to *Ṣoḍaśī: An Anthology of Contemporary Sanskrit Poets* (1992), Radhavallabh Tripathi writes:[13]

> Sanskrit is known for its classical literature, even though the creative activity in this language has continued without pause from the medieval age till today. [...] Consequently, contemporary Sanskrit writing suffers from a prevailing negligence.

Most current Sanskrit poets are employed as teachers, either pandits in *pāṭhaśāla*s or university professors.[13] However, Tripathi also points out the abundance of contemporary Sanskrit literature:

> On the other hand, the number of authors who appear to be very enthusiastic about writing in Sanskrit during these days is not negligible. [...] Dr. Ramji Upadhyaya in his treatise on modern Sanskrit drama has discussed more than 400 Sanskrit plays written and published during the nineteenth and twentieth centuries. In a thesis dealing with Sanskrit *mahākāvya*s written in a single decade, 1961–1970, the researcher has noted 52 Sanskrit *mahākāvya*s (epic poems) produced in that very decade.

Similarly, Prajapati (2005), in *Post-Independence Sanskrit Literature: A Critical Survey*, estimates that more than 3000 Sanskrit works have been composed in the period after Indian Independence (i.e., since 1947) alone. Further, much of this work is judged as being of high quality, both in comparison to classical Sanskrit literature, and to modern literature in other Indian languages.[14][15]

Since 1967, the Sahitya Akademi, India's national academy of letters, has had an award for the best creative work written that year in Sanskrit. In 2009, Satyavrat Shastri became the first Sanskrit author to win the Jnanpith Award, India's highest literary award.[16] Vidyadhar Shastri wrote two epic poems (*Mahakavya*), seven shorter poems, three plays and three songs of praise (*stavana kavya*), he received the *Vidyavachaspati* award in 1962. Some other modern Sanskrit composers include Abhiraj Rajendra Mishra (known as *Triveṇī Kavi*, composer of short stories and several other genres of Sanskrit literature), Jagadguru Rambhadracharya (known as *Kavikularatna*, composer of two epics, several minor works and commentaries on *Prasthānatrayī*).

23.8   See also

- Early Medieval literature

- Hindu scripture

- Indian literature

- Indian manuscripts

- List of Historic Indian Texts

- List of Sanskrit poets

- List of ancient Indian writers

- Sanskrit drama

- Telugu literature

- Yoga Vasistha

23.9   References

[1] P. 228 The *Sufis of Britain: an exploration of Muslim identity*

[2] P. 7 *Panchatantra — Five Strategies: Collection of animal fables complied before ...*

[3] Nair 2008, pp. 84-227.

[4] Joshi 1994, pp. 91-93.

[5] Useful for comparison: One of the first documents written in the Sumerian language on a stone plaque dates to c. the 31st century BCE, found at Jemdet Nasr; the Gezer calendar written in paleo-Hebrew on limestone dates from the 10th-century BCE.

[6] Amaresh Datta (1987). *Encyclopaedia of Indian Literature: A-Devo*. Sahitya Akademi. p. 540. ISBN 978-81-260-1803-1.

[7] Ohashi, Yukio. "Development of Astronomical Observation in Vedic and Post-Vedic India." Indian Journal of History of Science 28(3): 185-251, 1993.

[8] Cf. Burgess, Appendix by Whitney p. 439.

[9] (Hayashi 2003, pp. 122–123)

[10] Fallon, Oliver. 2009. Bhatti's Poem: The Death of Rávana (Bhaṭṭikāvya). New York: Clay Sanskrit Library. ISBN 978-0-8147-2778-2 I ISBN 0-8147-2778-6 I

`

[11] *Matsya Purana* 53.65

[12] Swami Abhayananda (1992, 2007). *Dattatreya: Song of the Avadhut: An English Translation of the 'Avadhuta Gita' (with Sanskrit Transliteration)*. Classics of mystical literature series. ISBN 0-914557-15-7 (paper), Source: (accessed: Monday February 22, 2010) p.10

[13] Radhavallabh Tripathi, ed. (1992), *Ṣoḍaśī: An Anthology of Contemporary Sanskrit Poets*, Sahitya Akademi, ISBN 81-7201-200-4

[14] S. Ranganath (2009), *Modern Sanskrit Writings in Karnataka*, ISBN 978-81-86111-21-5, p. 7:

> Contrary to popular belief, there is an astonishing quality of creative upsurge of writing in Sanskrit today. Modern Sanskrit writing is qualitatively of such high order that it can easily be treated on par with the best of Classical Sanskrit literature, It can also easily compete with the writings in other Indian languages.

[15] Adhunika Sanskrit Sahitya Pustakalaya, Rashtriya Sanskrit Sansthan:

> The latter half of the nineteenth century marks the beginning of a new era in Sanskrit literature. Many of the modern Sanskrit writings are qualitatively of such high order that they can easily be treated at par with the best of classical Sanskrit works, and they can also be judged in contrast to the contemporary literature in other languages.

[16] "Sanskrit's first Jnanpith winner is a 'poet by instinct'". *The Indian Express*. Jan 14, 2009.

5. ^ Bhattacharji Sukumari, History of Classical Sanskrit Literature, Sangam Books, London, 1993, ISBN 0-86311-242-0, p. 148.

23.10   Further reading

- Arthur Anthony Macdonell, A History of Sanskrit Literature, New York 1900

- Winternitz, M. A History of Indian Literature. Oriental books, New Delhi, 1927 (1907)

- J. Gonda (ed.) *A History of Indian Literature*, Otto Harrasowitz, Wiesbaden.

- Prajapati, Manibhai K. (2005), *Post-Independence Sanskrit Literature: A Critical Survey*, Standard Publishers (India)

- S. Ranganath, *Modern Sanskrit Writings in Karnataka*, Rashtriya Sanskrit Sansthan, 2009.

23.11   External links

- GRETIL: Göttingen Register of Electronic Texts in Indian Languages a cumulative register of the numerous download sites for electronic texts in Indian languages.

- Sanskrit Wikibooks

- TITUS Indica

- Sanskrit Literature

- Vedabase.net: Vaishnava literatures with word for word translations from Sanskrit to English.

- Official page of the Clay Sanskrit Library, publisher of classical Indian literature with facing-page texts and translations. Also offers numerous downloadable materials.

- Sanskrit Documents Collection: Documents in ITX format of Upanishads, Stotras etc., and a metasite with links to translations, dictionaries, tutorials, tools and other Sanskrit resources.

Shakuntala stops to look back at Dushyanta, Raja Ravi Varma (1848-1906), scene from Abhijñānaśākuntalam.

A 'Panchatantra' relief at the Mendut temple, Central Java, Indonesia.

Basohli painting (circa 1730 CE) depicting a scene from Jayadeva's Gita Govinda.

Chapter 24

Serbian epic poetry

Serb epic poetry (Serbian: Српске епске народне песме) is a form of epic poetry created by Serbs originating in today's Serbia, Bosnia and Herzegovina, Croatia, Macedonia and Montenegro. The main cycles were composed by unknown Serb authors between the 14th and 19th centuries. They are largely concerned with historical events and personages. The instrument in performing the Serbian epic is the Gusle.

24.1 History

In 1824, Vuk Karadžić sent a copy of his folksong collection to Jacob Grimm, who was particularly enthralled by The Building of Skadar. Grimm translated it into German, and described it as "one of the most touching poems of all nations and all times".[1][2]

24.2 Corpus

The corpus of Serbian epic poetry is divided into cycles:

- Non-historic cycle - poems about Slavic Mythology, particularly the Zmaj, Aždaja and Vilas

- Pre-Kosovo cycle - poems about events that predate the Battle of Kosovo

- Cycle of Kraljević Marko

- Kosovo cycle - poems about events that happened just before and after the Battle of Kosovo (no poem covers the battle itself)

- Post-Kosovo cycle - poems about post-Battle events

- Cycle of hajduks

- Cycle of uskoks

- Poems about the liberation of Serbia

- Poems about the liberation of Montenegro

Poems depict historical events with varying degrees of accuracy.

Kosovo Maiden *by Uroš Predić* Dying Pavle Orlović is given water by a maiden who seeks her fiancé; he tells her that her love, Milan, and his two blood-brothers Miloš and Ivan are dead.
—taken from the Serb epic poem

24.3   People of Serbian epic poetry

- Benedikt Kuripečič — 16th century diplomat who traveled trough Ottoman Bosnia and Serbia in 1530 and recorded that epic songs about Miloš Obilić are popular not only among Serbs on Kosovo but also in Bosnia and Croatia. He also recorded some legends about the Battle of Kosovo and explained that in the whole region new poetry on the topic was composed.[3]

- Dimitrije Karaman - the oldest known Serbian gusle player, c. 1551.

- Avram Miletić (1755 – after 1826) was a merchant and songwriter who is best known for writing the earliest collection of urban lyric poetry in Serbian.

- Old Rashko - one of the most important sources of the epic poetry recorded by Vuk Karadžić.

- Filip Višnjić (1767–1834), dubbed the "Serbian Homer" both for his blindness and poetic gift, was a *guslar* (*gusle* player).

- Tešan Podrugović (1783—1815) was Serbian hayduk, storyteller and gusle player (Serbian: guslar) who participated in the First Serbian Uprising and was one of most important sources for Serbian epic poetry.

- Živana Antonijević (Blind Živana) (died in 1822) was one of favorite female singers of Vuk Karadžić.

- Vuk Karadžić (1787—1864) was a Serbian philologist and linguist who was the major reformer of the Serbian language. He deserves, perhaps, for his collections of songs, fairy tales, and riddles to be called the father of the study of Serbian folklore.

- Petar Perunović (1880—1952), also known as 'Perun', he was a famous gusle player who played Gusle for Nikola Tesla and the first to record Serbian epic poetry in a studio.

24.4 Characters

Popular legendary villains of Serbian epic poetry who are depicted as enemies of Kraljević Marko are based upon historical persons:

- Musa Kesedžija - he is the result of merging several historical people including Musa Çelebi son of Bayezid I and Musa from the Muzaka Albanian noble family while Jovan Tomić believes he is based on the supporter of Jegen Osman Pasha

- Djemo the Mountaineer - a member of Muzaka noble family (Gjin Muzaka) or maybe Ottoman military person Jegen Osman Pasha

- General Vuča - Tanush Dukagjin, a member of Dukagjini noble family or Prince Eugene of Savoy or Peter Doci

- Philip the Magyar - Pipo of Ozora, an Italian condottiero, general, strategist and confidant of King Sigismund of Hungary.

Many other heroes of Serbian epic poetry are also based upon historical persons:

- Strahinja Banović — Đurad II Stracimirović Balšić

- Jug Bogdan — Vratko Nemanjić

- Beg Kostadin — Constantine Dragaš

- Sibinjanin Janko — John Hunyadi

- Petar Dojčin — Petar Doci

- Maksim Crnojević — Staniša Skenderbeg Crnojević

- Bajo Pivljanin - Bajo Nikolić

- Mihajlo Svilojević — Michael Szilágyi

- Janko od Kotara - Janko Mitrović

24.5 Excerpts

- Slavic antithesis:

- (Kraljević Marko speaks:)

-

-

Modern example of Serbian epics as recorded in 1992 by film director Paweł Pawlikowski in a documentary for the BBC *Serbian epics*; an anonymous *gusle* singer compares Radovan Karadžić, as he prepares to depart for Geneva for peace talk, to Karađorđe, who had led the First Serbian Uprising against the Turks in 1804:[6]

24.6   Quotes

-

Jacob Grimm

-

Charles Simic

24.7   Modern Serbian epic poetry

Serbian epic poetry is being made today in the same way. Some modern songs are published in books or recorded, and under copyright, but some are in public domain, and modified by subsequent authors just like old ones. There are new songs that mimic Serbian epic poetry, but are humorous and not epic in nature; these are also circulating around with no known author. In the latter half of the 19th century, a certain MP would exit the Serbian parliament each day, and tell of the debate over the Monetary Reform Bill in the style of epic poetry. Modern epic heroes include: Radovan Karadžić, Ratko Mladić and Vojislav Šešelj. Topics include: Balkan Wars of the 90s, 1999 Nato Bombing of Serbia, and the Hague Tribunal.

Popular Modern Serbian epic performers (Guslars):

- Milomir 'Miljan' Miljanić

- Djordjije 'Djoko' Koprivica

- Boško Vujačić

- Vlastimir Barać

- Sava Stanišić

- Miloš Šegrt

- Saša Laketić

- Milan Mrdović

24.8   See also

- Bugarštica

- Erlangen Manuscript

- List of national poetries

- The Building of Skadar

24.9   References

[1] Alan Dundes (1996). *The Walled-Up Wife: A Casebook*. Univ of Wisconsin Press. pp. 3–. ISBN 978-0-299-15073-0. Retrieved 1 March 2013.

[2] Paul Rankov Radosavljevich (1919). *Who are the Slavs?: A Contribution to Race Psychology*. Badger. p. 332. Retrieved 1 March 2013.

[3] Pavle Ivić (1996). *Istorija srpske kulture*. Dečje novine. p. 160. Retrieved 9 September 2013. Бенедикт Курипечић. пореклом Словенаи, који између 1530. и 1531. путује као тумач аустријског посланства, у свом Путопису препричава део косовске легенде, спомиње епско певање о Милошу Обилићу у крајевима удаљеним од места догађаја, у Босни и Хрватској, и запажа настајање нових песама.

[4] Политикин забавник 3147, p. 4

[5] *Black Lamb and Grey Falcon* by Rebecca West is the title of one of the best-known books in English on the subject of Yugoslavia.

[6] Judah, Tim (1997). *The Serbs - History, Myth and the Destruction of Yugoslavia*. New Haven and London: Yale University Press.

24.10   External links

- An article about Serbian oral tradition

- Songs from Kosovo cycle

- The Battle of Kosovo - Serbian Epic Poems Preface by Charles Simic *Swallow Press/Ohio University Press*, Athens 1987

- Heroic Ballads of Servia *translated by George Rapall Noyes and Leonard Bacon*, 1913

24.10.1   MP3s

-
  - Lesson in rhyme
  - Poem for Karadjordje
  - Fate of vizier Mahmud-pasha in the village of Krusa
  - Pit of Korich Part 2 Part 3

Chapter 25

Spanish poetry

25.1   Medieval Spain

Main article: Medieval Spanish literature
The Medieval period covers 400 years of different poetry texts and can be broken up into five categories

Primitive Lyrics

> Since the findings of the Kharjas, which are mainly two, three, or four verses, Spanish lyrics, which are written in Mozarabic dialect, are perhaps the oldest of Romance Europe. The Mozarabic dialect has Latin origins with a combination of Arabic and Hebrew fonts.[1]

The Epic

> Many parts of *Cantar de Mio Cid, Cantar de Roncesvalles*, and *Mocedades de Rodrigo* are part of the epic. The exact portion of each of these works is disputed among scholars. The Minstrels, over the course of the 1100s to the 1300s, were driving force of this movement. The Spanish epic likely originated from France. There are also indications of Arabic and Visigoth. It is usually written in series of seven to eight syllables within rhyming verse.[2]

Mester de clerecía

> The cuaderna vía is the most distinctive verse written in Alexandrine verse, consisting of 12 syllables. Works during the 1200s include religious, epics, historical, advice or knowledge, and adventure themes. Examples of such themes include the *The Miracles of the Virgin Mary, Poema de Fernán González, Book of Alexander, Cato's Examples*, and *Book of Apolonio*, respectively. Some works vary and are not necessarily mester de clerecía, but are reflective of it. Such poems are of a discussion nature, such as *Elena y María* and *Reason to Love*. Hagiographic poems include *Life of St. María Egipciaca* and *Book of the Three Wise Men*. Mature works, like *The Book of Good Love* and *Rhyming Book of the Palace*, were not included in the genre until the 1300s.[3]

Collection of verse (Cancionero)

> During this movement, language use went from Galician-Portuguese to Castilian. Octosyllable, twelve syllables, and verse of arte mayor were becoming the footing of verses. Main themes derive from Provençal poetry. This form of poetry was generally compilations of verses formed into books, also known as cancioneros. Main works include *Cancionero de Baena, Cancionero de Estuniga*, and *Cancionero General*. Other important works from this era include parts of *Dance of Death, Dialogue Between Love and an Old Man*, verses of *Mingo Revulgo*, and verses of the *Baker Woman*.[4]

The Spanish ballads

The romanceros have no set number of octosyllables, but these poems are only parallel in this form. *Romancero Viejo* consists of the oldest poems in these epochs, which are anonymous. The largest amount of romances comes from the 1500s, although early works were from the 1300s. Many musicians of Spain used these poems in their pieces throughout the Renaissance. Cut offs, archaic speech, and recurrent dialogue are common characteristics among these poems; however the type and focus were diverse. Lyrical romances are also a sizeable part of this era. During the 1600s, were recycled and renewed. Some authors still stayed consistent with the original format. By the 1900s, the tradition was still continued.[5]

25.1.1   Early Middle Ages

- Mozarab Jarchas, the first expression of Spanish poetry, in Mozárabe dialect

- Mester de Juglaría

  - Cantar de Mio Cid

- Mester de Clerecía

  - Juan Ruiz, Arcipreste de Hita
  - Gonzalo de Berceo

- Troubadours

- Xohán de Cangas

- Palla (troubadour)

- Paio Soares de Taveirós

25.1.2   Later Middle Ages

- Macías

- Pero Ferrus

- Juan Rodríguez de la Cámara

- Alfonso Martínez de Toledo, Arcipreste de Talavera

- Jorge Manrique

- Marqués de Santillana

25.2   Arabic and Hebrew poetry during the Moorish period

During the time when Spain was occupied by the Arabs after the early 700s, the Iberian Peninsula became dominated by the Arabic language in both the central and southern regions. Latin still prevailed in the north, but the two languages began to merge, forming several idioms called the Romance languages.[6] The Jewish culture had its own Golden Age through the span of the 900s to 1100s in Spain. Hebrew poetry was usually in the style of Piyyut; however, under Muslim rule in Spain, the style changed. These poets began to write again in what was the "pure language of the Bible". Beforehand, poems were written in Midrash. This change was a result of the commitment the Arabs had to the Koran. Tempos and secular topics were now prevalent in Hebrew poetry. However, these poems were only reflections of events seen by the Jews and not of ones practiced themselves.[7]

- The Alhambra Poets:

    - Ibn al-Yayyab

    - Ibn Zamrak

    - Ibn al-Khatib

- Ibn Sahl of Sevilla

- Ibn Hazm of Córdoba

- Ibn Gabirol

- Moses ibn Ezra

- Abraham ibn Ezra

- Ibn Quzman

- Ibn Arabi

25.3 After 1492

- Anonymous writers of the *Romancero*

- Juan Boscán

- Gutierre de Cetina

- Alonso de Ercilla

- Santa Teresa de Jesús

- San Juan de la Cruz

- Fernando de Herrera

- Garcilaso de la Vega

- Juan del Encina

- Fray Luis de León

- Diego Hurtado de Mendoza

- Lope de Rueda

- Jorge Manrique

- Ausiàs March (in Valencian)

- Sor Juana Inés de la Cruz

25.4 The Golden Age (*El Siglo de Oro*)

Main article: Spanish Golden Age

This epoch includes the Renaissance of the 1500s and the Baroque of the 1600s.[8] During the Renaissance, poetry became partitioned into culteranismo and conceptismo, which essentially became rivals.

- Culteranismo used bleak language and hyperbaton. These works largely included neologisms and mythological topics. Such characteristics made this form of poetry highly complex, making comprehension difficult.

- Conceptismo was a trend using new components and resources. An example of this new extension was the *Germanias*. Works included comparative and complex sentences. This movement derived from Petrarchanism.

During the Baroque period, Satire, Neostoicism, and Mythological themes were also prevalent.

- Satire tended to be directed to the elites, criticizing the defects of the society. This form of poetry often resulted in severe punishments being administered to the poets.
- Neostoicism became a movement of philosophical poetry. Ideas from the medieval period resurfaced.
- Mythological themes were more common in culteranismo. Not until the Generation of 1927 did these poems gain more importance. *La Fábula de Polifemo y Galatea* and *Las Soledades* are two key works.[9]

- Francisco de Quevedo y Villegas

- Luis de Góngora y Argote established culteranismo.

- Félix Lope de Vega Carpio

- Pedro Calderón de la Barca

- Saint John of the Cross

25.5 Romanticism

Germany and England were the large forces in this movement. Over the course of the late 1700s to the late 1800s Romanticism spread philosophy and art through Western societies of the world. The earlier part of this movement overlapped with the Age of Revolutions. The idea of the creative imagination was rising above the idea of reason. Minute elements of nature, such as bugs and pebbles, were considered divine. There were many variations of the perception of nature in these works. Instead of allegory, this era moved towards myths and symbols. The power of human emotion emerged during this period.[10]

- Manuel José Quintana

- José Zorrilla

- Gustavo Adolfo Bécquer

- Rosalía de Castro (in Galician and Spanish)

- José de Espronceda

- Miguel de Cervantes Saavedra

25.6   1898 until 1926

Spain went through drastic changes after the demise of Spain's colonial empire. French and German inspiration along with Modernism greatly improved the culture of Spain with the works of the Generation of 1898, which were mostly novelists but some were poets.[11]

- Antonio Machado

- Manuel Machado

- Ultraism

25.7   1927 until 1936

The Generation of 1927 were mostly poets. Many were also involved with the production of music and theatre plays.

- Rafael Alberti

- Vicente Aleixandre

- Dámaso Alonso

- Manuel Altolaguirre

- Luis Cernuda

- Gerardo Diego

- Manuel de Falla; influential on poets, for his vision of Moorish Spain

- Juan Ramón Jiménez

- Federico García Lorca

- Jorge Guillen

- Emilio Prados

- Pedro Salinas

25.8   1939 until 1975

Poets during the World War II and under General Franco in peacetime:

- Juan Ramón Jiménez received the Nobel Prize in Literature 1956, "For his lyrical poetry, which in Spanish language constitutes an example of high spirit and artistical purity". Was the last survivor of Generation of 1898. During the mid-1900s works steadily moved back to literary and political aspects.[12]

- Luis Buñuel

- Ángel Crespo

- Jaime Gil de Biedma

- Carlos Edmundo de Ory

- León Felipe

- Ángel González Muñiz

- Miguel Hernández

- José Hierro

- Lluis Llach

- Leopoldo Panero

- José María Pemán

25.9 1975 until present

These works became experimental, using themes, styles and characteristics of traditional poetry throughout Spain's time and combining them with current movements. Some poets remain more traditional, while others more contemporary.

Post-Franco and Contemporary Spanish Poets:

- Blanca Andreu

- Miguel Argaya

- María Victoria Atencia

- Felipe Benítez Reyes

- Carlos Bousoño

- Giannina Braschi

- Francisco Brines

- José Manuel Caballero Bonald

- Matilde Camus

- Antonio Colinas

- Aurora de Albornoz

- Luis Alberto de Cuenca

- Francisco Domene

- José María Fonollosa

- Gloria Fuertes

- Vicente Gallego

- Antonio Gamoneda

- Enrique García-Máiquez

- José Agustín Goytisolo

- Félix Grande

- Diego Jesús Jiménez

- Chantal Maillard

- Antonio Martínez Sarrión

- Carlos Marzal

- Bruno Mesa

- Juan Carlos Mestre

- Luis García Montero

- Luis Javier Moreno

- Lorenzo Oliván

- Salome Ortega

- Leopoldo María Panero

- Francisco Pino

- Juan Vicente Nuevo Piqueras

- Claudio Rodríguez

- Ángel Rupérez

- Jaime Siles

- Jenaro Talens

- Andrés Trapiello

- José Miguel Ullán

- José Ángel Valente

- Álvaro Valverde

- Luis Antonio de Villena

- Luisa Castro

- Isla Correyero

- Clara Janés

- Ana Rossetti

- Rafael Pérez Estrada

25.10   See also

- List of Spanish language poets

- Latin American poetry

- Arabic poetry

- List of Catalan language poets

25.11 Notes

[1] http://www.spanisharts.com/books/literature/i_lirica.htm

[2] http://www.spanisharts.com/books/literature/i_epica.htm

[3] http://www.spanisharts.com/books/literature/i_clerecia.htm

[4] http://www.spanisharts.com/books/literature/i_cancionero.htm

[5] http://www.spanisharts.com/books/literature/i_romancero.htm

[6] http://www.alhewar.net/Basket/Habeeb_Salloum_Spanish_Language.htm

[7] http://medievalhebrewpoetry.org/adelmanarticle.html

[8] http://www.spanisharts.com/books/literature/poetrygold.htm

[9] http://www.donquijote.org/spanishlanguage/literature/history/poesia.asp

[10] http://academic.brooklyn.cuny.edu/english/melani/cs6/rom.html

[11] http://www.answers.com/topic/spanish-literature

[12] http://www.nobelprize.org/nobel_prizes/literature/laureates/1956/press.html

25.12 Further reading

- D. Gareth Walters. *The Cambridge Introduction to Spanish Poetry: Spain & Spanish America.* (2002).

- Linda Fish Compton. *Andalusian Lyric poetry and Old Spanish Love Songs* (1976) (includes translations of some of the medieval anthology of love poems, compiled by Ibn Sana al-Mulk, the *Dar al-tiraz*).

- Emilio Garcia Gomez. (Ed.) *In Praise of Boys: Moorish Poems from Al-Andalus* (1975).

- Paul Halsall has a bibliography online, listing journal articles in English on medieval poetry in Spain.

- Carmi, T. (Ed.) *The Penguin Book of Hebrew Verse.* New York: Penguin Books (1981). ISBN 0-14-042197-1 (includes translations of Judah Al-Harizi, Nahmanides, Todros Abulafia and other Jewish poets from Spain).

- A. Robert Lauer, University of Oklahoma, on Spanish Metrification: the common structures of Spanish verse

Cantar de Mio Cid

Chapter 26

Telugu poetry

Telugu poetry is verse originating in the southern provinces of India, predominantly from modern Andhra Pradesh and some corners of Tamil Nadu and Karnataka.

26.1   Ori available

Telugu language literature is 3500 years old.[1] Though ambiguity exists in this regard, it might be even older than or even contemporary to the professed South Indian ancient languages. Archaeological work regarding its antiquity has been restrained because of poor funding to such authorities. There are books such as Gadha Sapta Shati dating back to 100 AD. Poetry from the language covers spiritual, mythological and secular writings. Earliest available poetry was found on the Epigraphs and Victory Inscriptions. Nonavailability of ancient literature despite the language being quite old is attributed to the little support that the language received from the pre-1000 AD rulers. During the period of patronage of Eastern Chalukya rulers in 1000 AD, the language attained its present script, rich vocabulary and grammar rules. This standardization led to development in the quantity and quality of literature of Telugu Language, which was predominantly composed of poetry. This phase of development reached its zenith under the rule of Sri Krishna Deva Raya of Vijayanagara Empire. Modern Telugu poetry has seen English transliterations. Sri Riasat Ali Taj (1930–1999), a prominent personality, poet, author, critic, writer, educationist, linguist and translator from Karimnagar, has made poetic translations (Manzoom Tarjuma in Urdu Rubaiyaat) published in popular Urdu magazines and newspapers in early 1950s.

26.2   Pandu

This era saw the beginning of the translation of the epic Mahabharata into Telugu by three great scholars Nannaya, Tikkana and Errana. These three scholars were reverently called as Kavitrayam (trinity of poets). They completed the great epic in three parts by adopting styles and setting standards, thereby paving way for the future writers. However, despite the best efforts of the scholars of this era, Telugu language used in the poetry included various words imported from Sanskrit and was thus out of reach of the common man.

26.3   Pre Prabandha era

This includes various poets such as Nanne Choda and Somanadha who concentrated on using more native words and styles such as Dwipada to reach common man. Srinatha famous for his famous works, *Sringara Naishadham*, *KasiKhandam* and *BhimaKhandam*. This era also saw the most widely quoted Telugu poet Potana and his poem Srimad Bhagavatam. A folk-style rendering of poems was also initiated by Annamayya during this period.

163

26.4   Prabandha era

This era includes writers such as Allasani Peddana, Tenali Ramalinga Kavi and Dhurjati. It is considered as the Golden Age for Telugu literature. Telugu language received patronage of the Vijayanagara Empire. Most of the masterpieces of Telugu literature, such as *Manu Charitra* and *Panduranga Mahatyam*, were written in this era.

26.5   Post Prabandha period

This era includes writers such as Pingali Surana who is famous for his *Kalaa Purnodayam* and *Raaghava Paandaveeyam* and Bhattumurthy / Ramarajabhushana, who wrote *Vasucharitra* and *Narasa Bhoopaaleeyam*.

26.6   Decline period

This era indicates degeneration of standards in the literature. Poets struggled for patronage and concentrated on styles such as Chitra Kavitvam and on composition of erotic literature to please their patrons. Some patrons tried to preserve the traditions but on the whole it was a dark age. There was some light seen at the end of tunnel when Tirupati Venkata Kavulu flourished at the end of this period. They started a new style of poetry Avadhanam and wrote *Krishna Raayabaaram* and *Devi Bhagavatam*.

26.7   Modern period

This started with Gurajada Apparao, who changed the face of Telugu poetry with his *Muthayala Saralu*, and was perfected by later writers in the Romanticism era including Rayaprolu and Devulapalli Krishna Sastri. Gurajada's attempt to reform Telugu poetry by shedding old rules and styles reached a zenith with Sri Sri. SriSri's famous work "Maha Prastanam" is an instant hit with every corners of society. Many writers followed his style and continue to enrich the literature.

26.8   Paryavaran Kavitodyamam

The Paryavaran Kavitodyamam movement started in 2008. It aims to bring awareness and concern among not only the elite class but also the masses through creative forms of literature. The Jagruthi Kiran Foundation initiated it under the leadership of Narayanam Narasimha Murthy, popularly known as *"Vidyavachaspati"*. The movement has literary activities including Harita Kata. Lot of literature has been produced by various poets, writers on Environment. Magazines such as *Malle Teega* and *Kadhakeli* are associated with Jagruthi Kiran Foundation. More than 500 poets and writers are involved in this movement.

26.9   Other forms

While the mainstream poetry based on rhythm and meter is growing up, Telugu literature also saw a rise in folk-poetry. Most famous were Satakam, Dwipada and Padalu. These were mainly used by Bhakti Reformers to reach the common man and spread their ideas. Some notable writers are Annamayya, Vemana, Ramadasu and Somanadha. Tyagaraja's Kritis and Muvva gopala Padalu cannot be missed in this list. Tyagaraja Kriti's are considered most important compositions in Carnatic Music.

Some famous satakams are listed below.

- Vemana Satakam

- Sumathi Satakam

- Sri Kalahastiswara Satakam

- Dasarathi Satakam

- Bhaskara Satakam

- Kumara Satakam

- Narasimha Satakam

- Sarveswara Satakam

- Kumara Satakam

- Kumari Satakam

- Andhra Nayaka Satakam

- Sri Kishna Satakam

- Bharthruhari Neethi Satakam

- Bharthruhari Vyragya Satakam

- Bharthruhari Srungara Satakam

- Daksharama Bhimeswara Sathakam

26.10   Awards

Ismail Award Given every Year for the first book of the poet, established in 2005.

CP Brown Award Given Every year for Translations and the people who has worked for Telugu literary activities

26.11   See also

- List of Telugu poets from India

26.12   References

[1] David Shulman, ed. (2002). *Classical Telugu Poetry: An Anthology*. Velcheru Narayana Rao (translator),. UC Press. ISBN 9780520225985.

26.13   External links

- vemana poems

- Modern Telugu poetry Book Review

Chapter 27

Thai poetry

Poetry has been featured extensively in Thai literature, and constituted the near-exclusive majority of literary works up to the early Rattanakosin period (early 19th century). It consists of five main forms, known as *khlong*, *chan*, *kap*, *klon* and *rai*; some of these developed indigenously while others were borrowed from other languages. Thai poetry dates to the Sukhothai period (13th–14th centuries) and flourished under Ayutthaya (14th–18th centuries), during which it developed into its current forms. Though many works were lost to the Burmese conquest of Ayutthaya in 1767, sponsorship by subsequent kings helped revive the art, with new works created by many great poets, including Sunthorn Phu (1786–1855). Prose writing as a literary form was introduced as a Western import during the reign of King Mongkut (1851–68) and gradually gained popularity, though poetry saw a revival during the reign of King Vajiravudh (1910–25), who authored and sponsored both traditional poetry and the newer literary forms. Poetry's popularity as a mainstream form of literature gradually declined afterwards, although it is still written and read, and is regularly employed ceremonially.

27.1 Forms

Thai poetic works follow established prosodic forms, known as *chanthalak* (Thai: ฉันทลักษณ์, pronounced [tɕʰǎntʰalák]). Almost all have rules governing the exact metre and rhyme structure, i.e. the number of syllables in each line and which syllable rhymes with which. Certain forms also specify the tone or tone marks of syllables; others have requirements of syllable "heaviness". Alliteration and within-line rhyming are also often employed, but are not required by the rules.

27.1.1 Khlong

The *khlong* (โคลง, [kʰlōːŋ]) is the among oldest Thai poetic forms. This is reflected in its requirements on the tone markings of certain syllables, which must be marked with *mai ek* (ไม้เอก, [máj èːk], อ่) or *mai tho* (ไม้โท, [máj tʰōː], อ้). This was likely derived from when the Thai language had three tones (as opposed to today's five, a split which occurred during the Ayutthaya period), two of which corresponded directly to the aforementioned marks. It is usually regarded as an advanced and sophisticated poetic form.[1]

In *khlong*, a stanza (*bot*, บท, [bòt]) has a number of lines (*bat*, บาท, [bàːt], from Pali and Sanskrit *pāda*), depending on the type. The *bat* are subdivided into two *wak* (วรรค, [wák], from Sanskrit *varga*).[note 1] The first *wak* has five syllables, the second has a variable number, also depending on the type, and may be optional. The type of *khlong* is named by the number of *bat* in a stanza; it may also be divided into two main types: *khlong suphap* (โคลงสุภาพ, [kʰlōːŋ sù.pʰâːp]) and *khlong dan* (โคลงดั้น, [kʰlōːŋ dân]). The two differ in the number of syllables in the second *wak* of the final *bat* and inter-stanza rhyming rules.[1]

Khlong si suphap

The *khlong si suphap* (โคลงสี่สุภาพ, [kʰlōːŋ sìː sù.pʰâːp]) is the most common form still currently employed. It has four *bat* per stanza (*si* translates as *four*). The first *wak* of each *bat* has five syllables. The second *wak* has two or four syllables in the first and third *bat*, two syllables in the second, and four syllables in the fourth. *Mai ek* is required for seven syllables and *Mai tho* is required for four, as shown below. "Dead word" syllables are allowed in place of syllables which require *mai ek*, and changing the spelling of words to satisfy the criteria is usually acceptable.

The following plan shows the rhyming structure of one stanza. Each letter represents a syllable; A and B (also C, D, E and F in other examples) represent rhyming syllables. Syllables shown by letters in parentheses are optional.

The following plan shows the tone mark requirements; each ก represents one syllable.

Example

> — Unknown, *Lilit Phra Lo* (ลิลิตพระลอ), c 15th–16th centuries

Transcriptions:

Translation:

> What tales, what rumours, you ask?
> Of whom is this praise being spread throughout the world?
> Have you two been asleep, having forgotten to wake up?
> You both can think of it yourselves; do not ask me.

27.1.2 Chan

The *chan* (ฉันท์, [tɕʰǎn] from Pali *chando*), is derived from Pali and Sanskrit metres, and based on the *Vuttodaya*, a Sri Lankan treatise on Pali prosody. It developed during the Ayutthaya period, and became a prominent poetic form, but declined afterwards until it resurfaced in a 1913 revival.[2]

The main feature of the *chan* is its requirements on the "heaviness" of each syllable. Syllables are classified as either "light" (*lahu*, ลหุ, [lahù]), those with a short vowel and open ending, or "heavy" (*kharu*, ครุ, [kʰarú]; See also Light and heavy syllables under Sanskrit prosody). The Thai metres follow their Pali/Sanskrit origins, with added rhyming schemes. Modern authors have also invented new forms for their compositions. Two traditional forms are shown here.[2]

Inthrawichian chan

The *inthrawichian chan* (อินทรวิเชียรฉันท์, [īn.tʰrá.wí.tɕʰīːan tɕʰǎn], from *Indravajra*, a form of Sanskrit poetry and meaning *Indra's thunderbolt*) has two *bat* per stanza, with eleven syllables in each *bat*, following the pattern HHLHH LLHLHH (H represents heavy and L represents light syllables):

The rhyming scheme (which is identical to that of *kap yani*, see below) is shown here in two stanzas:

Example

> — Chit Burathat (1892–1942), *Na Hat Sai Chai Thale Haeng Nueng* (ณ หาดทรายชายทะเลแห่งหนึ่ง, "At a Seaside Beach")

Transcription:

Translation:

> The evening settles as the sun crosses the sky.
> As it sets in the west, its light fades.
> Its last rays flicker, and the sky turns from red
> Into a clear glowing indigo, so bright and pure.

Wasantadilok chan

The *wasantadilok chan* วสันตดิลกฉันท์, [wá.săn.tà.dì.lòk tcʰăn], from Sanskrit *vasantatilaka*) has fourteen syllables per *bat*, with the pattern HHLHLLLH LLHLHH:

The following plan shows the rhyme structure in two stanzas.

Example

    — Phraya Sisunthonwohan (Phan Salak), *Inlarat Kham Chan* (อิลราชคำฉันท์), c 1913

Transcription:

Translation:

> The chofa stretches out as if it would fight the very sky.
> The roof crest-plates are such a grand beauty to look at; the spire of the stupa soars up high.

27.1.3 Kap

There are several forms of *kap* (กาพย์, [kàːp]), each with its specific metre and rhyming rules. The *kap* may have originated either from the Indic metres or from Cambodian forms.[3]

Kap yani

The *kap yani* (กาพย์ยานี, [kàːp jāː.nīː], or *yani sip et*, *sip et* meaning *eleven*, referring to the number of syllables per *bat*) has two *bat* per stanza. Each has two *wak*, with five and six syllables. It is slow in rhythm, and usually used to describe beauty and nature. The following plan shows the rhyming scheme in two stanzas; the spaces show the usual rhythmic breaks (not shown in writing).[3]

Example

    — Chaofa Thammathibet (1705–46), *Kap He Ruea* (กาพย์เห่เรือ พระนิพนธ์เจ้าฟ้าธรรมธิเบศร, *Kap* for the Royal Barge Procession)

Transcription:

Kap chabang

The *kap chabang* (กาพย์ฉบัง, [kàːp tcʰa.bāŋ], or *chabang sip hok*, *sip hok* meaning *sixteen*, the number of syllables per stanza) has three *wak* per stanza, with six syllables in the first and third, and four syllables in the second. It is often used for narratives, and often accompanies the *chan*. The following plan shows two stanzas.[3]

Example

— Phraya Sisunthonwohan (Noi Acharayangkun) (1822–91), Veneration of the Dhamma (บทนมัสการพระธรรมคุณ)

Transcription:

Translation:

> The Dhamma is the foundation of good, that which itself is good.
> Like a bright lantern,
> Of the great prophet-teacher, shining into each being's character,
> Bringing light to foolish hearts.

Kap surangkhanang

The *kap surangkhanang yi sip paet* (กาพย์สุรางคนางค์ 28, [kàːp sù.rāːŋ.kʰa.nāːŋ jîː sìp pèt], *yi sip paet* means *twenty-eight*) has seven *wak* per stanza, with four syllables in each *wak*. A less common form is *surangkhanang sam sip song* (thirty-two), with eight *wak* per stanza. Its rhythm is fast, and is used to describe anger and fighting. The following plan shows two stanzas of *surangkhanang 28*.[3]

27.1.4 Klon

In the generic sense, *klon* (กลอน, [klɔ̄ːn]) originally referred to any type of poetry. In the narrow sense it refers to a more recently developed form where a stanza has four *wak*, each with the same number of syllables. It is usually considered an original Thai form.[4] The *klon* metres are named by the number of syllables in a *wak*, e.g. *klon hok* (กลอนหก, [klɔ̄ːn hòk]) has six syllables per *wak* (*hok* means *six*). All metres have the same rhyming scheme, and there are also requirements on the tone of the final syllable of each *wak*. The *klon* is also divided into several types according to their manner of composition, with *klon suphap* (กลอนสุภาพ, [klɔ̄ːn sù.pʰâːp]) being the basic form.

The following plan shows the structure of *klon suphap* (two stanzas) in the most common eight-syllable variety, which was employed extensively by Sunthorn Phu, and is the most common form of the Rattanakosin period. The letters in parentheses represent alternative rhyming syllables. In practice, occasional *wak* with seven or nine syllables are also acceptable.

Example

— Sunthorn Phu, *Nirat Phukhao Thong* (นิราศภูเขาทอง, c 1828)

Transcription:

27.1.5 Rai

The *rai* (ร่าย, [râːj]) is probably the oldest Thai poetic form and was used in laws and chronicles. It is also the simplest. It consists of a continuing series of *wak* of unspecified number, usually with five syllables each, and with rhymes from the last syllable of a *wak* to the first, second or third of the next. Some variations don't specify the number of syllables per *wak* and are actually a form of rhymed prose. A composition consisting of *rai* alternating with (and ending with) *khlong* is known as *lilit* (ลิลิต, [lí.lít]), and suggests that the *khlong* developed from the *rai*. The following is the form of *rai* known as *rai boran* (ร่ายโบราณ, [râːj bōː.rāːn]).[5]

OOOA A(A)(A)OB B(B)(B)OC C(C)(C)OD D(D)(D)OE E(E)(E)OO ...

Example

> สรวมสวัสดิวิชัย เกริกกรุงไกรเกรียงยศ เกียรติปรากฏจรรขจาย สบายทั่วแหล่งหล้า ฝนฟ้าฉ่ำชุ่มชล ไพศรพณ์ผลพูนเพิ่ม
> เหิมใจราษฎร์บำเทิง...ประเทศสยามชื่นช้อย ทุกข์ขุกเข็ญใหญ่น้อย นาศไร้แรงเกษม โสตเทอญ
> — King Chulalongkorn, the *Nitra Chakrit* (ลิลิตนิทราชาคริต, 1879)

27.2 Reading

When read aloud, Thai poetry may be read conventionally, or in a melodic fashion known as *thamnong sano* (ทำนอง
เสนาะ, [tʰām.nɔ̄ːŋ sanɔ̄ʔ], lit. *pleasing melody*). *Thamnong sano* has many melodic styles, and there are also other specific
styles used for certain performances, such as sepha. *Thamnong sano* reading is often featured in student competitions,
along with other forms of language-related performances.

27.3 Notes

[1] In literary studies, *line* in western poetry is translated as *bat*. However, in some forms, the unit is more equivalent to *wak*. To
avoid confusion, this article will refer to *wak* and *bat* instead of *line*, which may refer to either.

27.4 References

[1] "โคลง Khloong". *Thai Language Audio Resource Center*. Thammasat University. Retrieved 6 March 2012. Reproduced form
Hudak, Thomas John (1990). *The indigenization of Pali meters in Thai poetry*. Monographs in International Studies, Southeast
Asia Series (87). Athens, Ohio: Ohio University Center for International Studies. ISBN 978-0-89680-159-2.

[2] "ฉันท์ Chan". *Thai Language Audio Resource Center*. Thammasat University. Retrieved 6 March 2012. Reproduced form
Hudak, Thomas John (1990). *The indigenization of Pali meters in Thai poetry*. Monographs in International Studies, Southeast
Asia Series (87). Athens, Ohio: Ohio University Center for International Studies. ISBN 978-0-89680-159-2.

[3] "กาพย์ Kaap". *Thai Language Audio Resource Center*. Thammasat University. Retrieved 6 March 2012. Reproduced form
Hudak, Thomas John (1990). *The indigenization of Pali meters in Thai poetry*. Monographs in International Studies, Southeast
Asia Series (87). Athens, Ohio: Ohio University Center for International Studies. ISBN 978-0-89680-159-2.

[4] "กลอน Klon". *Thai Language Audio Resource Center*. Thammasat University. Retrieved 6 March 2012. Reproduced form
Hudak, Thomas John (1990). *The indigenization of Pali meters in Thai poetry*. Monographs in International Studies, Southeast
Asia Series (87). Athens, Ohio: Ohio University Center for International Studies. ISBN 978-0-89680-159-2.

[5] "ร่าย Raay". *Thai Language Audio Resource Center*. Thammasat University. Retrieved 6 March 2012. Reproduced form Hudak,
Thomas John (1990). *The indigenization of Pali meters in Thai poetry*. Monographs in International Studies, Southeast Asia
Series (87). Athens, Ohio: Ohio University Center for International Studies. ISBN 978-0-89680-159-2.

Chapter 28

Urdu poetry

Urdu poetry (Urdu: اُردوشاعر *Urdū Shāʿirī*) is a rich tradition of poetry and has many different forms. Its basically an outcome of superimposition of Persian language poetry on Khari Boli with Sanskrit as its substratum. Many of the poetic forms and structures are of Arabic origin. Today, it is an important part of the cultures of South Asia. Meer, Dard, Ghalib, Anees, Dabeer, Iqbal, Zauq, Josh, Jigar, Faiz, Firaq, Shakeb Jalali, Ahmad Nadeem Qasmi, Shair, Mohsin, Faraz and Faizi are among the greatest poets of Urdu. The language of Urdu got its pinnacle under the British Raj when British perceived Persian language as the threat and replaced its official status with the Urdu and English languages. All famous writers of Urdu language including Ghalib and Iqbal were given British scholarships.[1] Following the Partition of India in 1947, it found major poets and scholars were divided along the nationalistic lines. However, Urdu poetry is cherished in both the nations. Both the Muslims and Hindus from across the border continue the tradition.

Its fundamentally a performative poetry and its recital, sometimes impromptu, is held in Mushairas (poetic expositions). Although its tarannum saaz (singing aspect) has undergone major changes in recent decades, its popularity among the masses remains unaltered. Mushairas are today held in metropolitan areas worldwide because of cultural influence of South Asian diaspora. Ghazal singing and Qawwali are also important expository forms of Urdu poetry. Bollywood movies have a major part in popularising Urdu poetry with younger generations.

28.1 Forms of Urdu poetry

The principal forms of Urdu poetry are:[2]

- **Ghazal**, is a set of two liner couplets, which strictly should end with the same rhyme and should be within one of the predefined meters of Ghazals.There has to be minimum of five couplets to form a Ghazal. Couplets may or may not have same thought. It is one of the most difficult forms of poetry as there are many strict parameters that one needs to abide by while writing Ghazal.

- **Hamd** is a poem in praise of Allah. The word "hamd" is derived from the Qur'an, its English translation is "Praise".

- **Marsiya** is an elegy typically composed about the death of Hasan, Husain, or their relatives. Each stanza has six lines, with the rhyme scheme aaaabb.[2] The famous marsia writers who inherited the tradition of Mir Anis among his successive generations are Mir Nawab Ali 'Munis', Dulaha Sahab 'Uruj', Syed Mohammed Mohsin (Jaunpuri), Mustafa Meerza urf Piyare Sahab 'Rasheed', Syed Muhammad Mirza Uns, Ali Nawab 'Qadeem', Syed Sajjad Hussain "Shadeed" Lucknavi, Allama, Dr.Syed Ali Imam Zaidi, "Gauher" Luckhnavi the great grandson of Mir Babber Ali Anis.

- **Masnavi** is a poem written in couplets in bacchic tetrameter with an iambus for last foot. The topic is often romance.[2] Mir Taqi Mir and Sauda wrote some of this kind. The Religious masnavi History of Islam (Tarikh-e-Islam Az Quran) written by Dr. Syed Ali Imam Zaidi Gauher Lucknavi.

- **Naat** is a poetry that specifically praises the Islamic prophet Muhammad.

- **Nazm** Urdu nazm is a major part of Urdu poetry. From Nazeer Akarabadi, Iqbal, Josh, Firaq, Akhtarul Iman to down the line Noon Meem Rashid, Faiz, Ali Sardar Jafri and Kaifi Azmi. They have covered common life, philosophical thinking, national issues and the precarious predecament of individual human being.As a distinct form of Nazm many Urdu poets influenced by English and other European poets took to writing sonnets in Urdu language.[3] Azmatullah Khan (1887-1923) is believed to have introduced this format to Urdu Literature.[4] The other renowned Urdu poets who wrote sonnets were Akhtar Junagarhi, Akhtar Sheerani, Noon Meem Rashid, Zia Fatehabadi, Salaam Machhalishahari and Wazir Agha.

- **Qasida**, usually an ode to a benefactor, a satire, or an account of an event. It uses the same rhyme system as the ghazal, but is usually longer.[2]

- **Qawwali**, is a form of Urdu poetry read along with devotional music, A Qawwali is almost always dedicated to particular Sufi.

- **Shayari**, a musical form of Urdu poetry, allows a person to express deep feelings through words. It lets one explain sentiments in all their forms through rhythmic words. In the Urdu and Hindi languages, Shayari, also known as poetry, consists of couplets, or Sher.[5] Like: Kabhi Kisi Ko Mukkamal Jahan Nahi Milta, Kahi Jameen To Kahi Aasmaan Nahi Milta.[6]

- **Ruba'i**, is a poetry style, the Arabic term for "quatrain". The plural form of the word, *rubā'iyāt*, often anglicised *rubaiyat*, is used to describe a collection of such quatrains.

- **Tazkira** is a biographical anthology of poetry.[2]

28.2 Collection forms of Urdu poetry

The principal collection forms of Urdu poetry are:[2]

- **Diwan**, a collection of gazals.[2]
- **Kulliyat**, a complete collection of poems by one author.[2]

28.3 Formation

Urdu poetry forms itself with following basic ingredients:

- Bait (بیت)
- Bait-ul-Ghazal (بیت الغزل)
- Beher (بحر)
- Diwan (دیوان)
- Husn-E-Matla (حسن مطلع)
- Kalam (کلام)
- Kulyat (کلیات)
- Maqta (مقطع)
- Matla (مطلع)

- Mavra (ماوراء)

- Misra (مصرع)

- Mushaira (مشاعره)

- Qaafiyaa (قافىیہ)

- Radif (ردیف)

- Sher (شعر)

- Shayar (شاعر)

- Shayari (شاعری)

- Tah-Tul-Lafz (تحت اللفظ)

- Takhallus (تخلص)

- Tarannum (ترنم)

- Triveni (تریوینی)

28.4 Genres

The major genres of poetry found in Urdu are:

- *Doha* (دوہا)

- *Fard* (فرد)

- *Geet* (گیت)

- *Ghazal* (غزل), as practiced by many poets in the Arab tradition. Mir, Ghalib, Dagh are well-known composers of *ghazal*.

- *Hamd* (حمد)

- *Hazal* (ہزل)

- *Hijv* (وجہ)

- *Kafi* (کافی)

- *Madah* (مدح)

- *Manqabat* (منقبت)

- *Marsia* (مرثیہ)

- *Masnavi* (مثنوی)

- *Munajat* (مناجات)

- *Musaddas* (مسدس)

- *Mukhammas* (مخمس)

- *Naat* (نعت)

- *Nazm* (نظم)

- *Noha* (نوحہ)

- *Qasida* (قصیدہ)

- *Qat'ā* (قطعہ)

- *Qawwali* (قوالی)

- *Rubai* (رباعی) (a.k.a. Rubayyat or Rubaiyat) (رباعیات)

- *Salam* (سلام)

- *Sehra* (ارہس)

- *Shehr a'ashob* (شہر آشوب)

- *Soz* (سوز)

- *Wasokht* (وسوخت)

Novel Foreign forms such as the sonnet, **azad nazm** or (Free verse) and haiku have also been used by some modern Urdu poets.

28.5 Pen names (*Takhallus*)

In the Urdu poetic tradition, most poets use a pen name called the Takhallus (تخلص) . This can be either a part of a poet's given name or something else adopted as an identity. The traditional convention in identifying Urdu poets is to mention the takhallus at the end of the name. The word *takhallus*[7] is derived from Arabic, meaning "ending". This is because in the ghazal form, the poet would usually incorporate his or her pen name into the final couplet (maqta) of each poem.

28.6 Scripts used in poetry

In Pakistan and Deccan region of India, Urdu poetry is written in the standard Nasta'liq calligraphy style of the Perso-Arabic script. However, in north India, where Urdu poetry is very popular, the Perso-Arabic is often found transliterated into the Devanāgarī script, as an aid for those Hindī-speakers, who can comprehend Urdu, but cannot read the Perso-Arabic script. With the dawn of the internet and globalisation, this poetry is often found written in Roman Urdu as well as in Hindi script. In India mostly it is known as Shayari.

28.6.1 Example of Urdu Ghazal

The following is a verse from an Urdu ghazal by Arif Farhad:

Roman Urdu:

> *Tum na aana waqt k darya main beh kar is taraf.*
> *Main to machli ki tarah uljha huwa hun jaal main*

English translation:

> Don't come towards this side in the river of time!
> I am captured in the net like a fish.

28.6.2   Example of some cool Hindi Shayari

The following are some verse of Hindi Shayari from unknown poet :

Hindi Love Shayari

" ▨▨▨▨▨▨ ▨▨ ▨▨ ▨▨▨▨▨,
▨▨ ▨▨▨▨ ▨▨ ▨▨ ▨▨▨▨,
▨▨▨ ▨▨▨ ▨▨ ▨▨ ▨▨▨,
▨▨ ▨▨ ▨▨▨▨ ▨▨ ▨▨ ▨▨ ▨▨▨▨. "

"▨▨▨ ▨▨ ▨▨▨▨▨ ▨▨ ▨▨ ▨▨▨ ▨▨▨ ▨▨▨
▨▨ ▨▨ ▨▨ ▨▨▨ ▨▨ ▨▨▨ ▨▨ ▨▨▨ ▨▨▨
▨▨▨▨ ▨▨▨ ▨▨▨▨ ▨▨▨▨▨ ▨▨▨▨
▨▨ ▨▨ ▨▨▨▨▨▨▨▨ ▨▨ ▨▨▨!"

" ▨▨▨▨▨ ▨▨▨▨▨▨ ▨▨▨▨▨ ▨▨▨ ▨▨▨▨,
▨▨▨ ▨▨▨▨▨ ▨▨ ▨▨▨▨▨▨ ▨▨▨▨,
▨▨▨▨▨▨ ▨▨ ▨▨▨ ▨▨▨▨ ▨▨ ▨▨▨▨▨,
▨▨▨▨▨▨ ▨▨▨▨▨ ▨▨▨▨▨▨▨ ▨▨▨▨!"

"▨▨▨▨▨▨▨▨▨ ▨▨▨▨▨ ▨▨▨ ▨▨▨▨,
▨▨▨▨▨ ▨▨▨▨ ▨▨ ▨▨▨ ▨▨▨ ▨▨▨▨,
▨▨ ▨▨▨ ▨ ▨▨ ▨▨▨ ▨▨▨ ▨▨▨ ▨▨▨▨,
▨▨ ▨▨▨▨ ▨▨ ▨▨ ▨▨▨▨▨▨ ▨▨▨ ▨▨▨ ▨▨▨▨.."

"▨▨ ▨▨▨▨▨ ▨▨▨▨▨▨ ▨▨ ▨▨▨▨▨ ▨▨▨▨ ▨▨▨▨
▨▨ ▨▨ ▨▨ ▨▨▨ ▨▨ ▨▨▨▨ ▨▨▨▨ ▨▨▨▨
▨▨▨▨ ▨▨ ▨▨▨ ▨▨▨▨ ▨▨▨▨▨ ▨▨▨,
▨▨ ▨▨ ▨▨▨ ▨▨▨▨▨ ▨▨ ▨▨▨ ▨▨▨ ▨▨▨▨

Source:

http://sms-hindi.in/forum_112331664.xhtml

28.7   See also

- Bait Bazi, a game using Urdu poetry

- Chaar bayt a folk art of singing.

- Maulvi Abdul Haq - father of Modern Urdu

- Rafiq Hussain was the first scholar in undivided India to obtain a Ph.D in Urdu Poetry of Allama Iqbal in 1943.

- List of Urdu poets

- Persian and Urdu

- Progressive Writers' Movement

- Rekhta

- Shayari

- Urdu Informatics

28.8   References

[1] *Language, religion and politics in North India.* Lincoln, NE: IUniverse. 2005. ISBN 978-0-595-34394-2.

[2] Bailey, Thomas Grahame (1932 & 2008). *A History of urdu literature* (PDF). Association press (Y.M.C.A.). ISBN 978-0-19-547518-0. Retrieved 15 July 2012. Check date values in: |date= (help)

[3] Encyclopedic dictionary of Urdu literature p.565 http://books.google.co.in/books?isbn=8182201918

[4] The Encyclopaedia of Indian Literature (Volume Five) p.4146 http://books.google.co.in/books?isbn=8126012218

[5] Hindi Shayari

[6] Shayari Network

[7] A Brief History of Persian Literature, by the Iran Chamber Society.

Template:Poetry/Shayari of different cultures and languages

Sad Poetry in urdu

Template:Hindi Shayari

Love Shayari in Hindi

Sad Shayari in Hindi

Chapter 29

Vietnamese poetry

Vietnamese poetry originated in the form of folk poetry and proverbs. Vietnamese poetic structures include *six-eight*, *double-seven six-eight*, and various styles shared with Classical Chinese poetry forms, such as are found in Tang poetry; examples include verse forms with "seven syllables each line for eight lines," "seven syllables each line for four lines" (a type of quatrain), and "five syllables each line for eight lines." More recently there have been *new poetry* and *free poetry*.

With the exception of free poetry, a form with no distinct structure, other forms all have a certain structure. The tightest and most rigid structure was that of the Tang Dynasty poetry, in which structures of content, number of syllables per line, lines per poem, rhythm rule determined the form of the poem. This stringent structure restricted Tang poetry to the middle and upper classes and academia.

29.1 History

29.1.1 Beginnings

The first indication of Vietnamese literary activity dates back around 500 BCE during the Dong Son Bronze-age civilization . Poetic scenes of sun worship and musical festivity appeared on the famous eponymous drums of the period. Since music and poetry are often inextricable in the Vietnamese tradition, one could safely assume the Dong Son drums to be the earliest extant mark of poetry.[1]

In 987 CE, Do Phap Than co-authored with Li Chueh, a Chinese ambassador in Vietnam by matching the latter's spontaneous oration in a four-verse poem called "Two Wild Geese".[2] Poetry of the period proudly exhibited its Chinese legacy and achieved many benchmarks of classical Chinese literature. For this, China bestowed the title of *Van Hien Chi Bang* ("the Cultured State") on Vietnam.[3]

All the earliest literature from Vietnam is necessarily written in Chinese (though read in the Sino-Vietnamese dialect[4]). No writing system for vernacular Vietnamese existed until the thirteenth century, when *chữ nôm* ("Southern writing", often referred to simply as *nôm*) — Vietnamese written using Chinese script — was formalized.[5] While Chinese remained the official language for centuries, poets could now choose to write in the language of their choice.

Folk poetry presumably flourished alongside classical poetry, and reflected the common man's life with its levity, humor and irony. Since popular poetry was mostly anonymously composed, it was more difficult to date and trace the thematic development of the genre.[6]

High-culture poetry in each period mirrored various sensibilities of the age. The poems of Lý dynasty (1010-1125) distinctively and predominantly feature Buddhist themes.[7] Poetry then became progressively less religiously oriented in the following dynasty, the Trần dynasty (1125-1400), as Confucian scholars replaced Buddhist priest as the Emperors' political advisers.[8] Three successive victorious defense against the Kublai Khan's Mongolian armies further emboldened Vietnamese literary endeavors, infusing poetry with celebratory patriotism.

巉 献 融 堁 趴 嗟
孖 才 孖 命 窖 羅 怙 饒
疧 戈 沒 局 㵢 椾
仍 調 頭 㪍 罵 刄 疽 悉
遌 之 彼 嗇 私 豐
㤼 青 慣 退 騙 紅 打 慳

The first 6 lines of The Tale of Kieu *by Nguyễn Du, exemplifying the* chữ nôm *script, in use from around the thirteenth through early twentieth centuries.*

29.1.2   Later Lê dynasty (1427-1788)

Literature in *chữ nôm* flourished in the fifteenth century during the Later Lê dynasty. Under the reign of Emperor Lê Thánh Tông (1460-1497), *chữ nôm* enjoyed official endorsement and became the primary language of poetry.[9] By this century, the creation of chu Nom symbolized the happy marriage between Chinese and vernacular elements and contributed to the blurring of the literary distinction between "high" and "low" cultures.[10]

Due to the civil strife between Trinh and Nguyen overlordship and other reasons, poetic innovation continued, though at a slower pace from the late fifteenth century to the eighteenth century. The earliest *chữ nôm* in *phu*, or rhymed verse,[11] appeared in the sixteenth century. Also in the same period, the famous "seven-seven-six-eight" verse form was also invented. Verse novels (truyen) also became a major genre. It was around the fifteenth century that people started linking the traditional "six-eight" iambic couplet verses of folk poetry together, playing on the internal rhyming between the sixth syllable of the eight line and the last syllable of the six line, so that end rhyme mutates every two lines.[12] Orally narrated verse novels using this verse pattern received immense popular support in a largely illiterate society.

In 1651 Father Alexandre de Rhodes, a Portuguese missionary, created a system to romanize Vietnamese phonetically, formalized as *quốc ngữ* ("the National Language") which, however, did not gain wide currency until the twentieth century.

29.1.3 Tây Sơn and Independent Nguyễn dynasty (1788-1862)

Itinerant performers recite these truyen, the most famous of which is the *Tale of Kieu* by Nguyễn Du, often said to be the national poem of Vietnam.[13] A contemporary of Nguyễn Du was Hồ Xuân Hương, a female author of masterful and boldly venereal verses.[14]

29.1.4 French colonial period (1862-1945)

Starting from the 1930s, *quốc ngữ* poems abounded, often referred to as *thơ mới* ("New Poetry"), which borrowed from Western traditions in both its free verse form as well as modern existential themes.[15]

Tản Đà (Nguyễn Khắc Hiếu), a transitional figure

Xuân Diệu

Hàn Mặc Tử (Nguyễn Trọng Trí)
Some prominent "New Poets"

29.1.5   Contemporary (1945-present)

The Second World War curbed some of this literary flourishing, though Vietnamese poetry would undergo a new period of development during the French resistance and the Vietnam War.[16]

29.2   Prosody

As in most metrical systems, Vietnamese meter is structured both by the *count* and the *character* of syllables. Whereas in English verse syllables are categorized by relative *stress*, and in classical Greek and Latin verse they are categorized by *length*, in Vietnamese verse (as in Chinese) syllables are categorized by *tone*. For metrical purposes, the 6 distinct phonemic tones that occur in Vietnamese are all considered as either "flat" or "sharp". Thus a line of metrical verse consists of a specific number of syllables, some of which must be flat, some of which must be sharp, and some of which may be either.

Like verse in Chinese and most European languages, traditional Vietnamese verse is rhymed. The combination of meter and rhyme scheme defines the verse form in which a poem is written.

Traditionally in Vietnamese 1 word = 1 character = 1 syllable. Thus discussions of poetry may refer, for example, to a seven-*word* line of verse, or to the tone of a *word*. In this discussion, *syllable* is taken to be the least-ambiguous term for the foundational prosodic unit.

29.2.1   Vowels and tones

Further information: Vietnamese phonology § Vowels and Vietnamese phonology § Tone

Vowels can be simple (*à, ca, cha, đá, lá, ta*) or compound (*biên, chiêm, chuyên, xuyên*), and one of six *tones* is applied to every vowel.

In order to correspond more closely with Chinese rules of versification, older analyses sometimes consider Vietnamese to have *eight* tones rather than six. However, the additional two tones are not phonemic in Vietnamese and in any case roll up to the same Sharp tone class as they do in a six-tone analysis.

29.2.2 Rhyme

Use of rhyme in Vietnamese poetry is largely analogous to its use in English and other European languages; two important differences are the salience of *tone class* in the acceptability of rhymed syllables, and the prominence of structural *back rhyme* (rhyming a syllable at the end of one line with a syllable in the middle of the next). Rhyme connects lines in a poem together, almost always occurring on the final syllable of a line, and sometimes including syllables within the line.

In principle, Vietnamese rhymes exhibit the same features as English rhymes: Given that every syllable consists of **CVC** — an optional initial consonant or consonant cluster + a vowel (simple or compound) + an optional final consonant or consonant cluster — a "true" rhyme comprises syllables with *different* initial **C** and *identical* **VC**. However additional features are salient in Vietnamese verse.

Rhyming syllables do *not* require identical tones, but must be of the same tone class: either all Flat (e.g. *dâu, màu, sầu*), or all Sharp (e.g. *đấy, cấy*). Flat rhymes tend to create a feeling of gentleness and smoothness, whereas Sharp rhymes create a feeling of roughness, motion, wakefulness.

Rhyme can be further classified as "rich" or "poor". *Rich rhyme* (not to be confused with Rime riche) has the same tone class, and the same vowel sound: Flat (*Phương, sương, cường, trường*) or Sharp (*Thánh, cảnh, lãnh, ánh*).

Lầu Tần chiều nhạt vẻ **thu**
Gối loan tuyết đóng, chăn **cù** giá đông[1]

> 1. ^ extracted from *Cung Oán Ngâm Khúc* - Nguyễn Gia Thiều (1741- 1798) - Poetry compilation *Tình bạn, tình yêu thơ* - Education Publisher 1987

Poor rhyme has the same tone class, but slightly different vowel sounds: Flat (*Minh, khanh, huỳnh, hoành*) or Sharp (*Mến, lẽn, quyện, hẽn*)

Người lên ngựa kẻ chia **bào**
Rừng phong thu đã nhuộm **màu** quan san[1]

> 1. ^ Nguyễn Du: *Truyện Kiều*, lines 1519-20.

Finally, poets may sometimes use a "slant rhyme":

Người về chiếc bóng năm **canh**
Kẻ đi muôn dặm một **mình** xa xôi[1]

> 1. ^ Nguyễn Du: *Truyện Kiều*, lines 1523-24.

29.3 Verse form

29.3.1 Regulated verse

The earliest extant poems by Vietnamese poets are in fact written in the Chinese language, in Chinese characters, and in Chinese verse forms[17] — specifically the regulated verse (*lüshi*) of the Tang dynasty. These strict forms were favored by the intelligentsia, and competence in composition was required for civil service examinations.[18] Regulated verse — later written in Vietnamese as well as Chinese — has continued to exert an influence on Vietnamese poetry throughout its history.

At the heart of this family of forms are four related verse types: two with five syllables per line, and two with seven syllables per line; eight lines constituting a complete poem in each. Not only are syllables and lines regulated, so are rhymes, Level and Deflected tones (corresponding closely to the Vietnamese Flat and Sharp), and a variety of "faults" which are to be avoided. While Chinese poets favored the 5-syllable forms, Vietnamese poets favored the 7-syllable forms,[19] so the first of these 7-syllable forms is represented here in its standard Tang form:[20]

> L = Level syllable; D = Deflected syllable; L**A** = Level syllable with "A" rhyme; / = pause.

The other 7-syllable form is identical, but with (for the most part) opposite assignments of Level and Deflected syllables. 5-syllable forms are similarly-structured, but with 2+3 syllable lines, rather than 2+2+3. All forms might optionally omit the rhyme at the end of the first line, necessitating tone alterations in the final three syllables. An additional stricture was that the two central couplets should be antithetical.[21]

Tang poetics allowed additional variations: The central 2 couplets could form a complete four-line poem (*jueju*), or their structure could be repeated to form a poem of indefinite length (*pailü*).[22]

While Vietnamese poets have embraced regulated verse, they have at times loosened restrictions, even taking frankly experimental approaches such as composing in six-syllable lines.[23] Though less prestigious (in part because it was not an element of official examinations), they have also written in the similar but freer Chinese "old style" (*gushi*).[24]

29.3.2 Lục bát

In contrast to the learned, official, and foreign nature of regulated verse, Vietnam also has a rich tradition of native, demotic, and vernacular verse. While lines with an odd number of syllables were favored by Chinese aesthetics, lines with an even number of syllables were favored in Vietnamese folk verse. *Lục bát* ("six-eight") has been embraced as the verse form *par excellence* of Vietnam. The name denotes the number of syllables in each of the two lines of the couplet. Like regulated verse, *lục bát* relies on syllable count, tone class, and rhyme for its structure; however, it is much less minutely regulated, and incorporates an interlocking rhyme scheme which links chains of couplets:

> • = any syllable; ♭ = Flat (*bằng*) syllable; ♯ = Sharp (*trắc*) syllable; ♭**A** = Flat syllable with "A" rhyme.
>
> ♭ *and* ♯ *are used only as handy mnemonic symbols; no connection with music should be inferred.*

The verse also tends toward an iambic rhythm (one unstressed syllable followed by one stressed syllable), so that the even syllables (those mandatorily Sharp or Flat) also tend to be stressed.[25] While Sharp tones provide variety within lines, Flat tones dominate, and only Flat tones are used in rhymes. Coupled with a predominantly steady iambic rhythm, the form may suggest a steady flow, which has recommended itself to narrative.[26] Poets occasionally vary the form; for example, the typically Flat 2nd syllable of a "six" line may be replaced with a Sharp for variety.

Lục bat poems may be of any length: they may consist of just one couplet — as for example a proverb, riddle, or epigram — or they may consist of any number of linked couplets ranging from a brief lyric to an epic poem.[27]

A formal paraphrase of the first six lines of *The Tale of Kiều* suggests the effect of syllable count, iambic tendency, and interlocking rhyme (English has no analogue for tone):

29.3.3 Song thất lục bát

Vietnam's second great native verse form intricately counterpoises several opposing poetic tendencies. *Song thất lục bát* ("double-seven six-eight") refers to an initial doublet — two lines of seven syllables each — linked by rhyme to a following lục bát couplet:

> • = any syllable; ♭ = Flat (*bằng*) syllable; ♯ = Sharp (*trắc*) syllable; ♯**A** = Sharp syllable with "A" rhyme.

In contrast to the *lục bát* couplet, the *song thất* doublet exactly balances the number of required Flat and Sharp syllables, but emphasises the Sharp with two rhymes. It bucks the tendency of even-syllabled lines in Vietnamese folk verse, calling to mind the scholarly poetic tradition of China. It necessitates the incorporation of anapestic rhythms (unstressed-unstressed-stressed) which are present but comparatively rare in the lục bát alone. Overall, the quatrain suggests tension, followed by resolution. It has been used in many genres, "[b]ut its great strength is the rendering of feelings and emotions in all their complexity, in long lyrics. Its glory rests chiefly on three works ... 'A song of sorrow inside the royal harem' ... by Nguyễn Gia Thiều, 'Calling all souls' ... by Nguyễn Du, and 'The song of a soldier's wife' ... [by] Phan Huy Ích".[28]

The *song thất* doublet is rarely used on its own — it is almost always paired with a *lục bát* couplet.[29] Whereas a series of linked *song thất lục bát* quatrains — or occasionally just a single quatrain — is the most usual form, other variations are possible. A sequence may begin with a *lục bát* couplet; in this case the sequence must still end with a *lục bát*. Alternatively, *song thất* doublets may be randomly interspersed within a long *lục bát* poem.[30] Poets occasionally vary the form; for example, for variety the final syllable of an "eight" line may rhyme with the 3rd — instead of the 5th — syllable of the initial "seven" line of the following quatrain.

29.3.4 Other verse forms

Stanzas defined only by end-rhyme include:

- **ABAB** (*alternate rhyme*, analogous to the Sicilian quatrain, or Common measure)

- **xAxA** (*intermittent rhyme*, analogous to many of the English and Scottish Ballads) Additional structure may be provided by the final syllables of odd lines ("x") being in the opposite tone class to the rhyming ones, creating a *tone class* scheme (though not a *rhyme scheme*) of **ABAB**.

- **ABBA** (*envelope rhyme*, analogous to the "In Memoriam" stanza) In this stanza, if the "A" rhyme is sharp, then the "B" rhyme is flat, and vice versa.

- **AAxA** (analogous to the Rubaiyat stanza)

- Couplets, in which flat couplets and sharp couplets alternate (for example Xuân Diệu's *Tương Tư Chiều*):

A poem in *serial rhyme* exhibits the same rhyme at the end of each line for an indefinite number of lines, then switches to another rhyme for an indefinite period. Within rhyming blocks, variety can be achieved by the use of both rich and poor rhyme.

Four syllable poetry

If second syllable is flat rhyme then the fourth syllable is sharp rhyme

Bão **đến** ầm ầm
Như **đoàn** tàu hỏa[1]

1. ^ Trích trong bài *Mặt bão* - Thơ Trần Đăng Khoa - Tác phẩm chọn lọc dành cho thiếu nhi - Nhà xuất bản Kim Đồng, 1999

The converse is true

Chim **ngoài** cửa **sổ**
Mổ **tiếng** võng **kêu**[1]

1. ^ Trích trong bài *Tiếng võng kêu* - Thơ Trần Đăng Khoa - Tác phẩm chọn lọc dành cho thiếu nhi - Nhà xuất bản Kim Đồng, 1999

However a lot of poems do not conform to the above rule:

Bão đi thong thả
Như **con** bò gầy

Five-syllable poetry

Similar to four-syllable poetry, it also has its own exceptions.

Hôm **nay** đi **chùa** Hương
Hoa **cỏ** mờ **hơi** sương
Cùng **thầy** me **em** dậy
Em **vấn** đầu **soi** gương[1]

1. ^ Trích trong bài *Chùa Hương* của Nguyễn Nhược Pháp (1914-1938) - Tập thơ *Mưa đèn cây* - nhà xuất bản phụ nữ - 1987

Six syllable poetry

Using the last syllable, với cách with rhyme rule like *vần tréo* or *vần ôm*:

Vần tréo

Quê hương là gì hở **mẹ**
Mà cô giáo dạy phải yêu
Quê hương là gì hở **mẹ**
Ai đi xa cũng nhớ nhiều

Đỗ Trung Quân - *Quê Hương*

Vần ôm

Xuân hồng có chàng tới **hỏi**:
-- Em thơ, chị đẹp em đâu?
-- Chị tôi tóc xõa ngang đầu
Đi bắt bướm vàng ngoài **nội**

Huyền Kiêu - *Tình sầu*

Seven syllable poetry

The influence of *Seven syllable, four line* in Tang poetry can still be seen in the rhyme rule of seven-syllable poetry. 2 kinds of line:

Flat Rhyme

Quanh **năm** buôn **bán** ở **mom sông**
Nuôi **đủ** năm **con** với **một chồng**
Lặn **lội** thân **cò** khi **quãng vắng**
Eo **sèo** mặt **nước** buổi **đò đông**[1]

1. ^ Trích bài *Thương vợ* - Trần Tế Xương (1871-1907) - Tuyển tập thơ *Tình bạn, tình yêu thơ* - Nhà xuất bản giáo dục 1987

Or more recently

Em ở thành Sơn chạy giặc về
Tôi từ chinh chiến cũng ra đi
Cách biệt bao ngày quê Bất Bạt
Chiều xanh không thấy bóng Ba Vì

Quang Dũng - *Đôi Mắt Người Sơn Tây*

Sharp Rhyme

Lẳng **lặng** mà **nghe** nó **chúc nhau:**
Chúc **nhau** trăm **tuổi** bạc **đầu râu**
Phen **này** ông **quyết** đi **buôn cối**
Thiên **hạ** bao **nhiêu** đứa **giã trầu**[1]

1. ^ Trích bài *Chúc Tết* - Trần Tế Xương (1871-1907)- Tuyển tập thơ *Tình bạn, tình yêu thơ* - Nhà xuất bản giáo dục 1987

Recently this form has been modified to be:

Ta về cúi mái đầu sương điểm
Nghe nặng từ tâm lượng đất trời
Cảm ơn hoa đã vì ta nở
Thế giới vui từ mỗi lẻ loi

Tô Thùy Yên - *Ta về*

Eight-syllable poetry

This form of poetry has no specified rule, or free rhyme. Usually if:

- The last line has sharp rhyme then word number three is sharp rhyme, syllable number five and six are flat rhyme

- The last line has flat rhyme then word number three is flat rhyme, word number five and six are sharp rhyme

But there are always exceptions.

29.3.5 Ca dao (folk poetry)

Ca dao[32] is a form of folk poetry that can be sung like other poems, and can be used to create folksongs. Cadao is actually a Sino-Vietnamese term. In *Folk Literature book', Dinh Gia Khanh noted:*   In Confucis, chapter Nguy Phong, Article Vien Huu says: "Tam chi uu huu, nga can tha dao"- or "My heart is sad, I sing and dao" Book Mao Truyen says ""Khúc hợp nhạc viết ca, đô ca viết dao"- or" The song with background music to accompany the lyrics is called "ca", singing a cappella, or without background music is called "dao" People used to call ca dao as phong dao because the ca dao reflects the customs of each locality and era. Ca dao can consist of four-syllable line, five-syllable line, six-eight or two seven six eight, can be sung wholecloth, without the need to insert fillers like when people ngam the typical poetry. For example, take the following six-eights

Đường vô xứ Nghệ quanh quanh
Non xanh nước biếc như tranh họa đồ

Or:

Tốt gỗ hơn tốt nước sơn
Xấu người đẹp nết còn hơn đẹp người

Vietnamese ca dao is romantic writing that serves as a standard for romance poetry. The love of the labourers are expressed in ca dao in many aspects: romantic love, family love, love for the village, love for the fields, love for the work, love for nature. Ca dao is also an expression of the intellectual struggle when we live in society, or when we meet with nature. Hence, ca dao reflects the emotional life, and material life of human, the awareness of working and manufacturing...in the social, economic and political milieu in a particular historical period. For example, talking about self-control of "four virtues, three conformity", women lament in songs:

Thân em như hạt mưa sa
Hạt vào đài các, hạt ra ruộng cày

Because their fate is more often than not decided by others and they have almost no sense of self-determination, the bitteness is distilled into poem lines that are at once humorous and painful:

Lấy chồng chẳng biết mặt chồng
Đêm nằm mơ tưởng, nghĩ ông láng giềng

Romantic love in the rural area is a kind of love intimately connected to rice fields, to the villages. The love lines serve to remind ourselves as well as our lovers:

Anh đi anh nhớ quê nhà
Nhớ canh rau muống, nhớ cà dầm tương
Nhớ ai dãi nắng dầm sương
Nhớ ai tát nước bên đường hôm nao!

The hard life, of "the buffalo followed by the plough"is also reflected in ca dao

Trâu ơi, tao bảo trâu này
Trâu ra ngoài ruộng, trâu cày với ta
Cày cấy vốn nghiệp nông gia,
Ta đây trâu đấy, ai mà quản công...

A distinctive characteristic of ca dao is the form which is close to rhyme rule, but still elegant, flexible, simple and light-hearted. They are as simple as colloquial, gentle, succinct, yet still classy and expressive of deep emotions. A sad scene:

Sóng sầm sịch lưng chừng ngoài bể bắc,
Hạt mưa tình rỉ rắc chốn hàng hiên...

Or the longing, missing:

Gió vàng hiu hắt đêm thanh
Đường xa dặm vắng, xin anh đừng về
Mảnh trăng đã trót lời thề
Làm chi để gánh nặng nề riêng ai!

A girl, in the system of tao hon, who had not learned how to tidy her hair, had to get married, the man is indifferent seeing the wife as a child. But when she reached her adulthood, things

Lấy chồng từ thủa mười lăm
Chồng chê tôi bé, chẳng nằm cùng tôi
Đến năm mười tám, đôi mươi
Tối nằm dưới đất, chồng lôi lên giường
Một rằng thương, hai rằng thương
Có bốn chân giường, gãy một, còn ba!...

Ca dao is also used as a form to imbue experiences that are easy to remember, for example cooking experiences:

Con gà cục tác: lá chanh
Con lợn ủn ỉn: mua hành cho tôi
Con chó khóc đứng khóc ngồi:
Bà ơi! đi chợ mua tôi đồng riềng.

Classical forms of ca dao

Phú form Phú means presenting, describing, for example about somebody or something to help people visualize the person or thing. For example:

Đường lên xứ Lạng bao xa
Cách một trái núi với ba quãng đồng
Ai ơi! đứng lại mà trông
Kìa núi Thành Lạc, kìa sông Tam Cờ.
Em chớ thấy anh lắm bạn mà ngờ
Bụng anh vẫn thẳng như tờ giấy phong...

Or to protest the sexual immorality and brutality of the reigning feudalism.

Em là con gái đồng trinh
Em đi bán rượu qua dinh ông nghè
Ông nghè sai lính ra ve..
"Trăm lạy ông nghè, tôi đã có con!".
- Có con thì mặc có con!
Thắt lưng cho giòn mà lấy chồng quan.

Tỉ form Tỉ is to compare. In this form, ca dao does not directly say what it means to say like in the phu, but use another image to compare, to create an indirect implication, or to send a covert message. For example:

Or

Or

Or

Hứng form Hứng (inspiration) originates from emotions, which can give rise to happy feelings or sad ones, to see externality inspires hung, making us want to express our feelings and situations.

Trên trời có đám mây vàng
Bên sông nước chảy, có nàng quay tơ
Nàng buồn nàng bỏ quay tơ,
Chàng buồn chàng bỏ thi thơ học hành...

Or:

Gió đánh đò dưa, gió đập đò dưa,
Sao cô mình lơ lửng mà chưa có chồng...

Six-eight   According to Vũ Ngọc Phan, Nguyễn Can Mộng:[33]

Rhymed verses in Vietnam is born of provers, then *phong dao* becoming melody, and *chuong* that can be sung. Six-eight literature, or two-seven all originate from here. The history of collecting and compiling proverbs, folk poetry and songs only started about 200 years ago. In mid-eighteenth century, Tran Danh An (hieu Lieu Am) compiled *Quốc phong giải trào* and *Nam phong nữ ngạn thi*. These compilers copied proverbs, folk poetry by vi:Nôm/Chinese transcribed Vietnamese words, then translated to Chinese words and noted, meaning to compare Vietnam folk poetry with Quoc Phong poems in Confucion odes of China.

At the end of the 19th century, beginning of 20th century, books about collected tuc ngu, ca dao written in Nom appear. Into 20th century, books collecting these heritages written in quoc ngu (Roman script) appear. Hence, it can be said that the six-eight form originated from proverbs and folk poetry. Rhyme is the bolded word. For example in *The Tale of Kieu*, when So Khanh tempted Kieu to elope with him out of lau xanh of Tu Ba:

> Đêm thu khắc lậu canh **tàn**[34]
>
> Gió cây trút lá, trăng **ngàn** ngậm **gương**
>
> Lối mòn cỏ nhợt mùi **sương** [35]
>
> Lòng quê[36] đi một bước **đường** một đau.

Six-eight is usually the first poetic inspiration, influencing many poets in their childhood. Through the lullaby of ca dao, or colloquial verses of adults. Like:

Cái ngủ mày ngủ cho ngoan
Để mẹ đi cấy đồng xa trưa về
Bắt được con cá rô trê
Thòng cổ mang về cho cái ngủ ăn

Due to the gentle musical quality of six-eight, this form of poetry is often used in poems as a refrain, a link or connection, from rough to smooth, gentle as if sighing or praising. For instance in the *Tiếng Hát Sông Hương* by Tố Hữu

Trên dòng Hương-giang
Em buông mái chèo
Trời trong veo
Nước trong veo
Em buông mái chèo
Trên dòng Hương-giang
Trăng lên trăng đứng trăng **tàn**
Đời em ôm chiếc thuyền **nan** xuôi dòng

Or Trần Đăng Khoa in epic[37] *Khúc hát người anh hùng*

Cô Bưởi lắng nghe tiếng gà rừng rực
Thấy sức triệu người hồi sinh trong lồng ngực
Và cô đi
Bên đám cháy

Chưa tàn
Lửa hát rằng:
Quê tôi - những cánh rừng **hoang**
Chính trong cơn bão đại **ngàn** - tôi **sinh**
Nuôi tôi trong bếp nhà **gianh**
Ủ là một chấm - thổi **thành** biển khơi...

29.3.6 Free poetry movement

The Vietnamese "free poetry" movement may have started from the poems translated from French by Nguyễn Văn Vĩnh, such as *La Cigale et la Fourmi* (from the fables of Jean La Fontaine) in Trung Bắc Tân văn (1928).

Ve sầu kêu ve ve
Suốt mùa hè
Đến kỳ gió bấc thổi
Nguồn cơn thật bối rối.

Poetry with no prosody, no rule, no limits on the number of words in the line, no line limits, appears to have been more adapted to a mass audience. .[38]

With the free poetry using the "dong gay" technique, presenting long lines and short, to create a visual rhythm, when read aloud, not according to line but to sentence, with the aim to hear properly the sound of each word. Visual rhythm is the most important thing, because through it, the reader can follow the analytic process to figure out the meaning of the poem. The word "free" can be understood as the escape from the restraint of poetry rules. The poets want to chase after his inspirations and emotions, using words to describe inner feelings instead of being constrained by words, by rules. They do not have to be constrained by criticism until they have to change the words, ideas until the poem becomes a monster child of their emotions. For example in Lưu Trọng Lư 's *Tiếng thu*

Năm vừa rồi
Chàng cùng tôi
Nơi vùng giác mộ
Trong gian nhà cỏ
Tôi quay tơ
Chàng ngâm thơ
Vườn sau oanh giục giã
Nhìn ra hoa đua nở
Dừng tay tôi kêu chàng...
Này, này! Bạn! Xuân sang
Chàng nhìn xuân mặt hớn hở
Tôi nhìn chàng, long vồn vã...
Rồi ngày lại ngày
Sắc màu: phai
Lá cành: rụng
Ba gian: trống
Xuân đi
Chàng cũng đi
Năm nay xuân còn trở lại
Người xưa không thấy tới
Xuân về.[1]

1. ^ Trích trong bài Phong trào thơ mới 1930-1945

which later becomes Hữu Thỉnh trong bài Thơ viết ở biển:

Anh xa em
Trăng cũng lẻ

Mặt trời cũng lẻ
Biển vẫn cậy mình dài rộng thế
Vắng cánh buồm một chút
đã cô đơn
Gió không phải là roi mà vách núi phải mòn
Em không phải là chiều mà nhuộm anh đến tím
Sông chẳng đi đến đâu
nếu không đưa em đến
Dù sóng đã làm anh
Nghiêng ngả
Vì em[1]

1. ^ Trích trong Tuyển tập thơ *Tình bạn, tình yêu thơ* - Nhà xuất bản giáo dục 1987

29.4 Poetical devices

The musical nature of Vietnamese poetry manifests in the use of onomatopoeic words like "ri rao" (rustling), "vi vut" (whistling), "am am" (banging), "lanh canh" (tinkling), etc. Word play abounds in Vietnamese poetry.

Imagery, or the use of words to create images, is another fundamental aspect of Vietnamese poetry. An example of imagery can be found in the national epic poem, *The Tale of Kieu* by Nguyễn Du (1765–1820):[39]

Cỏ non xanh tận chân trời
Cành lê trắng điểm một vài bông hoa

Due to the influence of the concept of visual arts in the times of the poet, Nguyễn Du usually employs "scenery description" style in his poems. Simple scenery, accentuated at certain points, gently sketched but irresistible. Another line by Bà Huyện Thanh Quan

Lom khom dưới núi tiều vài chú
Lác đác bên sông chợ mấy nhà

Or Nguyễn Khuyến:

Ao thu lạnh lẽo nước trong veo
Một chiếc thuyền câu bé tẻo teo
Sóng biếc theo làn hơi gợn tí
Lá vàng trước gió khẽ đưa vèo.

Or most recently Trần Đăng Khoa in *Nghe thầy đọc thơ*

Em nghe thầy đọc bao ngày
Tiếng thơ đỏ nắng, xanh cây quanh nhà
Mái chèo nghiêng mặt sông xa
Bâng khuâng nghe vọng tiếng bà năm xưa

These images are beautiful and tranquil, but they can also be non-static and lively. When objects are described in poetry, they are often personified. Using verbs for inanimate, insentient objects is akin to breathing life into the objects, making it lively in the mind of the reader. For instance, Tran Dang Khoa wrote in "*Mặt bão*":

Bão đến ầm ầm
Như đoàn tàu hỏa
Bão đi thong thả
Như con bò gầy

Or in *Góc Hà Nội*

Nắng tháng tư xỏa mặt
Che vội vàng nỗi nhớ đã ra hoa

...

Thành phố ngủ trong rầm rì tiếng gió
Nhà ai quên khép cửa
Giấc ngủ thôi miên cả bến tàu

Such lines contain metaphors and similes. Humorous metaphors are commonly seen in poetry written for children. Examples are these lines that Khoa wrote at 9 years old in *Buổi sáng nhà em*:

Ông trời nổi lửa đằng đông
Bà sân vấn chiếc khăn hồng đẹp thay

...

Chị tre chải tóc bên ao
Nàng mây áo trắng ghé vào soi gương
Bác nồi đồng hát bùng boong
Bà chổi loẹt quẹt lom khom trong nhà

However, these also appear in more mature poets' work. For example Nguyễn Mỹ in *Con đường ấy*:[40]

Nắng bay từng giọt - nắng ngân vang
Ở trong nắng có một ngàn cái chuông

Or Hàn Mặc Tử in *Một Nửa Trăng*

Hôm nay chỉ có nửa trăng thôi
Một nửa trăng ai cắn vỡ rồi

Particularly, the metaphors in Hồ Xuân Hương poetry causes the half-real, half-unreal state, as if teasing the reader as in "Chess"

Quân thiếp trắng, quân chàng đen,
Hai quân ấy chơi nhau đà đã lửa.
Thoạt mới vào chàng liền nhảy ngựa,
Thiếp vội vàng vén phứa tịnh lên.
Hai xe hà, chàng gác hai bên,
Thiếp thấy bí, thiếp liền ghểnh sĩ.

Or in *Ốc nhồi*

Bác mẹ sinh ra phận ốc nhồi,
Đêm ngày lăn lóc đám cỏ hôi.
Quân tử có thương thì bóc yếm,
Xin đừng ngó ngoáy lỗ trôn tôi.

The "tứ" (theme) of a poem is the central emotion or image the poem wants to communicate. "Phong cách" (style) is the choice of words, the method to express ideas. Structure of the poetry is the form and the ideas of the poems combined together.

29.4.1 Điệu (rhythm)

Điệu (rhythm)[41] is created by the sounds of selected words and cadence of the lines. Music in the poetry is constituted by 3 elements: rhyme, cadence and syllabic sound. "Six-eight" folk song is a form of poetry rich in musical quality.

- Cadence of lines: Cadence refers to the tempo, rhythm of the poem, based on how the lines are truncated into verses, each verse with a complete meaning. It is "long cadence" when people stop and dwell on the sound when they recite the line. Besides, in each verse, when reciting impromptu, we can also stop to dwell on shorter sounds at verses separated into components, which is called "short cadence"

Dương gian (-) hé rạng (-) hình hài (--)
Trời (-) se sẽ lạnh (-), đất ngai (--) ngái mùi(--)

- Cadence in poetry, created by the compartmentalization of the line and the words, similar to putting punctuations in sentence, so we pause when we read Nhịp (4/4) - (2/2/2/2)

Rhythm (4/4) - (2/2/2/2)

Em ngồi cành trúc (--) em tựa cành mai (--)
Đông đào (-) tây liễu (-) biết ai (-) bạn cùng (--)

Rhythm (2/2/2) - (2/2/2/2)

Trời mưa (-) ướt bụi (-) ướt bờ (-)
Ướt cây (-) ướt lá (--) ai ngờ (-) ướt em (--)

Rhythm (2/4) - (2/2/2/2)

Yêu mình (--) chẳng lấy được mình (--)
Tựa mai (-) mai ngã (--) tựa đình (-) đình xiêu (--)

Rhythm (2/4) - (4/4)

Đố ai (-) quét sạch lá rừng (--)
Để ta khuyên gió (--) gió đừng rung cây (--)

Rhythm (2/4) - (2/4/2)

Hỡi cô (-) tát nước bên đàng (--)
Sao cô (-) múc ánh trăng vàng (--) đổ đi (--)

Rhythm (4/2) - (2/4/2)

Trách người quân tử (-) bạc tình (--)
Chơi hoa (--) rồi lại bẻ cành (--) bán rao (--)

Rhythm (3/2/2) - (4/3/2)

Đạo vợ chồng (-) thăm thẳm (-) giếng sâu (--)
Ngày sau cũng gặp (--) mất đi dâu (-) mà phiền (--)

- Musical quality of words: according to linguistics, each simple word of Vietnamese is a syllable, which can be strong or weak, pure or muddled, depending on the position of the pronunciation in the mouth (including lips, air pipe and also the openness of the mouth) One word is pronounced at a position in the mouth is affected by 4 elements constituting it: vowel, first consonant, last consonant and tone. Hence words that have

    1. "up" vowel like : i, ê, e
    2. "resounding" consonant like: m, n, nh, ng
    3. "up sound" : level, sharp, asking tones

Then when the words get pronounced, the sound produced will be pure, high and up. On the other hand, words that have

    1. "down" vowel: u, ô, o,
    2. "dead-end" consonant: p, t, ch, c,

And "down" tone: hanging, tumbling and heavy tones then the word pronounced will be muddled and heavy

The purity of the words punctuate the line. Rhyming syllables are most essential to the musical quality of the poem.

Hôm qua (-) tát nước đầu đình (--)
Bỏ quên cái áo (-) Trên cành hoa sen (--)
Em được (--) thì cho anh xin (--)
Hay là (-) em để làm tin (-) trong nhà. (--)

Punctuating words and rhyming words in these lines generate a certain kind of echo and create a bright melody, all to the effect of portraying the bright innocence of the subject of the verse.

Nụ tầm xuân (-) nở ra xanh biếc. (--)
Em đã có chồng (--) anh tiếc (-) lắm thay. (--)

Sound "iếc" in the two words "biếc" và "tiếc" rhyming here has two "up" vowels (iê) together with up tone but rather truncated by the last consonant "c", are known as "clogged sound". These sounds, when read out loud, are associated with sobbing, hiccup, the music is thus slow, and plaintive, sorrowful. Hence, "iec" is particularly excellently rhymed, to express most precisely the heart-wrenching regret of the boy returning to his old place, meeting the old friends, having deep feelings for a very beautiful girl, but the girl was already married.

Yêu ai tha thiết, thiết tha
Áo em hai vạt trải ra chàng ngồi.

Sometimes to preserve the musical quality of the folklore poem, the sounds of the compound words can have reversal of positions. Like the above folklore, the two sounds "tha thiet" are reversed to become "thiet tha", because the 6-8 form of the poem only allows for flat rhyme. Poetry or folksongs often have "láy" words, whereby due to the repetition of the whole word or an element of it, "láy" word, when pronounced, two enunciations of the two words will coincide (complete "láy") or come close (incomplete "láy") creating a series of harmony, rendering the musical quality of poetry both multi-coloured and elegant.

29.5   Poetic riddles

29.5.1   Riddles

Like Ca Dao, folk poetry riddles, or Đố were anonymously composed in ancient times and passed down as a regional heritage. Lovers in courtship often used Đố as a challenge for each other or as a smart flirt to express their inner sentiments. [42] Peasants in the Red River and Mekong Deltas used Đố as entertainment to disrupt the humdrum routine of rice planting or after a day's toil. Đố satisfies the peasants' intellectual needs and allows them to poke fun at the pedantic court scholars, stumped by these equivocating verses. [43]

Mặt em phương tượng chữ diền,
Da em thì trắng, áo đen mặc ngoài.
Lòng em có đất, có trời,
Có câu nhân nghĩa, có lời hiếu trung.
Dù khi quân tử có dùng,
Thì em sẽ ngỏ tấm lòng cho xem. [1]

1. ^ Tục Ngữ - Phong Dao. Nguyễn Văn Ngọc. (Mặc Lâm. Yiễm Yiễm Thư Quán. Sàigòn 1967

My face resembles the character of "rice field"
My skin is white, but I wear a black shield
My heart (lit. bowel) harbors the earth, the sky
Words about conscience and loyalty
When you gentleman could use for me,
I will open my heart for you to see

The speaker refers to herself as "em," an affectionate, if not somewhat sexist, pronoun for a subordinate, often a female. Combined with the reference to the rice field, the verses suggest that the speaker is of a humble position, most likely a lowly peasant girl. Pale skin is a mark of beauty, hence the speaker is also implying that she is a pretty girl. She is speaking to a learned young man, a scholar, for whom she has feelings. The answer to the riddle is that the "I" is a book. In a few verses, the clever speaker coyly puts forth a metaphorical self-introduction and proposal: a peasant girl with both physical and inner beauty invites the gentleman-scholar's courtship.

29.5.2 Rhyming Math Puzzles

Yêu nhau cau sáu bổ ba,
Ghét nhau cau sáu bổ ra làm mười.
Mỗi người một miếng trăm người,
Có mười bảy quả hỏi người ghét yêu.[1]

  1. ^ Nguyễn Trọng Báu - (Giai thoại chữ và nghĩa)

If we love each other, we will divide the areca nut into three wedges
If we hate each other, we will divide the areca nut into ten wedges
One wedge per person, a hundred of us
With seventeen nuts, how many haters and lovers have we?

With just four rhyming verses, the riddle sets up two linear equations with two unknowns. The answers are 30 lovers and 70 haters. The numbers might seem irrelevant to the overall context of a flirty math puzzle, but one may see the proportions as a representation of the romantic dynamics of the couple, or the speaker himself or herself: 3 part love, 7 part despair.

29.6 See also

- Classical Chinese poetry forms

- Tang poetry

- Vè

- Tale of Kiều

- Chinh phụ ngâm

- Confucian scholar poets Trần Tế Xương, Nguyễn Khuyến, Bà Huyện Thanh Quan, Hồ Xuân Hương

29.7 Notes

[1] Nguyen 1975, p xv.

[2] Nguyen 1975, p 3.

[3] Nguyen 1975, pp xvi-xvii.

[4] Durand & Nguyen 1985, p 7.

[5] Nguyen 1975, p xviii.

[6] Nguyen 1975, p 39.

[7] Nguyen 1975, pp 4-5.

[8] Nguyen 1975, pp 10-11.

[9] Nguyen 1975, pp xviii-xix.

[10] Nguyen 1975, p 69.

[11] NB: "Rhymed verse" designates a specific form of verse, and should *not* be taken to mean that earlier Vietnamese verse was unrhymed. These earlier forms, like the Chinese forms they were based on, *were* rhymed.

[12] Nguyen 1975, p 88.

[13] Nguyen 1975, pp 112-13.

[14] Nguyen 1975, pp 117-18.

[15] Nguyen 1975, pp xx-xxi, 159.

[16] Nguyen 1975, p xxi.

[17] Echols 1974, p 892.

[18] Phu Van 2012, p 1519.

[19] Huỳnh 1996, p 7.

[20] Liu 1962, p 27.

[21] Liu 1962, p 26.

[22] Liu 1962, p 29.

[23] Huỳnh 1996, pp 6-7.

[24] Huỳnh 1996, p 3.

[25] Huỳnh 1996, p 9.

[26] Huỳnh 1996, p 11.

[27] Huỳnh 1996, pp 10-11.

[28] Huỳnh 1996, p 14.

[29] Huỳnh 1996, p 12.

[30] Huỳnh 1996, p 12.

[31] Xuân Diệu: *Tương tư chiều*, lines 1-9.

[32] Trích trong *Tục ngữ ca dao dân ca Việt Nam*, Vũ Ngọc Phan, nhà xuất bản Khoa học Xã hội Hà Nội - 1997

[33] Nguyễn Can Mộng, (hiệu: Nông Sơn; 1880 - 1954), , who wrote *Ngạn ngữ phong dao*

[34] *Khắc lậu*: ám chỉ cái khắc ở trên đồng hồ treo mặt nước chảy đi từng giọt mà sứt xuống; *canh tàn* là gần sáng.

[35] Cảnh đêm mùa thu - *Nhợt* là cỏ có sương bám vào, mùi nhời nhợt, chẳng hạn: *Lối mòn lướt mướt hơi sương*

[36] *Lòng quê*: Lòng riêng, nghĩ riêng trong bụng.

[37] *Trường ca là một tác phẩm dài bằng thơ có nội dung và ý nghĩa xã hội rộng lớn.* - *Đại từ điển tiếng Việt* - Nguyễn Như Ý chủ biên, NXB Văn hóa – Thông tin, Hà Nội 1998

[38] Trích trong Phê Bình Văn Học Thế Hệ 1932 - Chim Việt Cành Nam

[39] Nguyễn Du, *Kiều* Nhà xuất bản Thanh Niên, 1999

[40] Tập thơ *Mưa đèn cây* - nhà xuất bản phụ nữ - 1987

[41] Trích trong bài của Trần Ngọc Ninh

[42] http://chimviet.free.fr/40/nvtrn055_thotoan.htm

[43] http://ecadao.com/tieuluan/caudo/caudo.htm

29.8   References

- Durand, Maurice M.; Nguyen Tran Huan (1985) [1969], *An Introduction to Vietnamese Literature*, Translated by D. M. Hawke, New York: Columbia University Press, ISBN 0-231-05852-7

- Echols, John M. (1974), "Vietnamese Poetry", in Preminger, Alex; Warnke, Frank J.; Hardison, O. B., *The Princeton Encyclopedia of Poetry and Poetics* (Enlarged ed.), Princeton, NJ: Princeton University Press, pp. 892–893, ISBN 0-691-01317-9

- Huỳnh Sanh Thông (1996), "Introduction", *An Anthology of Vietnamese Poems: from the Eleventh through the Twentieth Centuries*, New Haven, CT: Yale University Press, pp. 1–25, ISBN 0-300-06410-1

- Liu, James J. Y. (1962), *The Art of Chinese Poetry*, Chicago: University of Chicago Press, ISBN 0-226-48687-7

- Nguyen, Dinh-Hoa (1993), "Vietnamese Poetry", in Preminger, Alex; Brogan, T.V.F., *The New Princeton Encyclopedia of Poetry and Poetics*, New York: MJF Books, pp. 1356–1357, ISBN 1-56731-152-0

- Nguyen Ngoc Bich (1975), *A Thousand Years of Vietnamese Poetry*, New York: Alfred A. Knopf, ISBN 0-394-49472-5

- Phu Van, Q. (2012), "Poetry of Vietnam", in Greene, Roland; Cushman, Stephen, *The Princeton Encyclopedia of Poetry and Poetics* (fourth ed.), Princeton, NJ: Princeton University Press, pp. 1519–1521, ISBN 978-0-691-13334-8

29.9   External links

- Chinh Phụ Ngâm Khúc - ny Đoàn Thị Điểm (1705–1748), originally by Đặng Trần Côn (1715?–1745)

- Poetry book vi:Góc sân và khoảng trời by vi:Trần Đăng Khoa - Information and Culture Publisher - 1998

- vi:Proverbs and folk poetry and songs of Vietnam by vi:Vũ Ngọc Phan - Hanoi Social Science Publisher- 1997

- New poetry movement 1930 - 1945

- GardenDigest.com, Extractions of commentary of poetry - by Michael P. Garofalo

- Evan.com, The 6th Poetry Day in Việt Nam, 2008 at Văn Miếu-Quốc Tử Giám

佳 人 遺 墨
GIAI-NHÂN DÍ-MẮC
Sự-tích và thơ-từ Xuân-Hương

Mà em vẫn giữ tấm lòng son.
XUÂN-HƯƠNG.

東 京 印 館
IMPRIMERIE TONKINOISE
14-16, Rue du Colon, 14-16
HANOI

Hồ Xuân Hương a witty and ribald poetess.

Chapter 30

Welsh poetry

Main articles: Welsh-language literature and Welsh literature in English

Welsh poetry may refer to poetry in the Welsh language, Anglo-Welsh poetry, or other poetry written in Wales or by Welsh poets.

30.1 History

Main article: Medieval Welsh literature

Wales has one of the earliest literary traditions in Northern Europe, stretching back to the days of Aneirin (fl. 550) and Taliesin (second half of the 6th century), and the haunting *Stafell Cynddylan*, which is the oldest recorded literary work by a woman in northern Europe.

In Welsh literature the period before 1100 is known as the period of *Y Cynfeirdd* ("The earliest poets") or *Yr Hengerdd* ("The old poetry"). It roughly dates from the birth of the Welsh language from Brythonic to the arrival of the Normans in Wales towards the end of the eleventh century.

From ca.1100 until ca.1600 Welsh poetry can be divided roughly into two distinct periods: the period of the Poets of the Princes (*Beirdd y Tywysogion*, also called *Y Gogynfeirdd*) who worked before the loss of Welsh independence in 1282 and the Poets of the Nobility (*Beirdd yr Uchelwyr*) who worked from 1282 until the period of the English incorporation of Wales in the 16th century.

The earliest poem in English by a Welsh poet dates from about 1470. More recently Anglo-Welsh poetry has become an important aspect of Welsh literary culture, as well as being influential on English literature.

Welsh poets often write under bardic names to conceal their identity in Eisteddfod competitions.

30.2 Forms

Since the later Middle Ages, the traditional Welsh poetic metres in strict verse consist of twenty four different metrical forms written in cynghanedd.

An awdl is a form of long poem, similar to the ode. The most popular metrical forms are the Cywydd, of 14th-century origin, and the several versions of the Englyn, a concise and allusive verse form similar to the Greek epigram and the Japanese haiku and as old as Welsh literature itself.

30.3   See also

- British literature

- List of Welsh language authors

- List of Welsh language poets

- Oxford Book of Welsh Verse in English

- Welsh literature

30.4   External links

- Welsh Poet

- Welsh Writers

- The Poetry of Wales, by John Jenkins, 1873, from Project Gutenberg

- The Welsh Poetry Competition, launched 2007

Chapter 31

Yakshagana poetry

Yakshagana poetry (Kannada:▯▯▯▯▯ ▯▯▯▯, pronounced as *yaksha-gaana prasanga*)(Yakshagana Padya or Yakshagana Prasanga) is a collection of Kannada poems used to enact a music dance drama called Yakshagana. The poems are composed in well known Kannada metres using the frame work of Yakshagana Raga and Yakshagana Tala. Yakshagana also has what is called a Yakshagana metre. The collection of Yakshagana poems forming a musical drama is called a Prasanga. Oldest surviving parasanga books are believed to have been composed in the 15th century.[1] Many compositions have been lost. There are evidences to show that oral compositions were in use before the 15th century.

There are more than 300 Yakshagana Prasanga books available today. Attempts are being made to preserve the texts by digitising them.

31.1 Some famous Prasangas

- **Gadhayuddha**
- **Krishna sandhana**
- **Basmasura Mohini**
- **Ratnavati Kalyana**
- **Bhishma Vijaya**
- **Chandrahasa Charitre**
- **Abhimanyu Kalaya**
- **Sudhanva Kalaga**
- **Sugreeva Vijayam** ((Andhra Yakshaganamu) Telugu - 1570) Kandukuru Rudra Kavi [2]

31.2 The Yakshagana poets

By far Muddana, Nagire Subba are the most well known Yakshagana poets. Muddana wrote the celebrated Ratnavati Kalyana.

> "...Nudiye ninnodeyana pesarodanudiye..."

> "...udu seneyadhipati baana tyajisuta nintanambinige..."

are his compositions.

- Purandaradasa (Anasooya Charitre)

- Nagire Subba

- Subba (son of venkata)

- Parthi Subba (a disputed author who lived in the 19th century)

- Kirikkadu Vishnu Master

- Halasinahalli Narasimha Shastri

- Devidasa

- Agari Srinivasa Bagavata

- Hattinangadi rama batta

- Kadandale

- Balipa Narayana Bagavata

- Kirikkadu Vishnu Bhat

- Bidirahalli Narasimha Murthy

- Vittappa Shanai

- Hosatota Manjunatha Bhagawatha

are few of the well known Yakshagana poets. There is a confusion regarding time and works of Parthi Subba who is believed to have written Ramayana in Yakshagana. While Muliya Timmapa and Govinda Pai have claimed that Parthi Subba (of Kumble) lived in the 19th century and wrote Ramayana prasangas, K. Shivaram Karanth vehemently rejects their opinion citing procedural lapse in their deduction. Karanth argued in his work 'Yakshagana Bayalata' that Parthi Subba, while was a Yakshagana poet or famous Bhagavatha in the 19th century, the Ramayana prasangas attributed to him are either written by an unknown poet or by a number of poets including Devidasa.

31.3   See also

- Kannada literature
- The Yakshagana Puppets Documentary Film

31.4   References

[1] Prof Sridhara Uppura, Diganta Sahitya publications, Managalore, 1998.

[2] Students' Britannica India By Dale Hoiberg, Indu Ramchandani, 2000 p80

31.5   External links

- A list of known compositions

Chapter 32

1270s in poetry

32.1   Major works

- The Codex Regius, the manuscript in which the Poetic Edda is preserved, is written.[1]

32.2   References

[1] Phillip Pulsiano; Kirsten Wolf (1993). *Medieval Scandinavia: An Encyclopedia*. Taylor & Francis. p. 100. ISBN 978-0-8240-4787-0.

Chapter 33

An Analytic History of Persian Modern Poetry

An Analytic History of Persian Modern Poetry (Persian: تاریخ تحلیلی شعر نو) is a research work on Persian contemporary poetry by Shams Langeroodi, first published in 1998.

33.1 Format

The book is in 4 volumes including the events in Iranian poetry from 1905 to 1979. It goes year by year starting with a brief description of political and social condition of the time following with a commentary on the literary criticism condition. A list of literary magazines and published poetry books is provided for each year. From each work, depending on its importance, it has a brief description, selected poems and includes different reviews.

Overall it includes seventy years of: bibliography of Persian modern poetry, Persian poetry publications (magazines, special issues, etc.) and a list of Persian poetry criticism.

Each volume covers the following years:

- *Volume. 1: 1905–1953*
- *Volume. 2: 1953–1962*
- *Volume. 3: 1962–1970*
- *Volume. 4: 1970–1979*

33.2 Importance

An Analytic History of Persian Modern Poetry was the first major research work on Persian modern poetry.

33.3 Notes

[1] Hafez Mousavi's interview with Shargh newspaper.

Chapter 34

The Call to Poetry

The Call to Poetry was a one-night performance art / international poetry gathering event held April 5, 2012 in Istanbul, near Taksim Square, widely promoted and heavily attended by international poets to celebrate the history of poetry with a dramatic reading of the world's oldest love poem, which is housed in the Istanbul Archaeology Museums.[1]

The Call to Poetry garnered significant interest in Istanbul, the greater Middle East and the US,[2] as did a portion of the evening dedicated to poetry of the Arab Spring.[3]

34.1 The World's Oldest Love Poem

Written on a 4,000-year-[4] old clay tablet known as İstanbul #2461, the Sumerian poem currently has its home at the İstanbul Archaeology Museum and was composed in the 21st century B.C. for the Sumerian king Shu-Sin, who ruled from 2037–2029 BC. The poem was intended for a spring fertility ritual and recited by one of his brides.[5]

34.2 Arab Spring Poetry

The Call to Poetry featured readings from contemporary Egyptian poet Hesham Al-Gak, a 2011 contestant on the Arab world's popular American Idol-style TV program based in Abu Dhabi called *Prince of Poets*. During the Egyptian revolution, Al-Gak used the competition to recite poems critical of Egyptian leaders and departed *Prince of Poets*'s Abu Dhabi studios to visit Cairo to compose and recite verse at the height of protests there.

34.3 Event Organizers

Call to Poetry organizer, American writer Dan Boylan cited Beat Generation figure Allen Ginsberg as an influence on the evening.[6] Having met Ginsberg as a teenager, Boylan premiered Istanbul-inspired sound poetry during the event, which included music and an over-capacity crowd that listened from outside the venue. American journalist David Trilling served as the first Call to Poetry's master of ceremonies and New Zealand Poet Fred Simpon released his book of verse, "Lucky Me!" during the event.

34.4 References

[1] "Istanbul to host celebration of world's oldest love poem". *Today's Zaman*. April 4, 2012.

[2] "Ancient Love Poem Sees Light of Day in Istanbul". *PRI's The World*. April 5, 2012.

[3] "Hesham Al-Gakh's Tahrir Square poetry honored in Istanbul". *The Daily News Egypt*. April 8, 2012.

[4] "Al Jakh is 'Prince of Poets' finalist". *The National (UAE)*. Feb 18, 2011.

[5] *Guinness World Records*.

[6] "Celebrating the World's Oldest Love Poem in Istanbul on April 5th, 2012". The Turkish Weekly Journal. Retrieved March 29, 2012.

Chapter 35

Classical reception studies

Classical reception studies refers to the scholarly enquiry regarding how the Classical world has been received in post-classical societies.

Influenced by reception theory within literature, it departs from the Classical tradition in various ways.

35.1 Definition

Lorna Hardwick and Christopher Stray asserted that Classical reception studies was devoted to examining "the ways in which Greek and Roman material has been transmitted, translated, excerpted, interpreted, rewritten, re-imaged and represented."[1] Charles Martindale thus noted that Classical reception "encompasses all work concerned with postclassical material".[2]

Hardwick and Stray asserted that scholars of reception studies held the relationship between the ancient and modern to be reciprocal, although acknowledged that others believed reception studies only shed light on the receiving society and not on the ancient text or context.[3]

35.2 References

35.2.1 Footnotes

[1] Hardwick & Stray 2008, p. 1.

[2] Martindale 2006, p. 1.

[3] Hardwick & Stray 2008, p. 4.

35.2.2 Sources

Hardwick, Lorna; Stray, Christopher (2008). "Introduction: Making Conceptions". *A Companion to Classical Receptions*. Lorna Hardwick and Christopher Stray (editors). Maldon and Oxford: Blackwell. pp. 1–9. ISBN 978-1405151672.

Martindale, Charles (2006). "Introduction: Thinking Through Reception". *Classics and the Uses of Reception*. Charles Martindale and Richard F. Thomas (editors). Maldon and Oxford: Blackwell. pp. 1–13.

Chapter 36

Classical tradition

Not to be confused with Classicism.

The Western **classical tradition** is the reception of classical Greco-Roman antiquity by later cultures, especially the

Vergil leading Dante on his journey in the Inferno, *an image that dramatizes the continuity of the classical tradition[1]* (Dante and Vergil in Hell *by Delacroix, 1823)*

post-classical West,[2] involving texts, imagery, objects, ideas, institutions, monuments, architecture, cultural artifacts, rituals, practices, and sayings.[3] Philosophy, political thought, and mythology are three major examples of how classical culture survives and continues to have influence.[4] The West is one of a number of world cultures regarded as having a classical tradition, including the Indian, Chinese, Judaic, and Islamic traditions.[5]

The study of the classical tradition differs from classical philology, which seeks to recover "the meanings that ancient texts had in their original contexts."[6] It examines both later efforts to uncover the realities of the Greco-Roman world and "creative misunderstandings" that reinterpret ancient values, ideas and aesthetic models for contemporary use.[7] The classicist and translator Charles Martindale has defined the reception of classical antiquity as "a two-way process ... in which the present and the past are in dialogue with each other."[8]

The beginning of a self-conscious classical tradition is usually located in the Renaissance, with the work of Petrarch in 14th-century Italy.[9] Although Petrarch believed that he was recovering an unobstructed view of a classical past that had been obscured for centuries, the classical tradition in fact had continued uninterrupted during the Middle Ages.[10] There was no single moment of rupture when the inhabitants of what was formerly the Roman Empire went to bed in antiquity and awoke in the medieval world; rather, the cultural transformation occurred over centuries. The use and meaning of the classical tradition may seem, however, to change dramatically with the emergence of humanism.[11]

Aeneas carrying his father and leading his son from fallen Troy, a popular image in the Renaissance for the retrieval of the past as a way to make possible the future; the figure of his wife, Creusa, who did not survive, represents that which was lost[12] (Federico Barocci, 1598)

The phrase "classical tradition" is itself a modern label, articulated most notably in the post-World War II era with *The Classical Tradition: Greek and Roman Influences on Western Literature* of Gilbert Highet (1949) and *The Classical Heritage and Its Beneficiaries* of R.R. Bolgar (1954). The English word "tradition," and with it the concept of "handing down" classical culture, derives from the Latin verb *trado, tradere, traditus*, in the sense of "hand over, hand down."[13]

Writers and artists influenced by the classical tradition may name their ancient models, or allude to their works. Often scholars infer classical influence through comparative methods that reveal patterns of thought. Sometimes authors' copies of Greek and Latin texts will contain handwritten annotations that offer direct evidence of how they read and understood their classical models; for instance, in the late 20th century the discovery of Montaigne's copy of Lucretius enabled scholars to document an influence that had long been recognized.[14]

36.1 See also

- Classics

- Classical republicanism

- Greek mythology in western art and literature

- Legacy of the Roman Empire

- List of films based on Greco-Roman mythology

- List of films based on Greek drama

- Matter of Rome

- Neoclassicism

- Quarrel of the Ancients and the Moderns

- Transmission of the Classics

36.2 References

[1] Anthony Grafton, Glenn W. Most, and Salvatore Settis, preface to *The Classical Tradition* (Harvard University Press, 2010), pp. viii–ix.

[2] Anthony Grafton, Glenn W. Most, and Salvatore Settis, preface to *The Classical Tradition* (Harvard University Press, 2010), pp. vii–viii.

[3] Grafton, Most, and Settis, preface to *The Classical Tradition*, p. viii.

[4] Grafton, Most, and Settis, entry on "mythology," in *The Classical Tradition*, p. 614 *et passim*.

[5] Grafton, Most, and Settis, preface to *The Classical Tradition*, p. x.

[6] Craig W. Kallendorf, introduction to *A Companion to the Classical Tradition* (Blackwell, 2007), p. 2.

[7] Grafton, Most, and Settis, preface to *The Classical Tradition*, p. vii; Kallendorf, introduction to *Companion*, p. 2.

[8] Charles Martindale, "Reception," in *A Companion to the Classical Tradition* (2007), p. 298.

[9] Kallendorf, introduction to *Companion*, p. 1.

[10] Kallendorf, introduction to *Companion*, p. 2.

[11] Kallendorf, introduction to *Companion*, pp. 1–2.

[12] Peter Gillgren, *Siting Federico Barocci and the Renaissance Aesthetic* (Ashgate, 2011), pp. 165–167.

[13] Kallendorf, introduction to *Companion*, p. 1.

[14] Kallendorf, introduction to *Companion*, p. 2.

36.3 Further reading

- Barkan, Leonard. *Unearthing the Past: Archaeology and Aesthetics in the Making of Renaissance Culture.* Yale University Press, 1999).

- Cook, William W., and Tatum, James. *African American Writers and Classical Tradition.* University of Chicago Press, 2010.

- Walker, Lewis. *Shakespeare and the Classical Tradition: An Annotated Bibliography 1961–1991.* Routledge, 2002.

Horatio Greenough's George Washington *(1840), modeled after a statue of Zeus*

Chapter 37

Dial-A-Poem

Dial-A-Poem is a phone-based service started in 1968 by poet John Giorno after a phone conversation with his friend William Burroughs. Fifteen phone lines were connected to individual answering machines; anyone could phone Giorno Poetry Systems and listen for free to a poem offered from various live recordings.

The venture was a success from 1969 on, and the poems dealt with numerous social issues such as the Vietnam War and the sexual revolution. Giorno claimed the service later influenced the creation of other information services over the telephone, such as banking, sports, and investing. It spawned a number of imitators. Eventually, all of them were eclipsed by the internet, most particularly by YouTube.

Chapter 38

Disjecta membra

Disjecta membra, also written *disiecta membra*, is Latin for "scattered fragments" (also scattered limbs, members, or remains) and is used to refer to surviving fragments of ancient poetry, manuscripts and other literary or cultural objects, including even fragments of ancient pottery. It is derived from *disiecti membra poetae*, a phrase used by Horace, a Roman poet.[1]

38.1 Ancient and medieval poetry, literature and manuscripts

Fragments of ancient writing, especially ancient Latin poetry found in other works are commonly referred to as *disjecta membra*.[2] The term *disiecta membra* or *disjecta membra* is paraphrased from the Roman lyric poet Horace (65 BC - 8 BC), who wrote of *disiecti membra poetae* in his *Satires*, 1.4.62, referring to the "limbs of a dismembered poet".[3] In full, the term originally appeared as *Invenias etiam disiecti membra poetae*, in reference to the earlier Roman poet Ennius.[4]

Although Horace's intended meaning remains the subject of speculation and debate, the passage is often taken to infer that if a line from poetry was torn apart and rearranged, the dismembered parts of the poet would still be recognisable. In this sense, in the study of literature, *disjecta membra* is often used to describe the piecing together of ancient fragments of an identifiable literary source. Similarly, isolated leaves or parts of leaves from ancient or medieval manuscripts may also be termed *disjecta membra*. Scholars have been able to identify fragments now held in different libraries that originally belonged to the same manuscript.

38.2 Pottery

Scholars have long referred to sherds of ancient Greek pottery as *disjecta membra*. They have studied fragments of ancient Greek pottery in institutional collections, and have attributed many such pieces to the artists who made them. In a number of instances they have been able to identify fragments now in different collections that belong to the same vase.[5]

38.3 References

[1] Oxford English Dictionary.

[2] Dictionary.com

[3] Online Etymology Dictionary. See also List of Latin Phrases (D)

[4] Horace, *Sermonum Liber Primus* (Satires), 1.4.62.

Disjecta membra *(a fragment of ancient Greek pottery).*

[5]   Aaron J. Paul, "Fragments of Antiquity: Drawing Upon Greek Vases", *Harvard University Art Museums Bulletin*, Vol. V, No. 2 (Spring 1997), pp. 4, 10.

Chapter 39

Spoken word

This article is about the performance art. For recordings of books or dialog, see Audiobook. For the 2009 film, see Spoken Word (film).

Spoken word involves performance-based poetry that focuses on the aesthetics of word play and story-telling, that originated from the poetry of African Americans in Harlem. It often includes collaboration and experimentation with other art forms such as music, theater, and dance. There is no mandatory manner in which to perform spoken word, however, certain aspects of the artistry indicate that it is, indeed, spoken word. Spoken word usually tends to focus on the performance of the words themselves, the dynamics of tone, gestures, facial expressions, and more. Performers can weave in poetic components - such as rhyme, repetition, slang, improvisation, and many more elements of poetry - to create an atmosphere for the audience to experience.

In entertainment, spoken-word performances generally consist of storytelling or poetry, as exemplified by artists like Hedwig Gorski, Gil Scott-Heron and Léo Ferré, and by the lengthy monologues of Spalding Gray.

39.1   History

The art of spoken word has existed for many millennia. The tradition of the spoken word is particular to cultures around the world when oral traditions were the means to pass on the genealogical, historical, cultural knowledge and traditions of different geographical sects of indigenous peoples and civilizations; it was particularly steeped in the African traditions that also included drumming and dancing as a means to reinforce cultural mores, spiritual incantations, social practices and world views. This can also be evidenced in Native American and Aboriginal cultures. The Ancient Greeks included Greek lyric which is similar to spoken-word poetry in their Olympic Games.[1][2] Similar exercises were encouraged in political and social discourse in what was then an ancient and thriving form of democracy.

Modern North American spoken-word poetry originated from the poetry of the Harlem Renaissance[3] and blues music as well as the 1960s beatniks.[4]

Modern-day spoken-word poetry became popular in the underground Black community in the 1960s with The Last Poets. The Last Poets was a poetry and political music group that was born out of the African-American Civil Rights movement.[5]

Dr. Martin Luther King's "I Have a Dream," Sojourner Truth's "Ain't I a Woman?" and Booker T. Washington's "Cast Down Your Buckets" have changed and also shaped the course of history.[6]

The artistic utilization of the spoken-word genre in black culture today draws on and reflects a rich literary and musical heritage, and the interaction among these genres, as in the past, has produced some of America's best-known art pieces. Like Langston Hughes and writers of the Harlem Renaissance were inspired by the feelings of the blues and the black spiritual, contemporary hip-hop and slam poetry artists were inspired by poets such as Hughes in their use of word stylings. Similarly, the experimental and often radical statements of the Black Arts Movement developed a great energy with cutting-edge jazz and funk music that would expand the boundaries of black cultural persona, and thereby provide space for increasingly alternative political ideologies to be raised, discussed, and acknowledged.[6]

Spoken-word poetry came more towards the mainstream in popularity a short time later when Gil Scott-Heron released his spoken-word poem *The Revolution Will Not Be Televised* on the album *Small Talk at 125th and Lenox* in 1970.[7]

In the meantime, artists from the rest of the world who came from a culture with a strong poetry tradition such as French singer-songwriters Léo Ferré or Serge Gainsbourg, made a personal use of spoken word over rock or symphonic music from the very beginning of the 1970s, in such albums as *Amour Anarchie* (1970), *Histoire de Melody Nelson* (1971) or *Il n'y a plus rien* (1973), and contributed to popularize this performing style in their cultural area without being related to the African American community or being influenced by its culture.

In the late 1970s Los Angeles poet Wanda Coleman brought modern spoken-word poetry into written form with the release of her poetry collection *Mad Dog, Black Lady* in 1979 on Black Sparrow Press.[8]

Many artists and poets have not published any of their works in book forms. Some use video and audio recording, the means used exclusively by Hedwig Gorski, who rejected what she called the "dull-drums" of book publishing in the 1980s.[9] Spalding Gray's film *Swimming to Cambodia* is a well-known example of spoken word, with Gray sitting at a desk, talking about his experiences during the filming of *The Killing Fields*.

The Nuyorican Poets Café on New York's Lower Eastside was founded in 1973 and is one of the oldest American venues for presenting spoken-word poetry. The Nuyorican Poets Café in 1989 held the first documented poetry slam.[10]

On the West Coast Da Poetry Lounge and The World Stage are two of the oldest venues for spoken-word poetry, The World Stage presenting the more literary side of the spoken-word tradition and Da Poetry Lounge embracing the more performance side of it.[11]

The Nuyorican Poets Café and Da Poetry Lounge have a close association with the poetry slam movement that was popularized by Russell Simmons' Def Poetry Lounge with both main hosts Bob Holman[12] and Shihan[13] appearing several times on the show.

MTV Unplugged creator Robert Small featured Spoke Word artist on episodes of MTV Unplugged prior to Def Poetry Jam. Bob Holman hosted with artist such as Danny Hoch, Gil-Scott Heron and Maggie Estep and many others. The show was considered ground breaking.

39.2   In media

Before the poetic catalyst of Russell Simmons' Def Poetry Jam in 2002, musical artists such as The Last Poets, Gil-Scott Heron, The Watts Prophets, and many more, were responsible for infiltrating spoken word into the media. Beginning as early as the 1960s, spoken word became an outlet to promote political frustrations and ambitions, such as civil rights.

Towards the late 1990s, movies and documentaries such as Slam (1998), and SlamNation (1998) were responsible for highlighting the evolution and implementation of spoken word in America's society. Both films' mentioned above feature artists such as Saul Williams, muMs da Schemer, Beau Sia, and Jessica Care Moore, who were fluent participants in the New York poetry slam scene, as well as members of the 1996 Nuyorican Poetry Slam Team.

Def Poetry catalyzed Spoken Word's presence in media along with the help of Brave New Voices (2008), a series focusing on the representation of America's youth in spoken word. The show was brought about after Def Poetry ceased to exist in 2007, in which HBO picked the series up with the help of Youth Speaks Inc., an organization internationally known for its involvement in inspiring and motivating young poet around the world. Directed by James Kass, the show highlighted the annual poetry slam competition at the Brave New Voices Festival, held by Youth Speaks Inc,. The docu-series didn't survive long; hence it was more of a feature program.

The yielding death of spoken word's presence on television, media's relationship with the genre of poetry has henceforth moved to the web. Poets such as Jefferson Bethke, Kai Davis, Sarah Kay, and others, are using outlets such as YouTube and Vimeo to display to the world their poetic and theatric talents.

39.3 Motivation

Since its inception, the spoken word has been an outlet for people to release their views outside the academic and institutional domains of the university and academic or small press. The spoken word and its most popular offshoot, slam poetry, evolved into the present-day soap-box for people, especially younger ones, to express their views, emotions, life experiences or information to audiences. The views of spoken-word artists encompass frank commentary on religion, politics, sex and gender, often taboo subjects in society.

Other alternative venues created for the dissemination of these works included The Virtual Free University and multimedia periodicals like Media Free Times[14] that were the de-design precursors of web-pages and E-zines.

Spoken word does elicit one's academic or particular viewpoints, but it is an art not solely meant to express those viewpoints. Rather, it can be an expression of viewpoints through the author's experiences in life through an unconventional manner of word use, allowing the viewer or listener to here such cases or views, comparatively, to the conventional means of average speech.

39.4 Feminist and LGBT movements

Spoken word events and publications are increasingly associated with feminist and LGBT movements.[15] The project of spoken word poetry requires an interfacing between poet and audience that mirrors the experience of an individual confronting the public. The poet is given space to re-imagine and claim ownership of their subject position in the performance of their work. Thus, spoken word is a genre that supports confessional writing and experimental restructuring of power relationships. Because of this, it is an attractive medium for demographics that are systematically marginalized and subordinated in existing power structures, like women, LGBTQ identified people, and persons of color. In the 21st century, radical feminist, black feminist, and islamic feminist movements have used spoken word poetry to re-conceptualize feminist politics typically associated with the 1970s second-wave feminist politics.[16]

39.5 Competitions

Spoken-word poetry is often performed in a competitive setting. Also known as slam poetry, these competitions began in 1986 when Marc Smith started a poetry slam in Chicago.[2]

In 1990, the first National Poetry Slam was held in San Francisco, California.[2] It is now held each year in different cities across the United States. It is the largest poetry slam competition event in the world.[17]

Other more popular poetry reading competitions include the Sunken Garden Readings in Connecticut[18] and the Dodge Festival in New Jersey which brings in over 10,000 people from around the country and globe.[18]

39.6 See also

- Hip hop
- Hip hop music
- List of performance poets
- Recitative

39.7 References

[1] "GREEK LYRIC" Retrieved 16-08-2014

[2] Glazner, Gary Mex. *Poetry Slam: The Competitive Art of Performance Poetry.* San Francisco: Manic D, 2000.

[3] Aptowicz, Cristin O'Keefe (2007), *Words in Your Face: a guided tour through twenty years of the New York City poetry slam.* New York: Soft Skull Press. 400 pp. ISBN 1-933368-82-9

[4] Neal, Mark Anthony (2003). *The Songs in the Key of Black Life. A Rhythm and Blues Nation.* New York: Routledge. 214 pp. ISBN 0-415-96571-3

[5] "last poet fragments".

[6] Folkways, Smithsonian. "Say It Loud". Smithsonian Institution. Retrieved 15 February 2013.

[7] Ben Sisario, "Gil Scott-Heron, Voice of Black Protest Culture, Dies at 62", *New York Times*, May 28, 2011.

[8] Wanda Coleman biography, Poetry Foundation.

[9] Hedwig Gorski website.

[10] "The History of Nuyorican Poetry Slam", Verbs on Asphalt.

[11] Amy Jo Nelson, "Spoken word poet Shihan inspires an awakening", *Sonoma State Star*, September 26, 2011.

[12] http://www.atlanticcenterforthearts.org/artresprog/resschedule/feb/b_holman.html

[13] The Poetry Lounge (2004).

[14] Media Free Times

[15] http://books.google.com/books?id=bw4LVNJqpToC&dq=feminist+%22spoken+word%22+poetry&lr=&source=gbs_navl_s

[16] http://repositories.lib.utexas.edu/handle/2152/22520

[17] Poetry Slam, Inc. Web. 28 Nov. 2012.

[18] Smith, Marc Kelly, and Mark Eleveld. *The Spoken Word Revolution: Slam, Hip-hop & the Poetry of a New Generation.* Naperville, IL: Source MediaFusion, 2003.

39.8 Text and image sources, contributors, and licenses

39.8.1 Text

- **National poetry** *Source:* https://en.wikipedia.org/wiki/National_poetry?oldid=652952152 *Contributors:* Dbachmann, Filiocht, Wikipedius, Man vyi, GK, ChristopherWillis, Logologist, DreamGuy, Pcpcpc, RHaworth, Eleassar777, Tabletop, DePiep, Quinlan Vos~enwiki, SmackBot, Jagged 85, Sadads, Bejnar, Rigadoun, Eliajha, Desapar, Silin2005, Fibo1123581321, Abiodun adekoya, Dcattell, Townblight, Yoonimelon, FrescoBot, Slowmoverz, Sp472105, Irvi Hyka, Righteousskills, Kmzayeem, TheNano7474 and Anonymous: 19

- **The History of English Poetry** *Source:* https://en.wikipedia.org/wiki/The_History_of_English_Poetry?oldid=682095120 *Contributors:* Charles Matthews, Rjwilmsi and Antiquary

- **History of poetry** *Source:* https://en.wikipedia.org/wiki/History_of_poetry?oldid=679869893 *Contributors:* Bearcat, Aetheling, JamesMLane, Discospinster, Art LaPella, RoyBoy, Spangineer, SteinbDJ, Camw, Afterwriting, DVdm, Bgwhite, RussBot, Jpbowen, Rob117, Meegs, DVD R W, Prodego, KnowledgeOfSelf, Jagged 85, Gilliam, Hmains, Sadads, JFQ, Mukadderat, SilkTork, Kyoko, Szfski, A Musing, Noroton, Midnightdreary, PhilKnight, Professor marginalia, Danielph23, R'n'B, Philip Trueman, Jsfouche, Macy, Dcattell, Denisarona, Mr. Granger, ClueBot, Arakunem, Sevilledade, Swanrizla, IamNotU, XLinkBot, Rror, Little Mountain 5, Addbot, Holt, D0762, MightySaiyan, Ajrv7i, Debresser, Евгений Пивоваров, Luckas-bot, Yobot, Tryptofish, FrescoBot, Levisque67, Wintonian, Poetic Minds, Savh, ClueBot NG, Satellizer, Wbm1058, BG19bot, Qtionary, Jdragonstyle, Iamthecheese44, Inkedhistorian, Arlo660, MusicAngels, Abdullah1237860 and Anonymous: 62

- **Table of years in poetry** *Source:* https://en.wikipedia.org/wiki/Table_of_years_in_poetry?oldid=618461856 *Contributors:* Topbanana, Alan Liefting, JustAGal, P64 and MerlIwBot

- **List of years in poetry** *Source:* https://en.wikipedia.org/wiki/List_of_years_in_poetry?oldid=675676015 *Contributors:* Delirium, Evertype, Kusunose, Jokestress, Woohookitty, Mandarax, Ground Zero, EamonnPKeane, Wavelength, TexasAndroid, Jpbowen, Pegship, Contaldo80, Stumps, Havocrazy, Chris the speller, Bob the ducq, Colonies Chris, Charivari, JeffW, Galo1969X, Keithh, A Musing, Chewy3326, JamesAM, Ichthys58, JustAGal, Nick Number, Jj137, Noroton, Modernist, Epeefleche, Magioladitis, Gwern, Keith D, Christian Storm, Hammersoft, Tavix, Psychless, Antiquary, SchreiberBike, Addbot, Fyrael, Ozob, Tassedethe, Luckas-bot, Yobot, ThaddeusB, Ulric1313, Reconsideration, INeverCry, FrescoBot, TRBP, Gamewizard71, Rwood128, George Dance, ClueBot NG, Ekkavi, Khazar2, ColonelHenry, Mogism, Rob at Houghton, Kazem91 and Anonymous: 26

- **Bengali poetry** *Source:* https://en.wikipedia.org/wiki/Bengali_poetry?oldid=675016192 *Contributors:* Edward, Big iron, Jiang, Ani07l, Sproy, Ragib, Chowbok, Utcursch, Beland, CALR, Rich Farmbrough, LindsayH, Aranel, Filiocht, Ogress, Ramashray, Alansohn, Woohookitty, Graham87, Sumanch, SchuminWeb, Bgwhite, RussBot, Anomie, Werdna, Nikkimaria, NeilN, Stumps, SmackBot, David Kernow, Jagged 85, Commander Keane bot, Hmains, Bluebot, Madmedea~enwiki, Roscelese, Sadads, Jwillbur, Amartyabag, Hippychickali, Tarikur, JHunterJ, Skinsmoke, Phuzion, DabMachine, Adambiswanger1, Courcelles, Ganeshbot, CmdrObot, KyraVixen, Ziaur2k, Annur, DumbBOT, A Musing, Aditya Kabir, Armanaziz, Auyon, Deeceec, Husond, Ekabhishek, MER-C, VoABot II, SDas, JamesBWatson, Jeroje, Edward321, Kaurab, NAHID, Ravichandar84, Tikiwont, Jeepday, Bonadea, CardinalDan, James Kidd, Ashiquemostafa, Anonymous Dissident, Susantab, KC Panchal, Aford2526, Moonriddengirl, Caltas, Steven Crossin, Nn123645, Townblight, Faizul Latif Chowdhury, Annthewriter, Bagworm, Binoyda, Jayantanth, Prokopenya Viktor, Suranjit, XLinkBot, Rrini.jhini, GDibyendu, Eeshitaa, CanadianLinuxUser, Fluffernutter, Mephiston999, Baffle gab1978, Tassedethe, Ratnajit ju, Yobot, Nishadhembram, Mattisjoti, Akash Kolkata, AnomieBOT, Noq, Jim1138, Bluerasberry, Ibrahim khan ali, Shakyasinha, Palashbose, Nirjhar Roy, Jodertio, Alvin Seville, Chandan Guha, FrescoBot, Nilanjan4346, Souptik, Reconsider the static, Orenburg1, Sneegdha, Generalboss3, Wintonian, John of Reading, GoingBatty, RA0808, Kkm010, KarunaDas, Dffgd, Shahinur Shaila, SporkBot, Amarkolkata, Chittoranjon Hira, Mangalkavya, Arzal, Maharshi Balmiki, Durmukh, Pranabbasuray, ClueBot NG, Nillohit, Nilsanka, Muktijoddha, Rahulghose, Karl 334, Amitabhadevchoudhury, Sudiptamunsi, Rajib 1969, Kunal71, Strike Eagle, Debashismaiti, Meatsgains, Smmmaniruzzaman, Lastbench, Squeamish Ossifrage, Z41N14Z, Khazar2, Kmzayeem, ColonelHenry, Shish Mohammad Zakaria, Ibrahim Husain Meraj, Amitava145, স্যা করণ, Nusaiba Tasnim, Farhana2012, Darpana Roy and Anonymous: 264

- **Biblical poetry** *Source:* https://en.wikipedia.org/wiki/Biblical_poetry?oldid=681529102 *Contributors:* RK, IZAK, Ihcoyc, Jiang, WouterVH, JASpencer, Uriber, Charles Matthews, Benwing, Tom harrison, Everyking, Jfdwolff, Wmahan, Andycjp, Antandrus, AlexG, Jaberwocky6669, Kwamikagami, Filiocht, DjR, Zawersh, Woohookitty, FeanorStar7, Jacobolus, Jeff3000, BD2412, Rjwilmsi, MZMcBride, TexasAndroid, RussBot, Justin Eiler, Dureo, Davidsteinberg, Theda, FDuffy, Stumps, SmackBot, Chris the speller, Sadads, Huji, Eliyak, RomanSpa, Fedallah, CharlesMartel, BeenAroundAWhile, ShelfSkewed, Cydebot, Doug Weller, A Musing, Ichthys58, WinBot, Fayenatic london, JAnDbot, Ekabhishek, Midnightdreary, R'n'B, Coin945, Curbrook, Java7837, Calwiki, Natg 19, Johnsondanl, StAnselm, Zaporozhian, Calatayudboy, Vanished user ewfisn2348tui2f8n2fio2utjfeoi210r39jf, ClueBot, Alwaysfair1, Niceguyedc, Excirial, Editor2020, Anticipation of a New Lover's Arrival, The, Addbot, AkhtaBot, R2dj2, OlEnglish, Yobot, Matanya, AnomieBOT, 9s, Jack Daniel Adams, I dream of horses, Linafelt, Difu Wu, EmausBot, WikitanvirBot, Wikipelli, ZéroBot, ClueBot NG, Helpful Pixie Bot, BattyBot, Cimorcus, Vieque, JudeccaXIII and Anonymous: 39

- **Biker poetry** *Source:* https://en.wikipedia.org/wiki/Biker_poetry?oldid=604744131 *Contributors:* D6, Dennis Bratland, SmackBot, Chris the speller, CmdrObot, R'n'B, Dawn Bard, XLinkBot, Delicious carbuncle, Redheylin, Yobot, ChildofMidnight, Johnnyturk888, FrescoBot, Anna Roy, Akbikerpoet, RoadrashBiker, Manytexts, Newyorkadam, American Biker Poet, WFF12 and Anonymous: 7

- **Cowboy poetry** *Source:* https://en.wikipedia.org/wiki/Cowboy_poetry?oldid=670632300 *Contributors:* Lou Sander, Hoss, Bearcat, Peterklevy, Orangemike, LindsayH, Bobo192, Frank101, Inky, Maltmomma, SmackBot, Evanreyes, Ohnoitsjamie, Jwillbur, SilkTork, SallyQ, DavidOaks, Billy Hathorn, Fvasconcellos, Cydebot, Firelookout, Elkoref, Midnightdreary, JMyrleFuller, FisherQueen, EDear, Libroman, Mcdav, Loganis, Chisoshorse, Jrl-mfa, ImageRemovalBot, ClueBot, Enchantingm, Niceguyedc, Richard E. Davies, Ozarkhighlands, Mike Moutoux, Zawadzke22, ChildofMidnight, FrescoBot, HamiltonLake, Plumadesabiduría, Pinethicket, John of Reading, Manytexts, Widr, Robmayes, CECrouch, Balaigne, Allenengel and Anonymous: 38

- **English poetry** *Source:* https://en.wikipedia.org/wiki/English_poetry?oldid=662844363 *Contributors:* Kpjas, Mav, Zundark, Rmhermen, Atorpen, Deb, Michael Hardy, Kwertii, Sannse, Paul A, Ihcoyc, Ahoerstemeier, Jdforrester, Alhuber, Susurrus, Jiang, Charles Matthews, Jwrosenzweig, Zoicon5, Tom Allen, Bevo, Raul654, Wetman, Owen, Sjorford, Seglea, Postdlf, Hoot, Dhodges, Aggelophoros, Cyrius, David

Gerard, Snobot, Fabiform, Haeleth, Lupin, Zigger, Everyking, Matthead, Bobblewik, Andycjp, Gdr, GeneralPatton, Anárion, Jokestress, Monk Bretton, Neutrality, Irpen, Ornil, Duja, Rich Farmbrough, Silence, YUL89YYZ, MeltBanana, Mjpieters, Paul August, Stbalbach, Hydrotaphia, Liuyao, CanisRufus, El C, Susvolans, Sortior, Duk, Filiocht, Man vyi, Rje, Officiallyover, Paul McMahon, Danski14, Alansohn, Monk127, Mac Davis, Helixblue, DanCupid, Aristides, Pcpcpc, Angr, Woohookitty, JeremyA, MONGO, Clemmy, BD2412, Jorunn, RobertG, Latka, Jak123, Alphachimp, Gdrbot, Satanael, Jimp, Brandmeister (old), RussBot, Splash, Pigman, Maris stella, Yrithinnd, Howcheng, Joelr31, Quillercouch, TransUtopian, Deville, Open2universe, Closedmouth, Fram, Tyrenius, JLaTondre, Mais oui!, Physicsdavid, Stumps, Smack-Bot, Malecasta, Yopie, Hmains, Betacommand, Bluebot, Sadads, Colonies Chris, Akhilleus, GuillaumeTell, Ceoil, John, TravisBrown, EdK, Neddyseagoon, Hu12, JoannaSerah, Ensak, Drinibot, Sopoforic, Ntsimp, Ssilvers, A Musing, Lo2u, Phoe, Kisa2674, Porqin, AntiVandal-Bot, Noroton, Husond, DuncanHill, AJokinen, Hut 8.5, PhilKnight, Magioladitis, Franciscrot, Theroadislong, 28421u2232nfenfcenc, Mrathel, DGG, MartinBot, R'n'B, J.delanoy, Christine E., Hubacelgrand, KickAssClown, Scribblingwoman, Bonadea, OriginalJay, Daimore, Moa-menam, NPrice, Shorn again, PGWG, Adransusy, AngryZionist, Dawn Bard, Gravitan, Bentogoa, SimonTrew, Svick, TonyBrit, Thedewil, WikiLaurent, Townblight, LarRan, Mr. Granger, ClueBot, Avenged Eightfold, EoGuy, Bagworm, Ottre, Brennos, Antiquary, Rclc, Doc9871, MystBot, Addbot, Groundsquirrel13, Tassedethe, LarryJeff, Tide rolls, Bebsch, Luckas-bot, Senator Palpatine, AnomieBOT, Jim1138, Arthur-Bot, Xqbot, Reconsideration, Mildboar, FrescoBot, Amartya ray2001, Lenathehyena50, SpacemanSpiff, Declan Clam, January, Andymcgrath, Chemyanda, Rwood128, Orphan Wiki, Bill.Roache, Princesscherry668, A930913, Mehfileranjan, LarkinToad2010, FrankieS17, Tomthumb1, Xanchester, ClueBot NG, SpikeTorontoRCP, Mark Arsten, 2bttrn, Jacqueline Starer, Preston stone, Jeremy112233, ChrisGualtieri, Khazar2, Webclient101, ColonelHenry, Farhana2012, SarahJamesorLeavesley, Nagy zsuzsa89, Mini-Martian and Anonymous: 187

- **Hebrew poetry** *Source:* https://en.wikipedia.org/wiki/Hebrew_poetry?oldid=551232111 *Contributors:* Ihcoyc, David Shay, Hadal, Woggly, D6, Brian0918, Grutness, ArbiterOne, Graham87, Makaristos, Davidsteinberg, Jmlk17, Jwy, John, DanieleProcida, A Musing, Dekimasu, Addbot, DrFO.Tn.Bot, Obersachsebot, Reconsideration, Rgcrgcrgc, ChrisGualtieri and Anonymous: 6

- **Indian poetry** *Source:* https://en.wikipedia.org/wiki/Indian_poetry?oldid=675813377 *Contributors:* RedWolf, Fennec, Ragib, CALR, Kdammers, Aranel, CanisRufus, Wiki-uk, Velella, Woohookitty, Graham87, CambridgeBayWeather, Jpbowen, Nlu, Stumps, SmackBot, Jagged 85, Blue -bot, Sadads, Bailbeedu, John, Shyamsunder, JHunterJ, Khatru2, Tkynerd, A Musing, הסרפד, Mattisse, Anupam, Nick Number, Big Bird, Storkk, Ekabhishek, Bakasuprman, Nkarthikeyanosho, Ilakkuvanar, Jeroje, Iitkgp.prashant, Gnanapiti, Drsrdesai, Coolkeg908, Vishu123, Sonasinghgill, Andres rojas22, Free intellect, Oysterdiver, Flyer22, Townblight, Icarusgeek, Aeja1370, Apparition11, XLinkBot, Addbot, AnomieBOT, Reconsideration, FrescoBot, DrilBot, John of Reading, Nuwanda360, Dewritech, Wikipelli, Soni Ruchi, Kkm010, Sahasrara, Anshudikshant, Chanan Dhillon, Titodutta, Avenugopalarao2011, DPL bot, John.kakoty, Mediran, SHRIPADVAIDYA, Tentinator, Xnhic2, Rajpbm, Sujeethaca, KH-1 and Anonymous: 47

- **Javanese poetry** *Source:* https://en.wikipedia.org/wiki/Javanese_poetry?oldid=575580656 *Contributors:* Bennylin, Keenan Pepper, Rjwilmsi, SmackBot, Stevage, Rigadoun, Corpx, JavierMC, AlleborgoBot, SieBot, Addbot and Anonymous: 3

- **Kannada poetry** *Source:* https://en.wikipedia.org/wiki/Kannada_poetry?oldid=679929817 *Contributors:* Danny, Rmhermen, Philip Taron, Sundar, Heavy chariot, Delip, HPN, Filiocht, Geschichte, GK, JohnyDog, Dr Gangrene, Shreevatsa, Raguks, Grammarbot, Tachs, NeilN, SmackBot, YellowMonkey, David Kernow, Martin.Budden, Commander Keane bot, Bluebot, Sadads, Dineshkannambadi, John, KNM, A Musing, Mattisse, Barticus88, Bot-maru, Husond, Ekabhishek, Gnanapiti, Haris04, Mercurywoodrose, Townblight, Studioartist, XLinkBot, Lightbot, AmritasyaPutra, GorgeCustersSabre, Sundeeppalavalli, Trsm1, ChrisGualtieri, Amortias and Anonymous: 15

- **Kashmiri language** *Source:* https://en.wikipedia.org/wiki/Kashmiri_language?oldid=681966680 *Contributors:* Zeno Gantner, Dcljr, Bogdan-giusca, Imc, Taxman, Secretlondon, Kukkurovaca, Gadfium, Utcursch, Icairns, Burschik, Muijz, Zeman, Demiurge, Jfpierce, Vsmith, Florian Blaschke, El C, Kwamikagami, Erauch, Prsephone1674, Peter Greenwell, Circeus, לערי ריינהארט, Jonsafari, HasharBot~enwiki, Ranveig, Jumbuck, Sl, Suruena, Garzo, Drbreznjev, Woohookitty, Jeff3000, Toussaint, Tombseye, Meji100, Eubot, RexNL, Codex Sinaiticus, Roboto de Ajvol, YurikBot, Al Silonov, Hairy Dude, RussBot, Hede2000, Rsrikanth05, Purodha, DeadEyeArrow, Bota47, Sagsaw, Malekhanif, Nikkimaria, Remus Lupin~enwiki, 5th Angel, Tropylium, David Straub, Imz, Martin.Budden, Unyoyega, Rueckk, Sebesta, Magicalsaumy, Sadads, D T G, Tamfang, Chlewbot, Grover cleveland, Maurice45, Khoikhoi, Megaman24, Andrew Dalby, Shyamsunder, JorisvS, Aarandir, JediScougale, Hvn0413, Meco, Espreon, Hu12, Norm mit, Iridescent, RaviC, WikiMarshall, CmdrObot, Alan Flynn, Cardreader, Rudjek, Onkoul, Doug Weller, Arvind Iyengar, Omicronpersei8, Thijs!bot, Anupam, Ahmed27, Escarbot, QuiteUnusual, Peh6n, MikeLynch, JAnD-bot, Deflective, Kuaichik, Jim Douglas, Avicennasis, Tuncrypt, CodeCat, Atulsnischal, MartinBot, Mermaid from the Baltic Sea, Dheeraj-soni, AgarwalSumeet, Abecedare, Karan9005, Idioma-bot, VolkovBot, Unmesh Bangali, TXiKiBoT, Dalgate74, Abtinb, PEHook, BotKung, Wikiisawesome, Shouriki, Erkin2008, Kashmirreporter, Andres65~enwiki, Kktor, Arjun024, SieBot, Phe-bot, Purbo T, Keilana, Fratrep, Abdelchi, Dcattell, CuteRobin, Michael Peter Fustumum, Townblight, Sitush, Vatsun, Voxpuppet, Pete unseth, Shovon76, Ordinaterr, Drag-onBot, Alexbot, Iohannes Animosus, G.broadwell, MelonBot, Khushamad, XLinkBot, Dthomsen8, WikHead, MystBot, GDibyendu, Qasima-likhawaja, Addbot, Abebambele, GSMR, Oniongas, Razimpatel, Download, Irfankshah, Numbo3-bot, 3swordz, Narayan, Luckas-bot, The-Suave, Amirobot, Kashmirspeaks, AnomieBOT, Rubinbot, Hunnjazal, Citation bot, TalkChat, Quebec99, Xqbot, HannesP, Anonymous from the 21st century, GrouchoBot, GhalyBot, Strider11, FrescoBot, Massagetae, DrilBot, HRoestBot, AmphBot, MastiBot, Nijgoykar, Shahmukhi, Sanjaytiku, Managerarc, Tim1357, Dsz4, كاشف عقیل, Zylbath, Rana A.R, Kamran the Great, EmausBot, Summydude, RA0808, Aakriti drake, ZéroBot, PotatoBot, Mar4d, Redav, Neechalkaran, H3llBot, ChuispastonBot, JstCse, Mjbmrbot, Socialservice, Khestwol, ClueBot NG, Chinaar, Helpful Pixie Bot, Koshurkott, Greatgeneral, Snaevar-bot, MKar, CityOfSilver, Orartu, Davidiad, Arjunkmohan, יהודה שמחה ולדמן, Jeremy112233, Graphium, Umaarshah, فرح دیسائی, VibhasKS, Hiftikar, Enock4seth, Granatoid, Wikiuser13, Saladin1987, Keshavrainadi-rector, Owais Khursheed, Jin khatama, Omar Irfan, PGCX864, Reza Sheikh, Praweenkprabhakar and Anonymous: 177

- **Korean poetry** *Source:* https://en.wikipedia.org/wiki/Korean_poetry?oldid=677751844 *Contributors:* PuzzletChung, (:Julien:), Rpyle731, Utcursch, Kdammers, Bender235, Cmdrjameson, Visviva, Mel Etitis, Woohookitty, BlankVerse, POofYS, Gurch, Benlisquare, Rincewind42, Appleby, Melchoir, Hmains, Betacommand, Bluebot, Sadads, Narco, Abbott75, Zadignose, John, Hemlock Martinis, A Musing, Object-man, TOMATOBOMB, VoABot II, Macmelvino, Erkan Yilmaz, Caspian blue, Heyheyheya, SentouYogensha, Azukimonaka, Designfabulous, Dusti, Jagello, Dcattell, Townblight, LarRan, Staticshakedown, Addbot, Lightbot, AnomieBOT, Doksuri, In ictu oculi, EmausBot, ClueBot NG, Argiecon, Andrea2016228 and Anonymous: 24

- **Latin American poetry** *Source:* https://en.wikipedia.org/wiki/Latin_American_poetry?oldid=675901721 *Contributors:* Rjwilmsi, RussBot, SmackBot, Chris the speller, Sadads, Colonies Chris, JHunterJ, Iridescent, Courcelles, CmdrObot, Qrc2006, Tkynerd, Alaibot, A Musing, Cool

Blue, MarshBot, PhilKnight, Anna Lincoln, Wikiisawesome, Todwyer, Calliopejen1, Jbmurray, Bien18, Tassedethe, Lightbot, Gail, Shadow-jams, FrescoBot, POESIA77, Leviatan1254, Arielllaura, Helpful Pixie Bot, Sarah Joy Jones, Redbutts, Historiadormundo and Anonymous: 26

- **Māori poetry** *Source:* https://en.wikipedia.org/wiki/M%C4%81ori_poetry?oldid=611511128 *Contributors:* Zigger, Gadfium, Woohookitty, Snori, JL-Bot, Niceguyedc and Addbot

- **Kantan Chamorrita** *Source:* https://en.wikipedia.org/wiki/Kantan_Chamorrita?oldid=663247238 *Contributors:* Xezbeth, Grutness, Smack-Bot, Sepa, Sadads, Adrigon, GRBerry, Ascidian, Good Olfactory, Addbot, Omnipaedista, Arthree, RjwilmsiBot, In ictu oculi, CitationCleaner-Bot, BattyBot and Anonymous: 1

- **Modern Hebrew poetry** *Source:* https://en.wikipedia.org/wiki/Modern_Hebrew_poetry?oldid=636189628 *Contributors:* Jason Quinn, Rich Farmbrough, Woohookitty, SmackBot, JustAGal, Dekimasu, Yobot, Davshul, Sasams, RjwilmsiBot, Dardar777, Helpful Pixie Bot and Jilfi

- **Old Norse poetry** *Source:* https://en.wikipedia.org/wiki/Old_Norse_poetry?oldid=654067052 *Contributors:* Sjc, Tkinias, Haukurth, Wiglaf, Bradeos Graphon, Dsmdgold, Golbez, Io usurped, Dbachmann, Anthony Appleyard, Megan1967, Pegship, Hayden120, Ciacchi, Sadads, Jml-dalton, John, Euchiasmus, JHunterJ, Clsc, Gizmo II, Blink484, A Musing, Berig, J.delanoy, ClueBot, Addbot, Lightbot, Þórður Breiðfjörð, Amirobot, Eisfbnore and Anonymous: 8

- •Pakistani poetry*Source:*https://en.wikipedia.org/wiki/Pakistani_poetry?oldid=662908350*Contributors:*Charles Matthews, Hajor, Manvyi , Woohookitty, Kbdank71, Welsh, Ged UK, Replicaa@hotmail.com, A Musing, Rasheedareejo, Sulaimandaud, Robina Fox, AtticusX,R' n'B, Mercurywoodrose, Smsarmad, Shujaat Ali Rahi, Mike robert, Apparition11, XLinkBot, Dthomsen8, MrOllie, Yobot, Ata Fida Aziz,J 04n, Cannolis, Tbhotch, Imranaraza, Mean as custard, Sarwarkhushk, A930913, Khani100, Soazkhwani, Nadeemaraza, Umais Bin Sajjad, Ro0o0my, Azhartokyo, Khalidk1558, Sleighsleigh, YameenKhan65, Shahid817, Tauqeer3430, Czeesh, Yasmeen Kh., Surgingpassions, Nomi -Writes and Anonymous: 68

- •Sanskrit literature*Source:*https://en.wikipedia.org/wiki/Sanskrit_literature?oldid=678310152*Contributors:*Yann, Topbanana, Phil Boswell,Re dWolf, Goethean, Ambarish, Wayland, Per Honor et Gloria, Kukkurovaca, Utcursch, LordSimonofShropshire, Estel~enwiki, GirolamoSav onarola, Sam Hocevar, RevRagnarok, CALR, Discospinster, Florian Blaschke, Dbachmann, Ashwatham, *drew, Kwamikagami, Shanes,War eh, Rramphal, NetBot, Jason One, Ramashray, Wiki-uk, RainbowOfLight, Shreevatsa, Raguks, Gryffindor, Ecelan, Mushin, Deeptrivia,Khira d, RussBot, Astorknlam, Equilibrial, SmackBot, Jagged 85, Devanampriya, ImpuMozhi, Sadads, R. Kevin Doyle, OrphanBot, GRuban,Iksvak u, Andrew Dalby, Sivasenani, Sreekanthv, Shyamsunder, JHunterJ, Interlingua, Skinsmoke, Rayfield, Bsskchaitanya, ShelfSkewed, Flam-mingo, VaporOne, Aristophanes68, Doug Weller, Mattisse, Mereda, Joy1963, Merbabu, Kaveri, Aadal, Ekabhishek, Magioladitis, VoABot II,SDas, S USHRUTA, Sindhutvavadin, SwiftBot, Tuncrypt, B9 hummingbird hovering, Abecedare, Victuallers, Asherek, Zerokitsune, Nagesh.adiga,Redti gerxyz, Philip Trueman, Andres rojas22, Buddhipriya, Madhero88, Smurali49, Ivan Štambuk, Ujjwol, Colfer2, Javierfv1212, Light-mouse, Townblight, Phil wink, Sandan222, ClueBot, PipepBot, PixelBot, Vegetarianchad3, Sun Creator, Galygal, Mhockey, Wikidas, Indopug,XLinkB ot, AgnosticPreachersKid, Ism schism, Addbot, Bennó, CarsracBot, Jonoikobangali, Sammod, Luckas-bot, Yobot, AnomieBOT,Adellefra nk, Materialscientist, Sarbeswar.meher, Xqbot, Aniljava, Opfallon, Verbum Veritas, FrescoBot, OgreBot, SpacemanSpiff, Kham-gatam, Jag gi81, Zaven2, Correctionwriter, Ansumang, Aoidh, Cowlibob, RjwilmsiBot, Generalboss3, Uanfala, EmausBot, WikitanvirBot, SoniRuchi, Pon ydepression, Katyayani Mohapatra, Dr.p.k.mishra, Zloyvolsheb, Bkrish68, StasMalyga, Sydney Ambrose, Brandmeister, Nagar-juna198, Ro cketrod1960, -revi, Encyclopedian Clerk, Aaron Booth, Rgimvl, Dream of Nyx, Wordboy121, Helpful Pixie Bot, Hrihr, BG19bot,Solomon7968 , Innuo, BattyBot, Amitrochates, Bharu12, Khazar2, Jaichetr, Srisharmaa, Faizan, Epicgenius, CsDix, Bodha2, WrobjexWiki,Coolgama, Ela queate, Robevans123, Wiki.authoring, Devendra.philo, Superguin17, Ksuriv and Anonymous: 98

- **Serbian epic poetry** *Source:* https://en.wikipedia.org/wiki/Serbian_epic_poetry?oldid=679070487 *Contributors:* Jiang, Nikola Smolenski, Joy, AnonMoos, Fredrik, Varlaam, Avala, FormatC, Nickj, Filiocht, Obradovic Goran, Hadžija, RJFJR, Bobrayner, Ninam~enwiki, Amor-row, Rjwilmsi, Orjen, GagHalfrunt, Gurch, Moe Epsilon, Gadget850, Ajdebre, Stumps, SmackBot, Zileselakovic, Well, girl, look at you!, F382d56d7a18630cf764a5b576ea1b4810467238, Sadads, Egsan Bacon, TenPoundHammer, John, IronGargoyle, Cydebot, A Musing, Mik-isRS, Voyaging, Vanjagenije, Методиje, Critikal1, StAnselm, Ivan Štambuk, Goustien, VVVladimir, Ostalocutanje, DumZiBoT, Addbot, Debresser, Yobot, Petkowsky, AnomieBOT, BenzolBot, Antidiskriminator, ZéroBot, Zoupan, Widr, BG19bot and Anonymous: 20

- •Spanish poetry*Source:*https://en.wikipedia.org/wiki/Spanish_poetry?oldid=676366402*Contributors:*Error, Jmabel, Neutrality, JPX7, Aranel ,WestonRuter, Giraffedata, Man vyi, Polylerus, Arthena, Rd232, Wdfarmer, BanyanTree, Fontgirl, Woohookitty, RussBot, Severa, SmackBot ,Vassyana, Hmains, Sadads, Krich, TenPoundHammer, John, Mattbr, Qrc2006, A Musing, JamesAM, Garcilaso, S710, RedCoat10, Tor -talus, R'n'B, Mathglot, Sblauvelt, Pablo.cantero, Anna Lincoln, Chickywiki, Metzby, Synthebot, Jbmurray, S711, ImageRemovalBot, Jenem e,Dthomsen8, Addbot, Yobot, AnomieBOT, Rczimler, Thartessos, Enantiotes, EmausBot, El Sud, Shiver59, ChuispastonBot, ClueBot N G,ThatAMan, Inkdream, Hmainsbot1, VoroSP, UAK8118 and Anonymous: 33

- •Telugu poetry*Source:*https://en.wikipedia.org/wiki/Telugu_poetry?oldid=681882075*Contributors:*HenkvD, Woohookitty, GregorB, Rjwilmsi ,Bgwhite, Anomalocaris, SmackBot, Devanampriya, Ohnoitsjamie, Bluebot, Sadads, JonHarder, Bsskchaitanya, Gnome (Bot), Alaibot, JodyB, Ekabhishek, Infrangible, Redtigerxyz, Rajasekhar1961, Raokasturi, Townblight, Kiranavs, XLinkBot, Materialscientist, Eumolpo, Velasub-ham, Vence1234, GorgeCustersSabre, FrescoBot, Cowlibob, Generalboss3, John of Reading, GoingBatty, N Ravi Kumar, Avenugopalarao2011, Pretty333 and Anonymous: 15

- **Thai poetry** *Source:* https://en.wikipedia.org/wiki/Thai_poetry?oldid=647598261 *Contributors:* Ahoerstemeier, Suphawut, Kwamikagami, Bgwhite, Marcus Cyron, Paul 012, Neelix, WereSpielChequers, Addbot, Snotbot, Helpful Pixie Bot, Ahora, ChrisGualtieri, Iyouwetheyhesheit and Anonymous: 2

- **Urdu poetry** *Source:* https://en.wikipedia.org/wiki/Urdu_poetry?oldid=682671539 *Contributors:* ZimZalaBim, Andries, Aalahazrat~enwiki, Katangoori, Gadfium, Utcursch, LordSimonofShropshire, Nograpes, Sam Hocevar, Mike Rosoft, Spiffy sperry, Arthur Holland, Aranel, El C, RoyBoy, IFaqeer, Filiocht, Giraffedata, Man vyi, GK, Gary, Wiki-uk, Geo Swan, Garzo, Grenavitar, Woohookitty, Uncle G, Alx-pl, Ian Lancaster, Seraphimblade, Indscribe, Sarabseth, Antiuser, Deeptrivia, RussBot, SpuriousQ, Gaius Cornelius, Matticus78, Mikeblas, Tachs, Szhaider, Sandstein, NeilN, Stumps, Veinor, SmackBot, YellowMonkey, Spasage, Zohab, Aksi great, M.Imran, Bluebot, Jungli, Maaa-jid, Jmlk17, Meetfazan, Kukini, Parasoft, Mukadderat, John, Park3r, Green Giant, Doc sameer, Ehheh, Aqdas Rizvi, Hu12, Twas Now, Chiesnick, Randhirreddy, Lalit Kumar, Hemlock Martinis, Synergy, A Musing, حسرف, Islescape, Anupam, Nick Number, Sluzzelin, Barek,

MER-C, Qateel Shifai, PhilKnight, Jay1279, JamesBWatson, Faizhaider, Az haris, JaGa, Shabu naqvi, R'n'B, Tgeairn, RockMFR, Numbo3, Shreewiki, Sarayuparin, Afgrewq, Itdevil, Barastert, Bonadea, CardinalDan, Malik Shabazz, Etvindia, Oaagha, Bibijee, Buddhipriya, Noor Aalam, Billinghurst, Oroosa, Vchimpanzee, Ibgte, Hgbasit, Ahmadnisarsayeedi, Skalam, Ghousebarq, Imnajam, Kumioko (renamed), Deewansahib, Townblight, Escape Orbit, WordyGirl90, ClueBot, Kaleemi, NickCT, Ameen Asim, Blanchardb, Isoft isoft, Bagworm, Robbie098, Ahmufti, NuclearWarfare, Iohannes Animosus, Tnxman307, Malikzafar, Pediaindia, JasonAQuest, Thingg, Dana boomer, Net2008, Apparition11, Editorviki, Azhar Hashmi, XLinkBot, Dthomsen8, Addbot, Noman.bokhari, MrOllie, Redheylin, Nolelover, Webguru, Yobot, Wiki-Dan61, Themfromspace, Ata Fida Aziz, AnomieBOT, APG, Jim1138, Hunnjazal, LilHelpa, JmCor, Rock wali, Runyourcar, J04n, Gorge-CustersSabre, SassoBot, Laddiweb, Alturka, Ahmed Nisar, A.amitkumar, FrescoBot, Saadi4u, Rayshade, AustralianMelodrama, Siddhartha Ghai, Monymirza, Shradha7, LogAntiLog, Lotje, Sehrasiddiqui, Diannaa, Rāmā, Sneegdha, Mohdajmal, Generalboss3, Zuner Ahmed, Emaus-Bot, Wahid alig, AlphaGamma1991, Soni Ruchi, Feronso, Michael R. Burch, Sarwarkhushk, Tarun marwaha, Mar4d, Odhikarjvd, Hrsuroor, Justice007, ClueBot NG, Freejokespoetry, Rezabot, Afreenkhundmiri, Omer123hussain, BG19bot, Gsyedk, Wasif121, Hallows AG, عدم عداده, Silvrous, Mrqd9, Kashmirarts, Savvy89, ChrisGualtieri, Demoakka, Delljvc, Sanjachetan, ASIF ALI IBRAHIM, Ngrewall, Pravesh101, Wamiq, Jatinnirmal, Rajpbm, Geoffsmile, Chand Rajput, Vehdani, Chaelhen, Rekhtashayari, QueenFan, Ufk iitk, Romanikase, Socialmedia77, NehaSharma1994, King756, Frazkathia, M.ad.qadri, Sprathmesh and Anonymous: 264

- **Vietnamese poetry** *Source:* https://en.wikipedia.org/wiki/Vietnamese_poetry?oldid=679142278 *Contributors:* Kaldari, Anthony Appleyard, SteinbDJ, Woohookitty, Tabletop, Grafen, SmackBot, YellowMonkey, Jwy, John, Itsmejudith, R'n'B, Dcattell, Phil wink, JL-Bot, Niceguyedc, Redheylin, Yobot, LilHelpa, A little insignificant, WIKIdesigner, Lotje, Hongtran0507, Ле Лой, In ictu oculi, John of Reading, GoingBatty, Active Banana, Jtle, KLBot2, Hungh3, PaintedCarpet, Lolax Marks and Anonymous: 9

- **Welsh poetry** *Source:* https://en.wikipedia.org/wiki/Welsh_poetry?oldid=637884798 *Contributors:* Mav, Charles Matthews, Hadal, Tagishsimon, Rich Farmbrough, LindsayH, Stbalbach, Aranel, Man vyi, Pcpcpc, Stemonitis, Woohookitty, Brighterorange, Seegoon, Mais oui!, Red-DragOn, Sadads, John, Drinibot, A Musing, JustAGal, Ghmyrtle, Enaidmawr, J.delanoy, Kumioko (renamed), Lightbot, Yobot, Johnbrondum, Rwood128, Dream of Nyx, Trystar12345, Khazar2, Arwel ap Dewi ap Siôn and Anonymous: 12

- **Yakshagana poetry** *Source:* https://en.wikipedia.org/wiki/Yakshagana_poetry?oldid=677407334 *Contributors:* DragonflySixtyseven, Raguks, Hmains, Sadads, Ekabhishek, Geniac, Uhai, GrahamHardy, WereSpielChequers, Redheylin, Yobot, LilHelpa, John of Reading, Mcmatter, Mandruss, Rushyasringeswara D C and Anonymous: 9

- **1270s in poetry** *Source:* https://en.wikipedia.org/wiki/1270s_in_poetry?oldid=654251146 *Contributors:* SimonP, Rich Farmbrough, Ladyof-Shalott, Alaibot, A Musing, KConWiki, Steven Crossin, Erik9bot, A conundrum, Moswento and Yjfstorehouse

- **An Analytic History of Persian Modern Poetry** *Source:* https://en.wikipedia.org/wiki/An_Analytic_History_of_Persian_Modern_Poetry?oldid=598014522 *Contributors:* Wiki-uk, Rjwilmsi, RussBot, Jpbowen, Vanished user sojweiorj34i4f, Sinarchive and DrilBot

- **The Call to Poetry** *Source:* https://en.wikipedia.org/wiki/The_Call_to_Poetry?oldid=630221499 *Contributors:* JackofOz, Tim!, Roscelese, Ekabhishek, Yobot, TYelliot, Snowysusan, Khazar2, Istanbularts and Anonymous: 1

- **Classical reception studies** *Source:* https://en.wikipedia.org/wiki/Classical_reception_studies?oldid=639951786 *Contributors:* Midnightblueowl and Omnipaedista

- **Classical tradition** *Source:* https://en.wikipedia.org/wiki/Classical_tradition?oldid=557220425 *Contributors:* Cynwolfe, JamesBWatson, Wiktic and Armbrust

- **Dial-A-Poem** *Source:* https://en.wikipedia.org/wiki/Dial-A-Poem?oldid=635376691 *Contributors:* Bearcat, Rpyle731, Cyberdat, Dawynn and Alvin Seville

- **Disjecta membra** *Source:* https://en.wikipedia.org/wiki/Disjecta_membra?oldid=666816712 *Contributors:* Bearcat, Ich, Ricky81682, Cloveapple, Cydebot, Ecphora, Te Irirangi, Addbot, Yobot, AnomieBOT, Jamietw, DexDor, Senator2029, Snotbot, PatHadley, Hmainsbot1, Litātiō and Anonymous: 1

- **Spoken word** *Source:* https://en.wikipedia.org/wiki/Spoken_word?oldid=682413270 *Contributors:* Lquilter, Karada, Delirium, Heidimo, Hyacinth, Bearcat, Anssix, Philwelch, Gyrofrog, Stevietheman, Gadfium, Andycjp, Slowking Man, Quadell, Cab88, Notinasnaid, Jpgordon, La goutte de pluie, Gbrandt, Eleland, Yamla, Ashlux, Woohookitty, RHaworth, Cuchullain, BD2412, Dwarf Kirlston, Captmondo, King of Hearts, DVdm, Roboto de Ajvol, YurikBot, Pigman, NawlinWiki, Daunrealist, Beanyk, Cybergoth, VAgentZero, Fanficgurl, That Guy, From That Show!, SmackBot, Dweller, Bobet, Herostratus, InverseHypercube, Cgt1998, C.Fred, Alex Ex, Jagged 85, Verne Equinox, Eskimbot, VickiZ, Gilliam, Bluebot, Joe.krisch, Shalom Yechiel, Darren Rankin, *Ria777*, Collaborator~enwiki, Jamieviva, Cybertooth85, SevenEightTwo, Tigertrouble, JzG, Euchiasmus, Gobonobo, Halaqah, Vanished User 03, Lablom, Sialo~enwiki, Phoenixrod, Tawkerbot2, Amaygarden, Cydebot, MantaRay, Bojackson, Torc2, Thijs!bot, Deja1818, Bobblehead, Neil916, The Fat Man Who Never Came Back, Natalie Erin, Dream Boat Guy, TribalMark, Tgevans, Teddywithfangs, Ingolfson, Poeticmic, 1000poems, Totemmaples, Matlloyd, Sahapi, RahadyanS, IanThal, JMyrleFuller, Iyaisoke, Tifsaleem, S3000, Laneketchey, TaylorAdams, Maxjett, Muslimpoet, InnocuousPseudonym, Ladiba, Dwcarless, Shawn in Montreal, AntiSpamBot, Nihongeorge, Candice L. Bledsoe, Rockcitytj, VolkovBot, Kevinccc, Soadnot, Thesoulenigma, Vipinhari, Technopat, Broadbot, Badly Bradley, Braincafe~enwiki, Mikez302, NS-ward, Pjt48, Closenplay, ShatteredThought, StAnselm, Onichiwa, BotMultichill, VVVBot, Artpoetry, Smsarmad, Pachon, Receleur, Nuttycoconut, Jdaloner, Kool D. J. Jeff Love, Apolloxtcy, Samuelmwils, Sanya3, HARLEMSUN05, Tuxfly, The Thing That Should Not Be, Raresoul, Art Warrior, Anapazapa, TheOldJacobite, Planed, Bagworm, Tlchicago, Jpennwiki, PixelBot, Benefit28, Pregnantbuffalo, Luisrodriguez, Qwfp, XLinkBot, Kaiwhakahaere, Addbot, Kiss Low, Roksta101, Ronhjones, Redheylin, Jtcarl, Lathamhj, Lulzmaster of Lulz, Tallulah13, Ekweisberg, Luckas-bot, Yobot, Fraggle81, Palladmial, O Wise 1, Lilyblak, AnomieBOT, Materialscientist, Sservb, ArthurBot, Tosin213, Msimon143, OONamasteOO, Nxguggenheim, Amaury, FrescoBot, Wikicanuser91, Khadija19, Gbern3, Sheila82, PulitzerBoard, PrincessofLlyr, Dhabolt, Mitohund, Digi ke, Reaper Eternal, Jbshields, Dalyricalpitbull, Alyssa Chica, Cluemaster25452, EmausBot, Acather96, KatDog22, Accuracy primo, Garybynumjr, Massmarkpro, Solarra, Winner 42, Wikipelli, K6ka, Traxs7, Brandmeister, ClueBot NG, Joefromrandb, Proscribe, Riolu66, Widr, Helpful Pixie Bot, 1635schl, BG19bot, Bonnieyhu, PTJoshua, Elderpops, Marcocapelle, Mark Arsten, Writenow921, Mmadonia, Hyperborée, Trossellini, Mediran, Acummins048, Alban Roger, Epicgenius, Mopoet2, Robinsonroc3, BenStein69, Rwe-wiki, Rustynail127, Abhikpal2509, Dalekslayer96, K1JAMS, Toridh, Espanadoggie, King's Rorschach, Wdonjuan, SpokkenMusiq, Brian heim composer and Anonymous: 295

39.8.2 Images

- **File:206ThoiLe_LeThanhTong.jpg** *Source:* https://upload.wikimedia.org/wikipedia/commons/f/f6/206ThoiLe_LeThanhTong.jpg *License:* Public domain *Contributors:* công cộng *Original artist:* không rõ

- **File:AUM_symbol,_the_primary_(highest)_name_of_the_God_as_per_the_Vedas.svg** *Source:* https://upload.wikimedia.org/wikipedia/commons/b/b7/Om_symbol.svg *License:* Public domain *Contributors:* ? *Original artist:* ?

- **File:Aeneas'{}_Flight_from_Troy_by_Federico_Barocci.jpg** *Source:* https://upload.wikimedia.org/wikipedia/commons/f/f7/Aeneas%27_Flight_from_Troy_by_Federico_Barocci.jpg *License:* Public domain *Contributors:* Web Gallery of Art, Uploaded to en.wikipedia 03:45 28 Jul 2004 by en:User:Wetman. *Original artist:* Federico Barocci

- **File:Ambox_important.svg** *Source:* https://upload.wikimedia.org/wikipedia/commons/b/b4/Ambox_important.svg *License:* Public domain *Contributors:* Own work, based off of Image:Ambox scales.svg *Original artist:* Dsmurat (talk · contribs)

- **File:Aphra_Behn_by_Mary_Beale.jpg** *Source:* https://upload.wikimedia.org/wikipedia/commons/2/29/Aphra_Behn_by_Mary_Beale.jpg *License:* Public domain *Contributors:* This image taken from http://belchetz-swenson.com/AphraBehn.php *Original artist:* Mary Beale

- **File:BengaliScriptKo.svg** *Source:* https://upload.wikimedia.org/wikipedia/commons/1/14/BengaliScriptKo.svg *License:* Public domain *Contributors:* ? *Original artist:* ?

- **File:Beowulf.firstpage.jpeg** *Source:* https://upload.wikimedia.org/wikipedia/commons/0/08/Beowulf.firstpage.jpeg *License:* Public domain *Contributors:* Originally uploaded to English Wikipedia by Jwrosenzweig. *Original artist:* ?

- **File:Books-aj.svg_aj_ashton_01.svg** *Source:* https://upload.wikimedia.org/wikipedia/commons/4/4b/Books-aj.svg_aj_ashton_01.svg *License:* CC0 *Contributors:* http://www.openclipart.org/cgi-bin/navigate/education/books (note: the link no longer works since reorganization of the OpenClipArt website). *Original artist:* Original author: AJ Ashton (on OpenClipArt). Code fixed by verdy_p for XML conformance, and MediaWiki compatibility, using a stricter subset of SVG without the extensions of SVG editors, also cleaned up many unnecessary CSS attributes, or factorized them for faster performance and smaller size. All the variants linked below are based on this image.

- **File:Brown-The_Seeds_and_Fruits_of_English_Poetry.jpg** *Source:* https://upload.wikimedia.org/wikipedia/commons/2/27/Brown-The_Seeds_and_Fruits_of_English_Poetry.jpg *License:* Public domain *Contributors:* Art Archive, kept in the Ashmolean Museum, Oxford *Original artist:* Ford Madox Brown

- **File:Calliope_Pio-Clementino_Inv312.jpg** *Source:* https://upload.wikimedia.org/wikipedia/commons/8/89/Calliope_Pio-Clementino_Inv3.jpg *License:* Public domain *Contributors:* Jastrow (2003) *Original artist:* Unknown

- **File:CanterdeMioCid.jpg** *Source:* https://upload.wikimedia.org/wikipedia/en/4/47/CanterdeMioCid.jpg *License:* PD *Contributors:* http://www.spanisharts.com/books/literature/ampliaciones/i_fot_cid1.htm *Original artist:* ?

- **File:Commons-logo.svg** *Source:* https://upload.wikimedia.org/wikipedia/en/4/4a/Commons-logo.svg *License:* ? *Contributors:* ? *Original artist:* ?

- **File:DSC00276_-_Processione_di_donne_-_570-550_a.C._-_Foto_G.** *Source:* https://upload.wikimedia.org/wikipedia/commons/1/10/DSC00276_-_Processione_di_donne_-_570-550_a.C._-_Foto_G._Dall%27Orto.jpg *License:* CC BY-SA 2.5 *Contributors:* uploader's own work *Original artist:* Giovanni Dall'Orto

- **File:Devimahatmya_Sanskrit_MS_Nepal_11c.jpg** *Source:* https://upload.wikimedia.org/wikipedia/commons/3/3f/Devimahatmya_Sanskrit_MS_Nepal_11c.jpg *License:* Public domain *Contributors:* Commentary: The Devimahatmya cropped from http://www.nb.no/baser/schoyen/5/5.20/ms2174.jpg; taken from: w:en:Image:Devimahatmya Sanskrit MS Nepal 11c.jpg *Original artist:* Anonymous

- **File:Disambig_gray.svg** *Source:* https://upload.wikimedia.org/wikipedia/en/5/5f/Disambig_gray.svg *License:* Cc-by-sa-3.0 *Contributors:* ? *Original artist:* ?

- **File:Edit-clear.svg** *Source:* https://upload.wikimedia.org/wikipedia/en/f/f2/Edit-clear.svg *License:* Public domain *Contributors:* The *Tango! Desktop Project. Original artist:*

  The people from the Tango! project. And according to the meta-data in the file, specifically: "Andreas Nilsson, and Jakub Steiner (although minimally)."

- **File:EdmundSpenser.jpg** *Source:* https://upload.wikimedia.org/wikipedia/commons/0/0d/EdmundSpenser.jpg *License:* Public domain *Contributors:* ? *Original artist:* ?

- **File:ElizabethBarrettBrowning.jpg** *Source:* https://upload.wikimedia.org/wikipedia/commons/5/59/ElizabethBarrettBrowning.jpg *License:* Public domain *Contributors:* ? *Original artist:* ?

- **File:Eugène_Ferdinand_Victor_Delacroix_006.jpg** *Source:* https://upload.wikimedia.org/wikipedia/commons/1/1d/Eug%C3%A8ne_Fer Victor_Delacroix_006.jpg *License:* Public domain *Contributors:* The Yorck Project: *10.000 Meisterwerke der Malerei.* DVD-ROM, 2002. ISBN 3936122202. Distributed by DIRECTMEDIA Publishing GmbH. *Original artist:* Eugène Delacroix

- **File:Flag_of_Guam.svg** *Source:* https://upload.wikimedia.org/wikipedia/commons/0/07/Flag_of_Guam.svg *License:* Public domain *Contributors:* ? *Original artist:* ?

- **File:Flag_of_India.svg** *Source:* https://upload.wikimedia.org/wikipedia/en/4/41/Flag_of_India.svg *License:* Public domain *Contributors:* ? *Original artist:* ?

- **File:Flag_of_Pakistan.svg** *Source:* https://upload.wikimedia.org/wikipedia/commons/3/32/Flag_of_Pakistan.svg *License:* Public domain *Contributors:* The drawing and the colors were based from flagspot.net. *Original artist:* User:Zscout370

- **File:Flag_of_Serbia.svg** *Source:* https://upload.wikimedia.org/wikipedia/commons/f/ff/Flag_of_Serbia.svg *License:* Public domain *Contributors:* From http://www.parlament.gov.rs/content/cir/o_skupstini/simboli/simboli.asp. *Original artist:* sodipodi.com

- **File:Quill_and_ink.svg** *Source:* https://upload.wikimedia.org/wikipedia/commons/c/c4/Quill_and_ink.svg *License:* CC BY-SA 2.5 *Contributors:* Own work *Original artist:* Ebrenc at Catalan Wikipedia

- **File:Radha_and_Krishna_in_Discussion.jpg***Source:*https://upload.wikimedia.org/wikipedia/commons/1/19/Radha_and_Krishna_in_Dis. jpg *License:* Public domain *Contributors:* http://chdmuseum.nic.in/art_gallery/indian_miniature_painting.html *Original artist:* Unknown

- **File:Ravi_Varma-Shakuntala_columbia.jpg***Source:*https://upload.wikimedia.org/wikipedia/commons/4/44/Ravi_Varma-Shakuntala_co lum.jpg*License:*Public domain*Contributors:*Downloaded fromColumbia University South Asian Studiesweb site by <a href='//en.wikipedia.org /wiki/User:Fowler%26fowler' class='extiw' title='en:User:Fowler,,&,,fowler'>Fowler&fowler</a><a href='//en.wikipedia.org /wiki/User_talk:Fowler%26fowler' class='extiw' title='en:User talk:Fowler,,&,,fowler'>«Talk»</a> 12:24, 21 October 200 7(UTC)*Original artist:*Raja Ravi Varma

- **File:Rigveda_MS2097.jpg** *Source:* https://upload.wikimedia.org/wikipedia/commons/0/02/Rigveda_MS2097.jpg *License:* Public domain *Contributors:* http://www.nb.no/baser/schoyen/5/5.20/ms2097.jpg *Original artist:* Unknown

- **File:Rossetti_selbst.jpg** *Source:* https://upload.wikimedia.org/wikipedia/commons/d/d2/Rossetti_selbst.jpg *License:* Public domain *Contributors:* http://www.abcgallery.com/ *Original artist:* Dante Gabriel Rossetti

- **File:Siang_Lue_Siang_Lao_Ang,_thamnong_sano.ogg** *Source:* https://upload.wikimedia.org/wikipedia/commons/d/d4/Siang_Lue_Siang_ Lao_Ang%2C_thamnong_sano.ogg *License:* CC0 *Contributors:* Own work *Original artist:* Paul_012

- **File:Siang_Lue_Siang_Lao_Ang.ogg** *Source:* https://upload.wikimedia.org/wikipedia/commons/4/4c/Siang_Lue_Siang_Lao_Ang.ogg *License:* CC0 *Contributors:* Own work *Original artist:* Paul_012

- **File:Stanza_from_Inlarat_Kham_Chan.ogg** *Source:* https://upload.wikimedia.org/wikipedia/commons/4/4f/Stanza_from_Inlarat_Kham_ Chan.ogg *License:* CC0 *Contributors:* Own work *Original artist:* Paul_012

- **File:Tagore3.jpg** *Source:* https://upload.wikimedia.org/wikipedia/commons/b/ba/Tagore3.jpg *License:* Public domain *Contributors:* Various, e.g. [1], published in 1914 in Sweden in Les Prix Nobel 1913, p. 60 *Original artist:* Unknown

- **File:TanDaNguyenKhacHieu.jpg** *Source:* https://upload.wikimedia.org/wikipedia/commons/c/cb/TanDaNguyenKhacHieu.jpg *License:* Public domain *Contributors:* Transferred from vi.wikipedia to Commons by Xiaoao. *Original artist:* The original uploader was Xiaoao at Vietnamese Wikipedia

- **File:Tanenuiarangi.jpg** *Source:* https://upload.wikimedia.org/wikipedia/commons/a/a0/Tanenuiarangi.jpg *License:* Public domain *Contributors:* ? *Original artist:* ?

- **File:Text_document_with_red_question_mark.svg** *Source:* https://upload.wikimedia.org/wikipedia/commons/a/a4/Text_document_with_ red_question_mark.svg *License:* Public domain *Contributors:* Created by bdesham with Inkscape; based upon Text-x-generic.svg from the Tango project. *Original artist:* Benjamin D. Esham (bdesham)

- **File:Three_stanzas_from_Nirat_Phukhao_Thong,_thamnong_sano.oga** *Source:* https://upload.wikimedia.org/wikipedia/commons/b/b0/ Three_stanzas_from_Nirat_Phukhao_Thong%2C_thamnong_sano.oga *License:* CC0 *Contributors:* Own work *Original artist:* Paul_012

- **File:Three_stanzas_from_Nirat_Phukhao_Thong.oga***Source:*https://upload.wikimedia.org/wikipedia/commons/8/89/Three_stanzas_fro m_Nirat_Phukhao_Thong.oga *License:* CC0 *Contributors:* Own work *Original artist:* Paul_012

- **File:Two_stanzas_from_Chant_in_honour_of_the_Dhamma.ogg** *Source:* https://upload.wikimedia.org/wikipedia/commons/d/d7/Two_ stanzas_from_Chant_in_honour_of_the_Dhamma.ogg *License:* CC0 *Contributors:* Own work *Original artist:* Paul_012

- **File:Two_stanzas_from_Kap_He_Ruea,_thamnong_sano.ogg***Source:*https://upload.wikimedia.org/wikipedia/commons/e/ee/Two_stanza s_from_Kap_He_Ruea%2C_thamnong_sano.ogg *License:* CC0 *Contributors:* Own work *Original artist:* Paul_012

- **File:Two_stanzas_from_Kap_He_Ruea.ogg** *Source:* https://upload.wikimedia.org/wikipedia/commons/0/05/Two_stanzas_from_Kap_He_ Ruea.ogg *License:* CC0 *Contributors:* Own work *Original artist:* Paul_012

- **File:Two_stanzas_from_Na_Hat_Sai_Chai_Thale_Haeng_Nueng,_thamnong_sano.ogg** *Source:* https://upload.wikimedia.org/wikipedia/ commons/6/6c/Two_stanzas_from_Na_Hat_Sai_Chai_Thale_Haeng_Nueng%2C_thamnong_sano.ogg *License:* CC0 *Contributors:* Own work *Original artist:* Paul_012

- **File:Two_stanzas_from_Na_Hat_Sai_Chai_Thale_Haeng_Nueng.ogg** *Source:* https://upload.wikimedia.org/wikipedia/commons/4/42/ Two_stanzas_from_Na_Hat_Sai_Chai_Thale_Haeng_Nueng.ogg *License:* CC0 *Contributors:* Own work *Original artist:* Paul_012

- **File:Two_stanzas_from_Veneration_of_the_Dhamma,_thamnong_sano.ogg** *Source:* https://upload.wikimedia.org/wikipedia/commons/ 5/5b/Two_stanzas_from_Veneration_of_the_Dhamma%2C_thamnong_sano.ogg *License:* CC0 *Contributors:* Own work *Original artist:* Paul_012

- **File:Vg_135,_Hassla.jpg** *Source:* https://upload.wikimedia.org/wikipedia/commons/1/13/Vg_135%2C_Hassla.jpg *License:* Public domain *Contributors:* Jungner, Hugo; Elisabeth Svärdström (1940-1971). Sveriges runinskrifter. V. Västergötlands runinskrifter. Stockholm: Kungl. Vitterhets Historie och Antikvitets Akademien. ISSN 0562-8016. p. 260 *Original artist:* Ulf Christofersson

- **File:Vietnamese_chu_nom_example.svg** *Source:* https://upload.wikimedia.org/wikipedia/commons/8/84/Vietnamese_chu_nom_example. svg *License:* CC0 *Contributors:* Refering to png file, Author newly created this. *Original artist:* 미달이.

- **File:Warton'{}s_History_of_English_Poetry.JPG** *Source:* https://upload.wikimedia.org/wikipedia/commons/8/8e/Warton%27s_History_ of_English_Poetry.JPG *License:* CC BY-SA 4.0 *Contributors:* Own work *Original artist:* Antiquary

- **File:Wiki_letter_w.svg** *Source:* https://upload.wikimedia.org/wikipedia/en/6/6c/Wiki_letter_w.svg *License:* Cc-by-sa-3.0 *Contributors:* ? *Original artist:* ?

- **File:Wiki_letter_w_cropped.svg** *Source:* https://upload.wikimedia.org/wikipedia/commons/1/1c/Wiki_letter_w_cropped.svg *License:* CC-BY-SA-3.0 *Contributors:*

- Wiki_letter_w.svg *Original artist:* Wiki_letter_w.svg: Jarkko Piiroinen

39.8.3 Content license

Made in the USA
Columbia, SC
11 October 2024